Psychological Testing and American Society

1890 – 1930

Michael M. Sokal, editor

PSYCHOLOGICAL

TESTING AND AMERICAN SOCIETY,

1890–1930

Psychological

Testing and American

Society

1890~1930

Edited by
MICHAEL M. SOKAL

RUTGERS UNIVERSITY PRESS   New Brunswick and London

First paperback edition, 1990

Library of Congress Cataloging-in-Publication Data

Psychological testing and American society, 1890–1930.
Originated at a symposium at the 150th National
Meeting of the American Association for the Advancement
of Science, held in New York on May 29, 1984.
Includes index.
1. Psychological tests—United States—History—
Congresses. 2. Intelligence tests—United States—
History—Congresses. I. AAAS National Meeting
(1984: New York, N.Y.) II. Sokal, Michael M.
BF176.P78 1987   153.9′3   86–11898
ISBN 0–8135–1193–3 (cloth)
ISBN 0–8135–1573–4 (pbk.)

British Cataloging-in-Publication Information Available.

Cover illustration: "Committee on Psychological
Examination of Recruits, 1917." Front (l. to r.): Edgar A.
Doll, Henry H. Goddard, Thomas H. Haines. Rear (l. to r.):
Frederick L. Wells, Guy M. Whipple, Robert M. Yerkes, Walter
V. Bingham, Lewis M. Terman. Robert M. Yerkes Papers
(Box 134; Folder 2270). Courtesy Yale University Library.

For
JOHN C. BURNHAM

CONTENTS

PREFACE

This volume had its origins in a symposium of the same title, organized and chaired by Michael M. Sokal, at the 150th National Meeting of the American Association for the Advancement of Science, held in New York on May 29, 1984. At this session, Leila Zenderland, James Reed, Henry L. Minton, and Franz Samelson presented earlier versions of their essays published here, and many of the relatively large number of psychologists, historians, and others who attended took part in lively and at times heated, lengthy discussions. As a result, the speakers at this session decided to implement earlier vague plans to expand their papers and seek publication of the symposium. The group subsequently invited several scholars who were writing about testing—including Richard T. von Mayrhauser, who had made some especially effective comments at the New York symposium—to join the project. All involved have benefited from the post-session discussion and from critical comments of the other authors, and all have learned much from the reports of anonymous Rutgers University Press referees. No one author agrees with all the statements made and the conclusions drawn by his or her colleagues, but each is pleased to be associated with the others. The group thus hopes this volume will stimulate further work on the history of testing in America and will inform the current debate on testing and its uses in the late twentieth century.

Each chapter's notes open with individual acknowledgments, but here we want to thank several individuals who made the whole volume possible. At Worcester Polytechnic Institute, Richard H. Gallagher (Dean of Faculty) and Jo Ann Manfra (Head of the Department of Humanities) not only wholeheartedly supported the editor's work, but also covered the cost of indexing the volume. Linda Cardani provided important college work-study assistance, Robert B. Percy III offered many useful editorial suggestions, and Margaret A. Brodmerkle and Penny J. Whiting contributed their secretarial services in a way that made revising almost pleasurable. In addition, while he worked on this volume, the editor benefited greatly from the extensive and very kind support of the Humanities, Science, and Technology Program of the National Endowment for the Humanities, through grant no. RH-20616-85. At Rutgers University Press, Editor-in-Chief Marlie Wasserman arranged for the insightful referee reports cited earlier and in other important ways helped us rework our original material into a unified whole. Managing Editor Eileen Finan and copy editor Alice Calaprice also helped us bring our chapters together, and their contributions to the volume well demonstrate why scholars need editors.

Despite the volume's origins at an American Association for the Advancement of Science symposium, in many ways it derives primarily from the contributors' discussions at past meetings of Cheiron, The International Society for the History of the Behavioral and Social Sciences. At these forums, scholars in many different fields present stirring papers and insightful formal commentaries, share exciting news about freshly opened manuscript collection, actively debate each other's interpretations and conclusions, and argue heatedly long into the night. These meetings greatly enrich most scholarship in the society's domain, and through Cheiron many of those studying the history of psychological testing have been able to build on each other's work. Several of the chapters in this volume contain arguments that institutions—by calling on particular psychologists for specific services, and by enabling others to extend their work—did much to shape ideas and practice. Cheiron's role in the development of historical studies of psychological testing may not parallel precisely that played by the New Jersey Training School for Feeble-minded Boys and Girls at Vineland in the development of testing itself. But analogies exist, and those of us writing in the field owe Cheiron much.

Finally, our dedication of this volume to John C. Burnham acknowledges a major debt owed by all those who study the history of American psychology. In the 1950s, when most who wrote on the subject did so primarily to seek support for their own psychological views, Burnham embarked on a series of exciting studies that revolutionized the field. Although it is difficult to summarize his achievement neatly because of its breadth, all of his work clearly approaches past science within the full cultural context in which it emerged, and this volume's title shows that its contributors have tried to follow his lead. Certainly the trail that he blazed is anything but narrow. By placing early American sociological thought within its intellectual context, he did much in 1956 to rescue significant ideas from enforced disciplinary obscurity.[1] By outlining the role of psychology and psychiatry in the Progressive Movement, his 1960 article on the interplay among the science, its medical analog, and the larger culture well demonstrated the importance of each for the development of the others.[2] By analyzing how Freudian ideas emerged (and did not emerge) in early twentieth-century America, he showed in 1967 that determined historical research, combined with a creative historical imagination, went further than either alone.[3] By sketching "The Origins of Behaviorism" in 1968, he laid bare the poverty of earlier historical interpretations that viewed the past solely in terms of the present.[4] By collecting a set of exciting documents on the history of American science in 1971, he opened new subjects to scholarship and thus helped stimulate the field to rapid growth.[5] By tracing the career of an American physician whose work involved many areas of medicine and psychoanalysis, he shed light in 1983 on all of these areas and provided a model for biographers of similar subjects.[6] Few scholars have influenced their fields as John C. Burnham has, and we are pleased and proud to dedicate this book to him.

NOTES

1. John C. Burnham, *Lester Frank Ward in American Thought* (Washington, D.C.: Public Affairs Press, 1956).
2. John C. Burnham, "Psychology, Psychiatry, and the Progressive Movement," *American Quarterly* 12 (1960): 457–465.
3. John C. Burnham, *Psychoanalysis and American Medicine, 1894–1918: Medicine, Science, and Culture,* monograph 20, *Psychological Issues* (New York: International Universities Press, 1967).
4. John C. Burnham, "On the Origins of Behaviorism," *Journal of the History of the Behavioral Sciences* 4 (1968): 143–151.
5. John C. Burnham, ed., *Science in America: Historical Selections* (New York: Holt, Rinehart and Winston, 1971).
6. John C. Burnham, *Jelliffe: American Psychoanalyst and Physician,* and *His Correspondence with Sigmund Freud and C. G. Jung,* edited by William McGuire (Chicago: University of Chicago Press, 1983).

ABBREVIATIONS

PSYCHOLOGICAL

TESTING AND AMERICAN SOCIETY,

1890–1930

MICHAEL M. SOKAL

1

Introduction: Psychological

Testing and Historical Scholarship—

Questions, Contrasts, and

Context

Science-based technologies have done much to shape late twentieth-century American society and culture. The assumptions of their developers and the implications of their use thus deserve, and have received, the serious attention of scholars, policy makers, and the public. In recent years, controversy over the use and influence of such technologies has mushroomed and, for example, the current debates over the plans and prospects of nuclear power and genetic engineering have attracted much national attention. On such issues both public and expert opinion varies greatly, and all but the most ideologically committed therefore welcome almost any information or point of view that sheds light on the questions at hand. No such technology, however, has been more controversial than standardized psychological testing, and all agree that it plays a major role in current American society, particularly with respect to education and employment practices. Its importance has led to well-publicized and often impassioned debates about all of its aspects, and major public figures have, at times, taken a full range of radically overstated positions on the meaning of the tests and their results, and on the testers' goals and assumptions. These extreme perspectives help define the boundaries of the controversy.

1

On one hand, for example, Americans have the views of Arthur R. Jensen of the University of California, Berkeley, and Richard J. Herrnstein of Harvard, who believe that tests reveal real differences in the ways in which individuals of different racial backgrounds function psychologically, and who argue therefore that the American educational system must take these differences into account.[1] Much more extreme are the statements of William Shockley, now at Stanford, a distinguished scientist and engineer, and one of the inventors of the transistor. A Nobel Prize winner and a major proponent of the proposed sperm bank for Nobel laureates, Shockley believes that many of the problems of modern American society stem from the mental limitations of large numbers of individuals. Going much further than Jensen and Herrnstein, he also argues that modern psychological tests reveal significant differences in mental ability between many members of at least one minority group, on one hand, and most members of the majority group, on the other. He therefore believes that the size of this minority population should be reduced. He carefully shuns any direct means of reduction as inconsistent with the foundations of American society and instead believes that members of this group should be offered incentives not to reproduce. He therefore proposes, as a "thinking exercise," that each "subnormal" black man or woman—or indeed each individual with "limited mental ability"—who undergoes voluntary sterilization be paid a bounty of $1,000 for each point that his or her IQ falls below the national average of 100.[2]

At the other extreme, several distinguished individuals in important media, academic, and policy-making positions deny that mental tests can shed light on anything of interest about any individual or social group. None have won Nobel prizes, but the national and legislative attention that some have attracted suggests that many others share their views. For example, Dan Rather's 1975 CBS documentary "The I.Q. Myth" brought the controversy before the nonreading public and left no uncertainty about its producers' negative opinions of the tests.[3] Among academics, Jerry Hirsch, a professor at the University of Illinois, has written perhaps the longest and bitterest attacks on Shockley's ideas—the most notable entitled "To 'Unfrock the Charlatans'"—that have received wide publicity and some Congressional attention, and his comments on the work of less extreme supporters of testing such as Jensen and Herrnstein are equally vehement.[4] Less in the public eye, but probably more influential, have been the decisions of a number of government officials. For example, in 1979 the Massachusetts state legislature passed a law that required that "the score of any group intelligence test administered to a student enrolled in a public school shall be removed from the record of said student at the end of the year in which such test was so administered." In the following year, Clifford Alexander, Jimmy Carter's Secretary of the Army, decided to purge every score of every psychological test from the records of every U.S. soldier.[5] The legislature's and Clifford's perspectives on tests clearly differ from Shockley's, and both were in a position to do something with their points of view.

Through the 1960s and 1970s, those most concerned about psychological testing stressed its implications for the problems of minority groups and for the many public and private programs designed to ease them. In the past decade, however, the changing social climate—sometimes seen as the rise of the Yuppies—has redirected this attention, resulting in widespread concerns about testing's implications for the largely white middle class. On this issue, too, testing is important, opinions vary, and the meaning and influence of psychological tests have been heavily debated. Educators and concerned parents thus closely follow the meaning of scores on the SAT (the Scholastic Aptitude Test of the Educational Testing Service) and the ACT (the American College Testing Program) and show their faith in such tests by praising teachers and teaching methods that raise the scores and condemning those that do not.[6] Meanwhile, books attacking this technology and castigating those who use it—with such titles as *The Testing Trap, None of the Above: Behind the Myth of Scholastic Aptitude,* and *The Reign of ETS: The Corporation That Makes Up Minds*[7]—call loudly for public attention and reinforce the views of those policy makers who favor abolishing such tests. Hundreds of other articles and speeches on both sides of the question are published and given yearly. Clearly, views on testing form no consensus, and debates on the issue still generate much heat.

Some general conclusions can be distilled from these arguments, however. Most, though not all, of the critics of testing express doubts as to the testers' ability to address policy issues with disinterest.

Many believe that the testers—like many intellectuals—identify themselves too closely with their work to be able to view it dispassionately. Some go further and see the testers as professional opportunists, seeking solely to reinforce their professional status and opportunistically claiming for themselves a unique expertise to which they really have no right.[8] Some—particularly several Marxist-influenced analysts of English testing—even argue that testers have often been motivated by an implicit (and at times explicit) desire to reinforce class and race distinctions.[9] Many critics thus cite the notorious work of Cyril Burt, the distinguished English tester whose publications supported the view that tests revealed significant differences in mental ability among individuals of different social classes. Recent investigative reporting and serious scholarship have both shown, however, that much of Burt's last work involved distortion of many kinds and represents a clearcut case of scientific fraud.[10] Some thus imply that Burt's professional sense of himself as a tester required that he continually reinforce through the 1950s the conclusions that he argued for in the 1920s and 1930s, while others see him unconsciously (or even consciously) seeking to provide support for the class distinctions that seemed to weaken in postwar Britain. Though I know of no critic who has accused the American testers cited here of fraud, many use the Burt case to dismiss all tests. After all, the argument goes, if Burt—the first psychologist to be knighted—acted fraudulently, why should less distinguished testers, even if they are American, be trusted?[11]

Others—especially critics of the Educational Testing Service and similar agencies—argue that even if the testers are disinterested, the relevance of their work for educational practice has yet to be demonstrated. That is, they argue that the tests simply do not work. These observers cite the relatively low correlation between results on the tests and later academic performance, and present accounts of high-scoring students who cannot complete a term in college and low-scoring students who head their institutions' Dean's lists.[12] They also point out major problems that at times beset even the best tests when they are administered—often by teachers with the barest acquaintance of testing procedures—and they tell horror stories of, say, normal children who were kept for years in classes for the mentally retarded because of testing errors.[13] For their own part, most testers readily admit their tests' imperfections and that, indeed, horror stories have occurred. They slight these problems, however, and seek to rectify them through calls for additional support for further test development and through arguments that only trained psychologists should administer most tests (perhaps another reason to call them professionally opportunistic).[14] More importantly, many psychologists stress testing as the creator of opportunity, which they believe, opens educational and employment doors for many whose true abilities would otherwise have been ignored.[15] The testers give much anecdotal evidence to support this conclusion and argue that, all things being equal, tests have helped individuals more than they have hurt them.

Because of such sharp disagreement, many concerned with the issues at hand have looked to the past and have sought a resolution—or at least illumination—in various recent historical studies of testing. Indeed, many significant questions about testing and its influence—with many implications for current practice—can be asked. For example, what forces led to the development of testing? Did testing emerge simply as the opportunistic ploy of psychologists seeking to bolster their professional status, or did others perceive a real social need that psychologists sought to meet? Have psychologists approached their testing programs dispassionately, or have they used their science-based technology to implement their personal views of proper social structure? Have the tests been truly useful and relevant, or has their continued use merely reflected the status and political power of psychologists? Have testers always agreed how their technology ought to be applied, or has the community of psychologists experienced debates like those that have wracked other professional groups? Has testing really influenced past policy making, or is this an incorrect assumption of psychologists and others? Has the actual practice of testing itself changed through time? Are psychologists today more (or indeed less) concerned with such factors as their subject's health on the day of a test than they were fifty years ago? Do they take more care in setting forth their instructions? How have various changes in the technology of testing—such as introduction of the multiple-choice question—influenced tests, and what are their implications? These questions and others suggest what history can bring to the current debate about testing and illustrate the sorts of questions that the essays included in this volume try to address.

Of course, this goal—of having the past illuminate the present—is nothing new; judges, legislators, and others who make public policy have also often looked to history to guide their deliberations. Typically, however, they simply do so to justify decisions already made, so that questions such as those sketched above often go unasked. Even when such individuals approach the past openly, they often know little or nothing of the canons of scholarship, and the historical understanding that they bring to their work thus has little real value. As, for example, two well-known historians have recently shown, policy makers sometimes base their decisions on outdated research, usually avoid the most valuable primary sources (like archival documents and manuscript collections) that trained historians depend upon, and, in drawing conclusions from the evidence they do consult, often ignore the simplest rules of logic.[16] Few studies of past testing exhibit all of these faults, but, unfortunately, most have apparently been written by those seeking to legitimate a previously held position—that is, by authors who know that testing lays bare an individual's (or group's) true social worth, or that the tests are useless at best and evidence of a conspiracy of some sort at worst. Dozens of such studies have appeared in recent years—primarily in response to Jensen's long 1969 article (which some believe reignited the current controversy on testing)[17]—and, though some have been reviewed widely, most have not received extensive attention.[18]

Despite this wealth of material, this essay cannot provide a comprehensive review of this literature. No one, for example, need suffer a review of the sections on testing in the dozens of history of psychology textbooks published during the past two decades,[19] and there is no need to cite each article on the topic published during the period. Nevertheless, the contents of the present book can perhaps best be appreciated when compared with earlier works in the field. Indeed, our primary goal is to bring before the public and scholarly community some of the best and latest research on the history of psychological testing in the United States. This scholarship responds at least to some of the questions presented here and will also further our understanding of several important historical topics. These include the development and application of science in twentieth-century America, the way in which individual scientists attempted to use their work to meet the social needs they perceived, and the concern and, at times, passion they brought to their studies. Most contributors to this volume also believe that their papers can clarify scientific and policy issues regarding testing and thus help the public and policy makers understand and evaluate the issues and respond to larger concerns.

In 1974, Leon J. Kamin of Princeton University published an insightful review of *The Science and Politics of I.Q.* that challenged much of the work on which Jensen had based his conclusions.[20] In doing so, he raised some of the first serious questions about the validity of Cyril Burt's studies. Despite his focus on fairly recent research, Kamin introduced his discussion with two chapters—published earlier in *Social Research*[21]—on "The Pioneers of I.Q. Testing in America" and "Psychology and the Immigrant," which dealt with pre-1930 American psychology. In particular, the second chapter raised questions about the influence of American psychologists in determining U.S. immigration policy in the early 1920s, when Congress introduced highly restrictive quotas. Kamin concluded that psychologists might "claim substantial credit" for these quotas, which he said "resulted in the deaths of hundreds of thousands of victims" of the Nazis. This analysis, however, cannot withstand logical and historical criticism, as Franz Samelson, one of the contributors to this volume, showed some time ago.[22] That is, while Kamin has no trouble demonstrating that the psychologists supported and spoke favorably of the immigration-restriction laws of the 1920s, and even that they testified on their behalf before Congress, he provides no evidence that the testers actually had any influence on the laws' passage. To be sure, psychologists like Robert M. Yerkes of Yale and Lewis M. Terman of Stanford—both subjects of chapters in this volume—later argued that their colleagues' work led directly to the laws. But historians have learned long ago to doubt such self-serving claims, and mere agreement of the political positions of two parties has never shown that one influenced the other. (Correlation, after all, does not prove causation.) Indeed, a critical review of the evidence shows that the testers' support for the laws was irrelevant at best. Almost all sectors of American society in the early 1920s supported immigration restriction, as workers feared that low-paid immigrants would take their jobs and, in the aftermath of the 1919 Red Scare and the 1921 Sacco-Vanzetti trial, employers feared aliens from southern and eastern Europe. Samelson's more detailed analysis, based in large part on research in the National Archives in Washington, D.C., revealed many other problems with Kamin's account, and his book's historical sections, though cited regularly by scholars, cannot be considered completely accurate.

This conclusion does not imply that books on the history of testing by testers stand up any better to critical readings. For example, May V. Seagoe's hero-worshipping biography of her teacher, *Terman and the Gifted*,[23] underrates most contemporaneous criticisms of her subject's work—a topic discussed extensively in chapter 5 of this volume—and ignores almost all of the recent excellent and highly relevant scholarship on Terman's teachers such as G. Stanley Hall of Clark University;[24] futhermore, she makes almost no use of the large cache of Terman papers at the Stanford University Archives. (Indeed, despite the wealth of archival material available on the history of testing—a recent *Guide to Manuscript Collections in the History of Psychology*[25] indexes twenty-eight collections with substantial numbers of documents on the subject—all too few authors have made use of these riches.) Surprisingly, Seagoe also sheds little light on how Terman's tests were administered by early twentieth-century psychologists. By ignoring the practice of testing in this way, Seagoe and most others who have written on the history of the subject have left untouched a major topic that has done much to help determine the influence of the tests and the ways in which they are used. But a more fundamental problem occurs as, throughout her analysis, Seagoe takes Terman's perspective as her own. She even adopts several of the heavily criticized methods that he used to estimate the intelligence of pre-twentieth-century individuals in an attempt to understand Terman's childhood. The book, though more than a hagiography and itself an important primary document representing the views of one mid-twentieth-century tester, has as many problems as Kamin's.

Though fairly well received by psychologists and others, Kamin's and Seagoe's books may not have gotten the national attention their authors had hoped for. One book on the history of testing that did, however, is Stephen Jay Gould's *The Mismeasure of Man*,[26] which attracted dozens of laudatory reviews and won the 1981 National Book Critics Circle Award for general nonfiction.[27] Gould is a well-known and highly respected Harvard scientist, and his work in paleontology and evolutionary theory—particularly his concept of punctuated equilibrium—has done much to reshape current ideas on the course of biological evolution. He also has, of course, an enviable public reputation for his columns and commentary on scientific subjects in such widely circulated publications as *Natural History* and *The New York Review of Books,* and his reading and reviews of some of Jensen's books [28] apparently convinced him that the topic of testing deserved his attention as well. The result is better than either of the other two books discussed above, but Gould's analysis still exhibits all too many faults common to other histories of testing. Its generally positive reception justifies its close examination here.

To be sure, Gould's own perspective is clear from the first page of his book. That is, while explicitly admitting that psychological tests can be useful for the diagnosis of individual learning disabilities and sensory disorders—a point missed and even denied by more than one reviewer—he believes strongly that tests have been and are being misused and have at times harmed individuals. He therefore sets out to analyze attempts during the past 150 years to assess human ability, all from the perspective of his "cardinal principle": that "science . . . is a socially embedded activity." The result reviews such nineteenth-century work as the craniometry of the American Samuel G. Morton and the Frenchman Paul Broca and the anthropometry of the Italian Cesare Lombroso, as well as the work of such twentieth-century mental testers as Alfred Binet (in France), Charles Spearman and Cyril Burt (in Britain), and Terman, Yerkes, Henry H. Goddard, and Louis L. Thurstone (in the United States). In doing so, he easily shows that science is part of the social world. Indeed, he admits that this conclusion "would . . . be accepted by nearly every historian of science." But in stressing several technical faults he finds in the testers' work, he sometimes seems to imply that scientists of the past should have escaped from their contexts and realized the limitations of their points of view. These implications especially mar his otherwise insightful discussion of such nineteenth-century science as Morton's studies.

Other implications are equally doubtful. For example, Gould suggests that Goddard's studies led to the passage of various state eugenical sterilization laws, and, like Kamin, strongly implies that the testers' work led to the quotas of the 1924 United States immigration law. Turning to England and the influence of Cyril Burt's work, Gould also argues that Burt's studies led to the infamous 11+ examination that has done much to stifle British secondary schooling. In doing so, he ignores not only Samelson's earlier studies, but also the excellent and highly praised biography of Burt that had appeared two years before his book.[29] To be sure, Gould admits that Burt was "not the architect" of the examination, but he still claims that "it hardly matters whether or not Burt's hand actually moved the pen." An analysis more in line with Gould's "cardinal principle" would argue that Goddard's work and the sterilization laws, Yerkes's tests and the immigration-restriction laws, and Burt's studies and the 11+ examination reflected in each case the shared perspectives of the testers and the policy makers. But Gould seems to want the scientists and not the larger society to plead guilty here. In many ways, Gould's lapse here is surprising, especially in view of the great insight he typically brings to most of his studies.

Gould's discussion, however, exhibits one major and unusual strength. That is, it recognizes that testing did not make its first appearance in the very late nineteenth century, and his discussions of Morton's, Broca's, and Lombroso's work are thus quite valuable. The book, however, slights the most influential techniques that nineteenth-century Americans used to analyze and record their mental abilities and characteristics. These stemmed primarily from the folk wisdom of physiognomy, which read an individual's character and temperament in his or her face; already in the eighteenth century, several Americans began to use the systematic physiognomy of Johann Caspar Lavater of Switzerland to study their friends and neighbors.[30] In many ways, the early nineteenth-century fashion for silhouettes represented an articulation of similar concerns[31]— especially as Americans often used these cuttings to recall their loved ones' characteristics. One of the most popular attractions of Charles Willson Peale's Philadelphia Museum was the physiognotrace, which preserved an individual's physiognomy forever.[32]

These techniques soon gave way to phrenology (which Gould mentions in passing), the most serious nineteenth-century approach to the study of individual mental ability.[33] In America, particularly, phrenology emerged as a popular technique for the reading of a person's psychological strengths and weaknesses, and for several decades before the Civil War, Americans often called upon the phrenologist for expert guidance. Throughout the period, itinerant phrenologists traveled throughout the country, providing mental examinations, psychological diagnoses, and practical professional advice to those who consulted them and paid their fee. The typical phrenological reading evaluated several categories of an individual's mental "powers"—including his or her domestic, selfish, and moral feelings; self-perceptive and reflective abilities; and intellectual and literary faculties—and it suggested several "business adaptations" for which he or she was best or least suited. It even spelled out the traits the subject should look for in a spouse.[34] The phrenologist thus served the early nineteenth century much as the consulting psychologist—using modern mental tests—serves the twentieth.

But unlike those who followed, the phrenologist clearly worked within the self-help style of reform of the period, which sought to alleviate the problems of the age by remaking the individual through moral suasion. That is, while later reformers worked primarily through institutions to shape society and sought to pass laws against this or that social ill, those of ante-bellum America addressed their attention to the individual and believed that, through education, he or she could be remade. Thus the early abolitionists sought to reeducate the slaveholder, and health reformers concentrated less on public health laws than on diet and dress reform.[35] Phrenology, with its precise readings of human strengths and weaknesses, and with the specific educational, career, and matrimonial advice its practioners gave, thus fit well within the pattern of an age that sought improvement not in the remaking of a society but rather in the remaking of the individual.

But in the disillusion with individual reform in the aftermath of the Civil War, Americans lost faith in phrenology. They approached reform more broadly and instead of reeducating the individual as their grandparents had, late nineteenth-century Americans built institutions and sought to pass laws to prevent evil, or at least to deter it. Archetypically, prohibition replaced temperance, and those opposed to alcohol refocused their attention from the individual drinker to the statehouse where laws were passed.[36] Phrenology—with its concern for an individual's character—had little to say to the new reformers and thus lost its authority. By the end of the century, phrenologists were often perceived simply as cranks, and the movement died. Scientifically, however, phrenology helped shape Morton's scientific craniometry (which Gould discusses) and mid-nineteenth-century investigators generalized this work into a physical anthropometry concerned with the quantitative study of all parts of the human body.[37] This science thrived in Britain and America, and its practitioners slowly broadened its focus to include the measurement of its subjects' minds as well as their bodies. One English anthropometrist, Francis Galton, looked to late nineteenth-century German psychological studies for techniques of mental measurement and thus stimulated the work of James McKeen Cattell, the subject of this book's second chapter. Phrenology thus led directly to what was perceived as mental testing. Perhaps more important, however, is the changing focus of reform that actually stimulated the growth of testing as such.

In using institutions as part of their "search for order" after the Civil War, Gilded Age reformers had special faith in schooling.[38] Millions of new immigrants—most with cultural backgrounds totally different from those of almost all earlier Americans—flocked yearly to the New World. The emerging giant trusts and the rapid industrialization of the period destroyed traditional paths of entry into an occupation and placed a heavy premium on standardized styles of work. This development, the vague and pervasive influence of social Darwinism, and the rise of new professions all led many Americans to search for formal and rationalized criteria for measuring "social efficiency" and for judging applicants for employment and university admission. Many reformers thus looked to education as an ordering, standardizing, and "Americanizing" process, and by 1900 most states had passed compulsory education laws. Among other effects, these laws brought to public attention the mentally disabled children who had previously remained within their family circles, and they helped stimulate concern for the welfare and evil influence of what were called the delinquent, dependent, and defective classes. This interest in turn led to new schools for the "feebleminded" to serve their needs and to "protect" the public.[39] Such developments did much to gain the interest of reformers in whatever tools could be used to sort individuals, and by the 1890s most had adopted a "Progressive" point of view that led them to seek guidance in the work of scientists. The new universities of the late nineteenth century had meanwhile begun to sponsor the emergence of a "new psychology"—based largely on "scientific" approaches to psychological questions and stimulated primarily by European-trained researchers—that went far beyond the faculty psychology that had long been taught in American colleges. Those who had learned in Germany the latest physiologically based techniques to study the mind had few qualms about applying their knowledge to measure the differences between people.[40] Here, then, is the context out of which mental testing grew—in which, as Gould would put it, testing was "socially embedded."

Some of the chapters that make up this volume approach several of the subjects previously treated by Kamin, Seagoe, and Gould. But in doing so the authors represented here go far beyond their predecessors in many ways, often by taking into account the context in which testing developed. For example, Henry L. Minton's discussion in chapter 5 of Terman's understanding of the "democratic ideal" and its relations to his goal for testing takes seriously both the psychological and the lay criticisms that Terman's work called forth, yet it conveys a full and sympathetic understanding of its subject. Similarly, James Reed's analysis in chapter 4 of the origins of his subject's approach to testing fits this activity into the complexity of Yerkes's entire career in psychology and thus illuminates the intellectual context in which at least one individual developed his tests. And much new light is shed on the institutionally diverse career of Henry H. Goddard—the subject of two chapters in this volume—as Leila Zenderland traces in chapter 3 the professional and practical concerns that led him to adapt Alfred Binet's tests for an American audience (at the New Jersey Training School for Feebleminded Boys and Girls at Vineland), and Hamilton Cravens shows in chapter 8 how Goddard's own ideas evolved as he faced different subjects in different settings (primarily at the Ohio Bureau of Juvenile Research). The other authors also treat their topics with originality. Though ignored by Kamin, Seagoe, and Gould, Walter Dill Scott of Northwestern University and James McKeen Cattell of Columbia—the subjects of chapters 7 and 2 by Richard T. von Mayrhauser and Michael M. Sokal, respectively—have received previous attention.[41] But no analysis yet in print approaches so completely the tests that either of these men originated, and none relates so clearly its subject's work to the developmental mainstream of testing. Finally, Franz Samelson's focus in chapter 6 on a "simple" technological innovation, the multiple-choice question, demonstrates the importance of supposedly "minor" figures—in this case Frederick J. Kelly of the State Normal School of Emporia, Kansas—and illustrates why historians cannot ignore the practical concerns of the people they study.

Indeed, this concern with practice and procedure—absent in almost all previous analyses of testing—highlights to one degree or another many of the articles that appear in this book. Certainly von Mayrhauser's discussion of Scott's rating scales illuminates Scott's reasons for setting his own course in the evolution of the tests. Zenderland's and Cravens's concern with the different "patient populations" that Goddard faced at different stages in his life makes clear just how and why he came to develop his tests and views. Similarly, the discussions of the institutional settings within which the testers worked—from traditional university, to state school for the feeble-minded, to insane asylum, to industrial consulting office, to state service bureau—demonstrate that this aspect of a tester's environment has important implications for his or her work. Certainly, as the respective authors show, the requirements of Yerkes's charge at the Boston Psychopathic Hospital led him to develop his own style of tests as effectively as did Goddard's and Scott's positions. These chapters thus concern themselves with the details of their topics—that is, with what has been called the "fine texture of the past"—and all illustrate just why such details are important for a satisfactory understanding of a subject. Certainly one would be hard pressed to comprehend fully the reasons for the failure of Cattell's tests without knowing just what they involved.

The deepening of understanding represented by these chapters rests largely on approaches and research techniques that no historian would consider revolutionary. First, the authors represented here have tried to approach their subjects dispassionately, hoping to understand testing, without making moralistic judgments. Perfect disinterest is of course impossible and probably undesirable, and each author has his or her own views on the tests and their use; after all, they came to write on the subject because each believes that psychological testing warrants serious critical attention. But none of the authors here is an ideologue; none is committed either to the elimination of tests from our world or, say, to their use in determining an individual's reproductive future. To be sure, few who have written on the history of testing would argue for either extreme, though their books and articles could easily mislead readers, and their passionate criticisms of the testers' lack of disinterest might raise an eyebrow. More prosaically, in basing their discussions on careful readings and extensive work in a wide range of manuscript collections, the authors of these chapters hope that future scholars will be alerted to the value of primary sources.

Yet the essays that comprise this volume do not ignore previous accounts of testing. Most, for instance, recognize the importance of their subjects' character and temperament, and thus, for example, Cravens's sketch of Goddard's political naiveté conveys quite clearly an important reason for the special history of the Ohio Bureau of Juvenile Research. Similarly, von Mayrhauser's insightful contrast of Scott's and Yerkes's temperaments adds much to our understanding of the development of their distinctive testing styles. Indeed, the entire volume can serve as a comparative study of the development of different tests by individuals in different settings, thereby illustrating that previous analyses that approached "testing" as an undifferentiated whole are fatally flawed.

More broadly, all of the authors adopt the viewpoint that Gould identifies as his "cardinal principle," which he admits would be recognized by almost all historians of science: that "science . . . is a socially embedded activity." The authors discuss science and technology as part of the national society and culture in which they were developed and as the product of a particular local "community" setting—an approach by which they stress the varying important institutional contexts previously mentioned. In addition, most authors place their tests and testers within the context of Progressivism, which shaped most aspects of American society and political thought during the first years of the twentieth century. Indeed, Cravens's claim of an emerging belief that science should influence policy, and the actual appeal to science by policy makers as discussed in most of the following essays, can in many ways be taken as the "essence of Progressivism." All too many past discussions of testing have ignored this point, or (like studies by various critics of the American educational "establishment") have made it without actually examining the work of the testers in detail, or without differentiating among the different testers and their varying goals.[42]

More generally, what can the authors claim that this volume shows about testing? Certainly, they cannot claim to have answered all, or even most, of the questions posed earlier, but their essays do make a start on some of them. Each author presents his or her own conclusions, but several overarching and interrelated points can be distilled from all. For example, there are discussions of the major influence of changes in the technology of testing (such as the introduction of the multiple-choice question); the overstated claims that testing has deeply influenced past policy decisions; the serious disagreements among testers on various scientific points and, especially, on the applications of their technology; the continuing importance of social and cultural contexts for the development of testing; and the serious concern with which most testers approached their work. These last two points are inextricably intertwined, as the settings within which the testers' lived helped determine their hopes and goals, and so it follows that no tester ever approached his or her work with total disinterest. But as noted earlier, past implications that the testers should have been able to escape their social worlds deny Gould's "cardinal principle,"[43] and, as these essays show, they usually tried to apply their tests fairly and carefully. Terman's work, for example—though often criticized for its antidemocratic implications—emerged directly from his view of the democratic ideal, and Goddard used his tests at Vineland in a real effort to serve the children in his care. The testers usually worked to serve others; they believed themselves to be altruists.

Perhaps the major contribution of this book is to show the importance of the practical realities faced by the testers, a point typically ignored by those who have previously written about testing. That is, the defenders of the tests seem to feel that they can be carried out fairly and with relatively little effort, and that with proper training for those who administer the tests most problems could easily be avoided. More serious is the fact that many opponents of testing seem to believe that the tests serve no social role other than to support the testers' inflated claims to a unique professional expertise. But as this book demonstrates, testing itself emerged and evolved in response to real problems, as American society changed rapidly and the Progressives looked to science for guidance. Attacks on the testers' personal integrity and attempts to denigrate their goals thus unfairly distort the past,[44] and if this volume does nothing more than encourage historians to take the testers' own concerns seriously, it will have done much.

NOTES

1. Arthur R. Jensen, "How Much Can We Boost IQ and Scholarstic Achievement?" *Harvard Educational Review* 39 (1969): 1–123, and Richard J. Herrnstein, "I.Q.," *The Atlantic*, September 1971, 43–64, are the best-known statements of these positions. More recent and detailed explications are Jensen, *Bias in Mental Testing* (New York: Free Press, 1980), and Herrnstein, *I.Q. in the Meritocracy* (Boston: Little-Brown, 1973).
2. William Shockley summarizes his views clearly in "The Apple-of-God's-Eye Obsession," *The Humanist* 32, no. 1, (January-February 1972): 16–17. The most complete list of his publications on the subject appears in the notes to Jerry Hirsch, "To 'Unfrock the Charlatans,'" *Sage Race Relations Abstracts* 6, no. 2 (May 1981): 1–65. Michael Rogers, "Brave New William Shockley," *Esquire*, January 1973, 130, 150–153, presents an interesting popular view.
3. See Diane Ravitch, "'The I.Q. Myth'—Criticisms, Complexities, Contradictions," *The New York Times*, April 20, 1975, sec. II, 29.
4. Besides the detailed arguments of "To 'Unfrock the Charlatans,'" see, for example, Jerry Hirsch, "Jensenism: The Bankruptcy of 'Science' Without Scholarship," *Educational Theory* 25 (1975): 3–27; reprinted in the *Congressional Record* in May 1976.
5. See the Associated Press story, published in the *Worcester Telegram* as the "King Lets IQ-Score Bill and Four Others Slip Into Law Unsigned," April 28, 1979, 28; and the *Washington Star Service* story, published in the *Worcester Telegram* as "Intelligence Test Scores Stricken From GI Files," August 9, 1980, 27.
6. For example, see Lawrence Biemiller, "SAT Scores Rise 3 Points in Math, 1 on Verbal Test," *The Chronicle of Higher Education*, September 26, 1984, 1, 11, and "Composite Scores on ACT Test Rise Slightly," ibid., 3.
7. Andrew J. Strenio, *The Testing Trap* (New York: Rawson, Wade, 1981); David Owen, *None of the Above* (Boston: Houghton Mifflin, 1985); Allan Nairn and Associates, *The Reign of ETS*, The Ralph Nader Report on the Educational Testing Service (Washington, D.C.: Ralph Nader, 1980).
8. Such is the thrust of Nairn, *The Reign of ETS*, and Owen, *None of the Above*. See also, for example, Christopher Lasch's more general attacks on claims of professional expertise, as collected in *The Minimal Self: Psychic Survival in Troubled Times* (New York: Norton, 1984).

9. For example, see Brian Evans and Bernard Waites, *IQ and Mental Testing: An Unnatural Science and Its Social History* (Atlantic Highlands, N.J.: Humanities Press, 1981), and Brian Simon, *Intelligence, Psychology, and Education* (London: Lawrence and Wishart, 1978). Even Gillian Sutherland, a much less ideologically committed historian who stressed throughout her analysis of *Ability, Merit and Measurement: Mental Testing and English Education 1880–1940* (Oxford: Clarendon Press, 1984) the testers' attempts to destroy class distinctions, concluded (on p. 287) that "altogether it is easier to characterise the elitism of the English educational system as aristocratic rather then meritocratic." See also Adrian Wooldridge, "Mental Measurement and the Meritocratic Ideal in England 1880–1980," unpublished paper, American Historical Association, New York, December 1985.

10. L. S. Hearnshaw, *Cyril Burt, Psychologist* (Ithaca, N.Y.: Cornell University Press, 1979).

11. Evans and Waites's analysis in *IQ and Mental Testing* clearly carries this implication. Others have been more explicit and have used Burt's fraud to dismiss much American testing. See, for example, Andrew Hacker, "Creating American Inequality," *The New York Review of Books*, March 20, 1980, 20–28.

12. See, for example, Nairn, *The Reign of ETS*, passim.

13. See, for example, Strenio, *The Testing Trap*, 20–23.

14. Jensen, *Bias in Mental Testing*, certainly carries this implication.

15. Lee J. Cronbach, "Mental Tests and the Creation of Opportunity," *Proceedings of the American Philosophical Society* 114 (1970): 480–487, represents this view most effectively.

16. See Wilcomb E. Washburn, "The Supreme Court's Use and Abuse of History," *Organization of American Historians Newsletter* 11, no. 3 (August 1983): 7–9; Yehoshua Porath, "Mrs. Peters's Palestine," *The New York Review of Books*, January 16, 1986, 36–39.

17. See, for example, Raymond E. Fancher, *The Intelligence Men: Makers of the IQ Controversy* (New York: Norton, 1985).

18. But see Michael M. Sokal, "Approaches to the History of Psychological Testing," *History of Education Quarterly* 24 (1984): 419–430.

19. Perhaps the worst of these is William S. Sahakian, *History and Systems of Psychology* (New York: Schenckman Publishing Company, 1975), 129–133, which discusses "The I.Q. and the Era of Testing" in a chapter headed "Berlin: Physiological Psychology Makes Its Appearance."

20. Leon J. Kamin, *The Science and Politics of I.Q.* (Potomac, Md.: Erlbaum, 1974).

21. Leon J. Kamin, "The Science and Politics of I.Q.," *Social Research* 41 (1974): 387–425.

22. Franz Samelson, "On the Science and Politics of the IQ," *Social Research* 42 (1975): 467–488.

23. May V. Seagoe, *Terman and the Gifted* (Los Altos, Calif.: William Kaufman, 1975).

24. For example, see Dorothy Ross, *G. Stanley Hall: The Psychologist as Prophet* (Chicago: University of Chicago Press, 1972).
25. Michael M. Sokal and Patrice A. Rafail, *A Guide to Manuscript Collections in the History of Psychology and Related Areas* (Millwood, N.Y.: Kraus, 1982).
26. Stephen Jay Gould, *The Mismeasure of Man* (New York: Norton, 1981).
27. For example, see Jeremy Bernstein, "Who Was Christy Matthewson?" *The New Yorker*, April 12, 1982, 144–153.
28. For example, see Stephen Jay Gould, "Jensen's Last Stand," *The New York Review of Books*, May 1, 1980, 38–44.
29. Hearnshaw, *Cyril Burt, Psychologist.*
30. J. C. Lavater, *Physiognomische Fragmente*, 4 vols. (Leipzig: Weidmann und Reich, 1775); idem, *Essays on Physiognomy: Designed to Promote the Knowledge and Love of Mankind*, 3 vols., trans. by H. Hunter (London: J. Murray, 1789–1798); *The Pocket Lavater, or The Science of Physiognomy* (Hartford, Conn.: Andrus and Judd, n.d.).
31. Emily Nevill Jackson, *The History of Silhouettes* (London: The Connoisseur, 1911), 38–40, 62.
32. Charles Coleman Sellars, *Mr. Peale's Museum: Charles Willson Peale and the First Popular Museum of Natural Science and Art* (New York: Norton, 1980), 153, 192.
33. The vast literature on American phrenology is typically uncritical and historically uninformed. Much more insightful are Madeleine B. Stern, *Heads and Headlines: The Phrenological Fowlers* (Norman: University of Oklahoma Press, 1971), and John M. O'Donnell, *The Origins of Behaviorism: American Psychology, 1870–1920* (New York: New York University Press, 1985), 67–80.
34. Few phrenologists were charlatans, and they often based their readings on their impression of all of their subjects' traits, including speech, dress, and manner. A more detailed analysis of phrenological advice would view the phrenologist as sort of a Clever Hans, who could sense his subjects' unconscious reactions to his diagnoses, would cite what twentieth-century psychologists call the Barnum Effect, and would consider the anxieties of early nineteenth-century Americans. But such an analysis belongs elsewhere.
35. See Lawrence J. Friedman, *Gregarious Saints: Self and Community in American Abolition* (New York: Cambridge University Press, 1983); Ronald L. Numbers, *Prophetess of Health: A Study of Ellen G. White* (New York: Harper and Row, 1976).
36. William R. Brock, *Investigation and Responsibility: Public Responsibility in the United States* (New York: Cambridge University Press, 1984).
37. Paul A. Erickson, "Phrenology and Physical Anthropology: The George Combe Connection," *Current Anthropology* 18 (1977): 92.
38. Michael B. Katz, "From Voluntarism to Bureaucracy in American Education," *Sociology of Education* 44 (1971): 297–332.
39. This paragraph summarizes many years of scholarship on the social his-

tory of American ideas. See Robert H. Wiebe, *The Search for Order* (New York: Hill and Wang, 1967); Henrika Kuklick, "The Organization of Social Science in the United States," *American Quarterly* 28 (1976): 124–141; Burton J. Bledstein, *The Culture of Professionalism: The Middle Class and the Development of Higher Education in America* (New York: Norton, 1978).

40. On the origins of the new psychology in the United States, see, for example, Ross, *G. Stanley Hall*, 103–206, and Michael M. Sokal, ed., *An Education in Psychology: James McKeen Cattell's Journal and Letters from Germany and England, 1880–1888* (Cambridge, Mass.: MIT Press, 1981), 6–11, 333–335. On psychologists' quick response to calls for application, see O'Donnell, *The Origins of Behaviorism,* esp. 137–141.

41. For example, see Thomas M. Camfield, "Psychologists at War: The History of American Psychologists and the First World War" (Ph.D. diss., University of Texas at Austin, 1969).

42. For example, see Clarence J. Karier, "Testing for Order and Control in the Corporate Liberal State," *Educational Theory* 22 (1972): 154–180, reprinted in *Roots of Crisis: American Education in the Twentieth Century,* edited by Clarence J. Karier, Paul C. Violas, and Joel H. Spring (Chicago: Rand McNally, 1973), 108–137, and "Intelligence Testing and the Efficient Society," chapter 3 in Edgar Gumbert and Joel H. Spring, *The Superschool and the Superstate: American Education in the Twentieth Century, 1918–1970* (New York: Wiley, 1974), 86–112.

43. More generally, see Michael M. Sokal, "James McKeen Cattell and American Psychology in the 1920s," *Explorations in the History of Psychology in the United States,* edited by Josef Brozek (Lewisburg, Pa.: Bucknell University Press, 1984), 273–323.

44. See especially J. David Smith, *Minds Made Feeble: The Myth and Legacy of the Kallikaks* (Rockville, Md.: Aspen Systems, 1985), which judges Goddard's work from a late twentieth-century perspective.

2

James McKeen Cattell and Mental

Anthropometry: Nineteenth-Century

Science and Reform and

The Origins of Psychological

Testing

Historians of psychology, especially those who have examined the origins of mental testing, write ambivalently about James McKeen Cattell and his role in the development of testing. On one hand, all realize that his work in the field in the 1890s was among the earliest, and that it did much to bring the potential of an applicable psychology to the attention of the American public.[1] On the other hand, most also realize that Cattell's tests just did not work; that is, they told the tester and his subjects nothing of value or even of interest, and by the very early twentieth century, Cattell abandoned his program. Consequently, various presentist accounts ignore Cattell and his work, implying that they had no influence on the tests and testers that followed. Others used Cattell's tests and their fate simply as an example of the way in which science improves with time. Some who have written on the topic ignore what must be called Cattell's failure, in order to trace what they see as the unbroken evolution of testing as an important and influential applied science.

Such accounts ignore the many more significant historical questions that can emerge from a study of Cattell's work. For example:

What were the sources of his approach to testing, and how did these influences shape his program? What role did he envision for his tests, and how was this role reflected in the procedures he adopted? Just how, and why, did his tests differ from those developed by others in the early twentieth century? What led to the failure of his tests? Despite its failure, what influence did his program have? To be sure, these questions recognize that Cattell's work was unsuccessful, a point of view that to many historians implies a presentist bias. And if an explanation of Cattell's failure would involve an appeal to late twentieth-century scientific understanding, such a charge would be appropriate. But answers to all of these questions can be found in the nineteenth-century scientific ideology that shaped Cattell's work, in the early twentieth-century context that influenced those who criticized his tests, and especially in a comparison of the two. Consequently, the nineteenth-century focus of this chapter does much to clarify the evolution of early twentieth-century testing.

Unlike the other testers discussed in this volume, Cattell was a child of the nineteenth century, and he remained rooted in it long after 1900. His important series of directories, *American Men of Science*, clung to the genteel term used by those who avoided the neologism "scientist";[2] it continues today—suitably modified for the late twentieth-century—as *American Men and Women of Science*. The journal *Science*, which he owned and edited until his death in 1944, reflected many nineteenth-century views of science.[3] Most importantly, the way in which Cattell actually did science—from his first experiments with G. Stanley Hall at Johns Hopkins in the early 1880s, through his apprenticeship with Wilhelm Wundt at Leipzig in the mid-1880s, to his psychophysical experiments at the University of Pennsylvania in the early 1890s—reflected a scientific ideology already out of date by the time he learned it. Even his program of mental testing at Columbia in the 1890s rested on old conceptions of the social use and social organization of science.[4] Consequently, if Cattell's—and the nineteenth century's—legacy for American mental testing is to be understood, his education and the forces that shaped it must be reviewed.

James McKeen Cattell was born in 1860 in Easton, Pennsylvania, where his father, William C. Cattell, was professor of ancient languages at Lafayette College.[5] Cattell's early life revolved around this college, especially after 1863, when his father became its president. He never attended public school, but read and was tutored in his father's library. He also traveled with his father, spending thirteen months in Europe during 1869–1870. At fourteen, he began auditing classes at Lafayette, and in September 1876 he matriculated there as a freshman. He graduated with honors in 1880; what he learned at college shaped his later scientific career.

Lafayette, like many American colleges of the period, sought to develop "discipline and piety" among its students within a Presbyterian religious framework of improving their mental faculties.[6] By the late 1870s, however, this Scottish realist approach to higher education was elsewhere losing its hold, and Lafayette was clearly not on the cutting edge of educational innovation. Its faculty did include several distinguished scholars, most notably Francis A. March, an outstanding philologist and the most important American contributor to the *Oxford English Dictionary.* But even he worked within the older tradition and, by doing so, influenced many generations of Lafayette students.

March was especially influential on Cattell, who took several courses with him and who later praised him as "the great teacher, the great scholar, and the great man."[7] March admired Francis Bacon's philosophy, which he reduced to an empiricism based on an exhaustive collection of data without regard to hypotheses. His greatly oversimplified understanding of Baconianism and his "vulgar utilitarianism" were widespread in the United States at the time, and like all other Baconian explicators of the period, March did not ask how empirical knowledge would lead to useful results.[8] His early essay, "The Relation of the Study of Jurisprudence to the Origin and Progress of Baconian Philosophy," made this debt explicit. His greatest philological work, *A Comparative Grammar of the Anglo-Saxon Language: In which its Forms are Illustrated by those of the Sanskrit, Greek, Latin, Gothic, Old Saxon, Old Norse, and Old High Gothic,*[9] was described by one of his students as built of "thousands of interrelated details." In his lectures, March honored Bacon as "the prophet of inductive science," arguing that "we should seek the truth . . . for generation, for fruit, and for comfort."[10] In 1878–1879, March took the junior class, with Cattell in it, through his annual exegesis of Bacon's essays.[11] In later life, Cattell became the kind of Baconian that March was: empirical, inductive, and convinced that science would lead directly to utility.

Formal philosophy was also part of the curriculum. March taught mental philosophy, and the professor of rhetoric taught moral philosophy. Both courses introduced Scottish common-sense realism, deriving from Thomas Reid, which had close ties with Presbyterianism and the goals of the college. In Scotland this philosophy was developed subtly, often in conjunction with a sophisticated understanding of Baconianism.[12] In the United States, however, this faculty psychology had deteriorated by the 1860s into mere scholastic disputation over precise terminologies as, for example, the classification of human desires under the headings of hunger, thirst, and sex.[13] Neither of the two most distinguished textbooks of the period satisfied Cattell: Joseph Haven's *Mental Philosophy* and, for moral philosophy, Mark Hopkins's *An Outline Study of Man.*[14] In March's class, students were required to write essays on such topics as "Is there any such thing as immediate perception?" Cattell's essay began, "I do not know, and I doubt if anyone else knows." Cattell also questioned Hopkins's classification of human desires, and, when informed of Cattell's objections, Hopkins responded: "Young Cattell is sharp, and the President is to be congratulated on having such a son. I agree with the suggestion he makes."[15]

Cattell's dissatisfaction with Scottish realism reflected the feelings of many other young Americans of the period. Cattell had access to the post-Darwinian literature through the excellent libraries that Lafayette and his father had been building since the 1850s. By 1880 he was studying the positivism of Auguste Comte, and his honorary philosophy oration at the commencement that year treated "The Ethics of Positivism." No copy of the talk has been found, but Cattell would have known that Comte stressed the authority of scientific (or positive) thought, and argued that each science should be as mathematical as its practitioners can make it. But Comte knew that not all disciplines could be reduced to mathematical formulation, and he left a major role for empiricism. This emphasis on both quantification and empiricism meshed well with Cattell's Baconianism, though he would add his own experimentalist and utilitarian twist.[16] This scientific ideology formed the basis for Cattell's sixty-year career.

Soon after graduation from Lafayette, Cattell traveled to Europe, toured for a while, and spent the 1880–1881 winter semester at the University of Göttingen, where he heard Hermann Lotze lecture. Lotze impressed him greatly, as he saw in his philosophical system a way of combining the ethical concerns of his father's Presbyterianism with his own belief in the value of scientific forms of thought. He planned to follow Lotze when he accepted a call to Berlin, but Lotze's death and Cattell's family concerns led him to Leipzig, where he heard Wilhem Wundt lecture on psychology. Wundt was clearly his second choice, and he did not impress Cattell at this time. He prepared an essay on Lotze's philosophy, which helped him win a fellowship in philosophy at Johns Hopkins for the 1882–1883 academic year. Returning to the United States, he looked forward to at least a year at America's premier research university.[17]

At Johns Hopkins, Cattell thrived.[18] He had been subject to bouts of depression in Europe, but these dissipated in Baltimore. More importantly, he began to experience nineteenth-century scientific empiricism. In October 1882 he conducted his first experiments in the Johns Hopkins physiological laboratory under the direction of H. Newell Martin, professor of biology. He also began using hashish, morphine, opium, and other psychedelic and narcotic drugs, in part for the sensation and in part out of interest in what they do to the mind. One of the first notations he made under the influence of hashish expressed his commitment to experimental science: "I seemed to be two persons, one of whom could observe and even experiment on the other." In February 1883 he entered G. Stanley Hall's brand new psychological laboratory and soon had some results: he had measured in milliseconds the time it took to recognize the letters of the Latin alphabet for each of nine subjects. This quantitative data was followed by the utilitarian recommendation that the least distinct letters be modified in certain ways to make them easier to read.[19] Despite this work, his fellowship was given to John Dewey in May 1883 for the following year, in part because of Cattell's constant bickering with the university's faculty and administration, and in part because of his competitor's superiority as a philosopher.

Cattell decided to return to Europe to earn a doctorate with Wundt in experimental psychology. He spent almost three full years at the University of Leipzig, from November 1883 through June 1886.[20] He carried out numerous reaction-time experiments, and when he disagreed with Wundt's views he modified the procedures extensively and adopted Sigmund Exner's interpretation of mental chronometry.[21] Contrary to the thrust of most history-of-psychology textbook discussion of Cattell, he showed little interest at this time in individual differences between the two experimental subjects whose reaction times he measured.[22] He directed his effort to the collection of exclusively mathematical data, measuring the reaction times under different conditions of, for instance, attention, practice, and fatigue, without concern for their meaning. Wundt tried to force him to interpret his experiments psychologically; for instance, his doctoral dissertation was appropriately titled "Psychometrische Untersuchungen," whereas he called the report in English "The Time Taken up by Cerebral Operations."[23] He preferred a physicalistic interpretation of his results.

Cattell initially looked to a career in neurology as a means of capitalizing on this early work. Thus from Leipzig he went to St. John's College, Cambridge, to study medicine. However, his father soon arranged for him a lectureship in psychology at the University of Pennsylvania, and he quickly abandoned his medical studies. He matured socially during his time at Cambridge, from October 1886 through December 1887 and from April through December 1888;[24] he became engaged to a young English woman whom he had met while she studied music at Leipzig; and he spent much time making acquaintances among the intellectual aristrocracy.[25] Most importantly, he fell under the direct influence of one of the members of the group, Francis Galton. Although he never studied formally with Galton, the rest of his career reflected in many ways Galton's understanding of science.

Galton's interests were wide-ranging.[26] By the 1860s, he was devoting most of his attention to the study of individual and racial differences. Biological variation was an important basis for the theory of natural selection developed by his cousin, Charles Darwin. Galton's emphasis on the heredity of human traits led him to develop the concept (and ideology) of eugenics, the systematic biological improvement of the human race.[27] In order to collect data about the differences between people, he established his Anthropometric Laboratory at the International Health Exhibition in 1884.[28] After the exhibition closed, he transferred the laboratory to the South Kensington Museum, from which evolved the later Science Museum. At the laboratory, for a fee of three pence, individuals could have a full range of bodily measurements taken, in addition to measures of their abilities to perform certain physical tasks (see Figure 1). His final schema for anthropological measurements in fact included two reaction-time determinations, proof that he had the idea of using reaction times before he met Cattell, although Cattell introduced him to some specific procedures.

Despite the fact that Cattell had read Galton's articles as early as January 1884, Galton apparently made the first contact between the two men.[29] His earliest anthropometric work had concentrated on physical and physiological characteristics, and he soon looked beyond these for a way to investigate psychological differences. For several years he had considered the reaction-time experiment as such a technique.[30] Perhaps Galton found Cattell's name in the literature, or perhaps mutual acquaintances such as Alexander Bain mentioned the young American to him. In any event, by October 1885 the two men had exchanged letters about reaction-time apparatus at the Anthropological Institute.[31]

Despite Galton's use of Cattell's apparatus, he was not greatly influenced by the young American. But his influence on Cattell was unbounded. Cattell later wrote that Galton had been "the greatest man I have ever known", and is reputed to have remarked that his career had been shaped by three men named Francis: Bacon, March, and Galton.[32] Galton provided him with a scientific goal—the measurement of the psychological differences between people—that made use of the experimental procedures he had developed at Leipzig. Cattell could collect quantitative data that might eventually be useful without relying on any systematic view of the mind; curiously, he showed little interest in the statistical foundation of Galton's work, the law of normal distribution.

To be sure, a native American anthropometric tradition had grown out of early nineteenth-century phrenology and craniometry, and in post-Civil War America it had become an important part of the emerging physical-education movement.[33] Despite Cattell's interest in athletics, his acquaintance at Johns Hopkins with Edward M. Hartwell (a leading physical educator who carried out many important anthropometric studies), and the fact that others perceived similarities between their work and his, he appears not to have drawn on this tra-

MR. FRANCIS GALTON'S ANTHROPOMETRIC LABORATORY.

The Laboratory communicates with the Western Gallery containing the Scientific Collections of the South Kensington Museum. Admission to the Gallery is free. It is entered either from Queen's Gate or from Exhibition Road.

Date of Measurement.	Initials.	Birthday Day.	Birthday Month.	Sex.	Single, Married, or Widowed?	Page of Register.
11 Aug't 88	J M K C	25	5 · 6	m	Single	626

Head length, maximum from root of nose.	Head breadth maximum.	Height standing, less heels of shoes.	Span of arms from opposite finger tips.	Weight in ordinary clothing.	Eye Color.	Color Sense.
Inch. Tenths.	Inch. Tenths.	Inch. Tenths.	Inch. Tenths.	lbs.	Grey	? Normal.
7	5 8½	66 7	68 · 9	144		Yes

Length of elbow to finger tip left arm.	Length of middle finger of left hand.	Strength of squeeze. Right hand.	Strength of squeeze. Left hand.	Breathing capacity.	Keenness of Eyesight. Distance of reading diamond numerals. Right eye.	Keenness of Eyesight. Left eye.	Snellen's type read at 20 feet. No. of Type
Inch. Tenths.	Inch. Tenths.	lbs.	lbs.	Cubic inches.	Inches.	Inches.	
21 1	17 7	89	82	238	16	12	218

Height of top of knee, when sitting, less heels.	Height sitting above seat of chair.	Keenness of hearing.	Highest audible note. Vibrations per second.	Reaction time. To sight. Hundredths of a second.	Reaction time. To sound. Hundredths of a second.	Judgment of Eye. Error in dividing a line of 10 inches in half. Per cent.	Judgment of Eye. Error in dividing a line of 10 inches in thris in thris. Per cent.	Error in degrees, estimating an angle of 90°	Error in degrees, estimating an angle of 60°
Inch. Tenths.	Inch. Tenths.	? Normal.							
24 8	34 3	Yes	19,000	30	20	0	3	1	10

One page of the Register is assigned to each person measured, in which his measurements at successive periods are entered in successive lines. No names appear on the Register. The measurements that are entered are those marked with an asterisk (*). Copies of the entries can be obtained through application of the persons measured, or by their representatives, under such conditions and restrictions as may be fixed from time to time.

FIGURE 1. James McKeen Cattell's record at Francis Galton's Anthropometric Laboratory, 1888.

dition.[34] From 1889, when he left England, to the end of the century, Cattell devoted himself to an extension of Galton's anthropometric program into what he called mental testing.

On January 1, 1889, Cattell was appointed to a professorship of psychology at the University of Pennsylvania, which he later erroneously claimed to be the world's first. His father's advocacy and his European scientific pedigree no doubt played a part in this high honor for a 29-year-old. Within a year, he had established a laboratory, begun to train students, and sketched out a research program on "mental tests and measurements," which he later claimed coined the term "mental tests" now in common use.[35] He explicitly ignored the simple measurements of bodily dimensions that had been so much a part of Galton's program; instead, he concentrated on procedures to examine both physiological and psychological characteristics.

Cattell's 1890 program of tests was carried out sporadically on his students at the university and included the following

1. Dynamometer Pressure, or strength of squeeze
2. Rate of Movement
3. Sensation Areas, or the minimum distance between two points at which the skin senses them as two
4. Pressure Causing Pain
5. Least Noticeable Difference in Weight
6. Reaction-Time for Sound
7. Time for Naming Colors
8. Bisection of a 50 cm Line
9. Judgment of a 10 sec time
10. Number of Letters Repeated on One Hearing

In setting forth this series, Cattell established as his goal the measurement of individual differences, or variation among organisms of the same species. As such, his program invoked Galton's Darwinian concerns, and clearly Cattell adopted an evolutionary perspective throughout his work. But in doing so he clearly remained Baconian, arguing the "what the individual variation may be, and what influences may be drawn from it, cannot be foreseen." Galton himself amplified this point in a series of comments, comparing Cattell's testing to "sinking shafts . . . at a few critical points." He admitted that one goal of Cattell's procedures was exploratory, to determine "which of the measures are the most instructive." Cattell also revealed his Baconian belief that utility would follow immediately from knowledge and hinted at a public need for his work when he commented that the tests might be "useful in regard to training, mode of life or indication of disease." [36]

Late nineteenth-century Americans were anxious to know more about themselves and their world. In the social confusion and chaos that followed the Civil War, many engaged in a "search for order" that sought replacements for the traditional sources of authority that had crumbled through the last third of the century. [37] In doing so, throughout the period they looked for cures for the problems exemplified by the millions of immigrants who they believed to be in need of Americanization, seen in the demands of the newly industrialized workplace, discussed by the popular social Darwinists, and often summarized by reference to the delinquent, dependent, and defective classes. In such an atmosphere, people began looking to science for answers as never before, and the implicit promise of Cattell's testing program—vague as it was—received great attention.

Cattell was not alone in sensing a public need that could be tapped by mental testing in the 1890s. By that decade, some scientists working in physical anthropometry began to claim that they could measure "The Physical Basis of Precocity and Dullness," and though others, like anthropologist Franz Boas, disputed their claim, [38] their studies continued throughout the decade. [39] Within the discipline that was just beginning to identify itself as psychology, testing boomed. At Clark University, for example, Edmund C. Sanford extended his colleague Franz Boas's anthropometric studies of schoolchildren. At the University of Nebraska, Harry K. Wolfe, Wundt's second American doctoral student in experimental psychology, urged the adoption of mental tests in the local public schools. Like Cattell, he admitted that he was not sure what he was studying, and he reminded teachers "not [to] be uneasy because the meaning of any peculiarities is obscure." At Yale, another of Wundt's students, Edward Wheeler Scripture, tried out various mental testing procedures and even published a paper on fencing as an indication of mental ability. [40]

Most important in legitimating the new discipline in the public eye was the work of Joseph Jastrow. He had earned a Ph.D. degree with G. Stanley Hall at Johns Hopkins in 1886. He began corresponding with Francis Galton about his anthropometric interest in 1887, and he became professor of psychology at the University of Wisconsin in 1888. By 1890 his concern with mental testing paralleled Cattell's; early in 1892 he published a proposal for "Some Anthropologic and Psychologic Tests on College Students" based almost completely on Galton's program.[41] He also used tests to investigate differences between the sexes, clashing with Mary Whiton Calkins, the distinguished Wellesley psychologist, about the meaning of the differences revealed by his tests.[42]

Under Jastrow's direction in 1893, the two streams of interest in anthropometric mental testing converged at the World's Columbian Exposition in Chicago. At this World's Fair, Frederic Ward Putnam, curator of the Peabody Museum of American Archaeology and Ethnology at Harvard University, planned a Department of Ethnology that was to include a Section of Physical Anthropology under the direction of Franz Boas. Part of Boas's plan was to carry out a program of anthropometric measurements on visitors to the fair, including as many foreign visitors as possible, and on the members of the Indian tribes brought to Chicago for the occasion. Jastrow, Boas, and Putnam saw no reason to limit the program to physical anthropometry and extended it to include mental tests.[43] The result was to be an outgrowth of Galton's Anthropometric Laboratory, and Jastrow wrote to Galton in 1892, asking for suggestions about procedures and apparatus. He even went before the preliminary meeting of the American Psychological Association and asked the cooperation of all the members for the Section of Psychology at the World's Fair and invited correspondence on the matter.[44] Using a schedule of tests that resembled Galton's and Cattell's, Jastrow tested thousands of individuals with the help of the army of graduate student volunteers he had assembled for the occasion.

Despite this flurry of interest in testing that he had in large part set off, Cattell could not devote much time to this work between 1891 and 1894. Around the time he published his "Mental Tests and Measurements" paper, he began to commute to New York from Philadelphia to lecture about one day a week at Columbia College. In 1891 Cattell accepted an appointment at Columbia that forced him to give up his program of testing at Pennsylvania. He devoted the next three years to establishing the psychological laboratory at Columbia, completing two major experimental studies[45] and planning the *Psychological Review*. He did find time to review books on anthropometry for other psychologists, and Cattell's interest in testing led the editor of the *Educational Review* to invite him to write a popular article on the subject for the journal.[46] Teachers facing new educational challenges had heard about Cattell's tests and wanted to learn more about them, hoping the tests could provide significant help and insights.

In January 1893, Cattell wrote to the president of Columbia "concerning the possibility of using tests of the senses and faculties in order to determine the condition and progress of students, the relative value of different courses of study, etc." Beneath his rationale for educational efficiency, he had to admit that he did not have specific tests designed for specific purposes; he compared his program of testing with the work of researchers in electricity fifty years earlier: "They believed that practical applications would be made, but knew that their first duty was to obtain more exact knowledge." He carried this argument to its Baconian conclusion: "The best way to obtain the knowledge we need is to make the tests, and determine from the results what value they have."[47]

It was not, however, until September 1894 that Cattell finally received authorization for the testing program he wanted. He was granted permission to examine every student entering Columbia College and the Columbia School of Mines for the next four years, and in fact he tested students throughout the 1890s and into the twentieth century. Cattell, his junior colleage Livingston Farrand, and all their graduate students were deeply involved in the testing program, which soon began to attract national attention. The scope of their reputation may be appreciated from the diversity of their audiences. Cattell and Farrand described their work in papers presented at meetings of the New York Schoolmasters' Association, the New York Academy of Sciences, the American Psychological Association, and the American Association for the Advancement of Science.[48] The day had yet to come when errors in the Scholastic Aptitude Test were front-page news, but the clipping service to which Cattell subscribed certainly kept busy.

The schedule of tests that Cattell prepared at Columbia was explicitly concerned with both physical and mental measurements, and included all of the tests that he proposed several years earlier at Pennsylvania. He enlarged the series, however, by including various craniometric measurements and tests of pitch perception, and by increasing the number and variety of reaction-time and memory tasks that the subject was asked to perform. For example, the individual being tested was presented with one hundred letters arranged in a 10 × 10 matrix in which ten A's were embedded, and told to strike out the A's as quickly as possible. His first published report on the tests was based on very few results, and Cattell stressed that he did not "wish to draw any definite conclusions" from them, going so far as to characterize them as "mere facts." But being a positivist, he noted that "they are quantitative facts and the basis of science." He concluded with the pragmatic resolution that "there is no scientific problem more important than the study of the development of man, and no practical problem more urgent than the application of our knowledge to guide this development." The questions he hoped to answer were:

> To what extent are the several traits of body, of the senses and of mind interdependent? How far can we predict one thing from our knowledge of another? What can we learn from the tests of elementary traits regarding the higher intellectual and emotional life?[49]

Within a few years, Cattell's testing program provided answers to at least the last two of these questions, but they disappointed him greatly. His testing program brought together a large set of procedures through which he could measure an individual's capacity to perform a number of carefully defined tasks. Like his Pennsylvania program, it was Darwinian in the sense that by determining the way in which individual organisms differed from one another, it measured variation. But in focusing on an essentially random set of operations and behaviors, it missed those capacities required for life in the world and survival, and thus ignored another and perhaps more important aspect of the Darwinian perspective: function. In France, Alfred Binet picked up on Darwin's functional implications in the early twentieth century, as did, significantly, most of the later twentieth-century American testers discussed in other chapters of this book. They could thus do more with their tests than Cattell.

More important, perhaps, is that these other testers all worked through the institutions that had come to dominate American life in the first third of the twentieth century, and through them used their tests to help improve the fit between individuals and these institutions. Cattell, on the other hand, thought his procedures would directly benefit individuals and always wrote of the uses to which the person being examined would put the results of his tests. In many ways, then, he resembled the mid-nineteenth-century phrenologists who tried to change the world by remaking those who lived in it, and whose influence waned as legal action replaced moral suasion as the primary technique of reform. Cattell would have denounced any attempt to classify his work with that of the phrenologists, whom he saw as little more than frauds. But throughout his life he remained a nineteenth-century man in more than his vocabulary.

Interest in anthropometric mental testing in the United States reached a peak in December 1895, when the American Psychological Association, meeting under Cattell's presidency, appointed a committee "to consider the feasibility of cooperation among the various psychological laboratories in the collection of mental and physical characteristics." The committee charged itself to "draw up a series of physical and mental tests which are regarded as especially appropriate for college students."[50] It consisted of Cattell, Jastrow, Sanford, and two other psychologists, James Mark Baldwin of Princeton University and Lightner Witmer of the University of Pennsylvania. Witmer had been Cattell's student at Pennsylvania, and had earned a Ph.D. with Wundt, at Cattell's insistence. He then succeeded Cattell to the chair of psychology at Pennsylvania, and in many ways his approach to psychology was similar to Cattell's.[51] Baldwin, by contrast, was broadly educated in philosophy and, though he had experimented, was not convinced that the laboratory provided the best approach to a full understanding of individuals. Instead, he worked on broader functional questions and in 1895 published his *Mental Development in the Child and the Race.*[52] As such, he was the only member of the committee to come to the problem of testing without a commitment to an anthropometric approach to the study of human differences.

The committee presented a preliminary report in December 1896 and a detailed report in December 1897, and both accounts stressed mental anthropometry as a preferred method. Sanford, for example, wrote that he "approved the Columbia schedule as it stands." Jastrow did recognize that at least three categories of tests could be developed, namely, those of "(a) the senses, (b) the motor capacities, and (c) the more complex mental processes." But he argued that the last category should be ignored and that "it is better to select, even if in part arbitrarily, one part of a certain sense capacity" than a broader, more functional aspect of mental life.[53]

But the report of the committee was not unanimous. Baldwin presented a minority report in which he agreed that tests of the senses and motor abilities were important, but he argued that such essentially physiological tests had received too great a place in a schedule developed by a committee of the American Psychological Association. He asked for additional tests of the higher mental processes and discussed several possible approaches, all more functional than the others suggested, that could be used in testing memory. He concluded by arguing for "giving the tests as psychological a character as possible."[54]

Baldwin's criticisms of the anthropometric tests were the first, but not the last. Some of the critiques took the form of attacks on the assumptions made by the testers. Hugo Münsterberg, for example, director of the psychological laboratory at Harvard, wrote about the "danger" of believing that psychology could ever help educators. More directly, he attacked Scripture's work and the scientific assumptions that underlay much of the test, claiming that "I have never measured a psychical fact, I do not believe that in centuries to come a psychical fact will ever be measured."[55] To be sure, there were other reasons for Münsterberg's attack,[56] and it went beyond the criticisms that most psychologists would make about the testers' procedures. Furthermore, it was not directed at Scripture solely as a tester and, if Baldwin's criticisms were taken seriously, it was not clear that the testers were trying to measure psychological quantities. But to deny that psychological processes were in principle measurable was to undercut Cattell's positivistic assumption that quantifiable data were the only type worthy of scientific attention.

Other critics were to compare Cattell's tests with those then being developed in France by Alfred Binet and his collaborators, which were explicitly concerned with the functional higher mental processes.[57] Cattell knew of Binet—who was a cooperating editor of the *Psychological Review*—and of his work. He even cited Binet's work in his major paper on anthropometric tests. There he noted that he and his coauthor "fully appreciate the arguments urged by . . . M. M. Binet and Henri in favor of making tests of a strictly psychological character," but he stressed that "measurements of the body and of the senses come as completely within our scope as the higher mental processes." They went even further, noting that "if we undertake to study attention or suggestibility"—psychological traits of functional importance—"we find it difficult to measure definitely a definite thing."[58] In other words, Cattell's stress on quantification led him to avoid investigating that which was difficult to quantify and to concentrate on what he could measure. The positivistic Baconianism that formed his scientific ideology therefore led him to avoid what he knew was more important—or at least what his colleagues told him was more important—to focus on that which he could work with easily. He was like the man who lost a quarter one night in the middle of the block, but who looked for it at the corner, because the light was better there.

One psychologist who explicitly compared Cattell's work with Binet's was Stella Emily Sharp, a graduate student of Edward Bradford Titchener at Cornell. In 1898 she published her doctoral dissertation in which she compared the theories of "individual psychology"— the phrase is Binet's—of the American and French testers. In it she stressed that "the American view is founded upon no explicit theory," a conclusion with which Cattell would have agreed entirely, and she presented Binet's view as the belief that "the complex mental processes . . . are those mental characteristics whereby individuals are commonly classed." She did not describe her classification scheme but informally tried out some of Binet's suggested procedures on several of her graduate-student classmates. In doing so, she selected Binet's more functional and less sensory operations and, for example, asked them to remember sentences (rather than Cattell's series of letters) and to describe a picture they had seen sometime before (rather than reproduce the length of a line seen earlier). Her results for some tests seemed to form "a basis of a general classification of the individuals," but she also found that "a lack of correspondences in the individual differences observed in the various tests was quite as noticeable as their presence." She therefore concluded that she had demonstrated the "relative independence of the particular mental activities under investigation" and thus showed the uselessness of Binet's procedures. But she went further. If Binet's tests—with their functional perspective—did not give a good picture of the variations among individuals, then, she argued, "mental anthropometry," which ignored function and lacked any theoretical superstructure, could not yield results of any value either.[59]

Sharp's results are still quoted today,[60] but other events of the late 1890s had more to do with the failure of anthropometric mental testing. At least two were personal. At Yale, Scripture's temperament had led him into conflicts with most of his colleagues, and in the last years of the decade he was too busy fighting for his academic life to continue testing. Jastrow, meanwhile, had given up his struggle to publish the results of his testing program; this effort had led to conflicts with the officials at the Exposition and contributed to his nervous breakdown in the mid-1890s.[61] Scripture's and Jastrow's abandonment of anthropometric mental testing left Cattell and Witmer the only prominent psychologists working in the area, and Witmer's attention was soon focused on narrow applications of tests in his clinical psychology. Cattell was therefore left alone with his tests, which he continued throughout the decade, and by the late 1890s he was able to subject the data he collected to a new form of analysis. And this analysis, carried out by one of his graduate students, led most directly to the failure of his testing program.

Clark Wissler was an 1897 graduate of Indiana University who had come to Columbia as a graduate student primarily to work with Cattell on his anthropometric testing program. At Columbia, he was especially impressed by Franz Boas, the distinguished anthropologist whom Cattell had brought to the university, and soon became interested in the anthropological implications of Cattell's work. He later had an important career as an anthropologist, but his studies with Boas in the late 1890s had a more immediate effect. Cattell was mathematically illiterate—his addition and subtraction were often inaccurate—but Boas, with a Ph.D. in physics, was mathematically sophisticated. Cattell knew that Galton had developed mathematical techniques to measure how closely two sets of data were related, or were correlated, and he made sure that Wissler learned these procedures from Boas. He then had Wissler apply these techniques to the data collected during his decade-long testing program at Columbia.[62]

Wissler calculated the correlation between the results of any one of Cattell's tests and the class grades of the students tested, and between the grades earned in any one class and those earned in any other. His results showed that there was almost no correlation among the results of the various tests. For example, in calculating the correlation between the results of the reaction-time test and the marking-out-A's test, Wissler found that 252 students took both tests, and he measured the correlation between the results of the two tests as -0.05. Consequently, despite the fact that the two tests might appear to be closely related, "an individual with a quick reaction-time [was] no more likely to be quick in marking out the A's than one with a slow reaction-time." Furthermore, Wissler's analysis showed that there was no correlation between the results of any of Cattell's tests and the academic standing of any of the students tested. In contrast, Wissler found that academic performance in most subjects correlated very well with that in other subjects. Even "the gymnasium grade, which [was] based chiefly on faithfulness in attendance, correlated with the average class standing to about the same degree as one course with another."[63] In all, Wissler's analysis struck most psychologists as definitive, and with it, anthropometric mental testing, as a movement, died.

Cattell, of course, abandoned his career as an experimental psychologist, but he continued his activity within the American psychological community. For example, in the 1920s he founded The Psychological Corporation. From about 1900 on, he was better known as an editor and as an entrepreneur of science than he was as a psychologist. In many ways, his later career is more interesting than his earlier one, though as his experience with The Psychological Corporation shows, it may not have been any more successful.[64]

Despite the death of the anthropometric testing movement as such, anthropometric mental testing itself—in many ways the product of a nineteenth-century scientific ideology—continued into the first years of the twentieth century. As Americans sought sources of social authority, they perceived mental testing as too valuable a tool to be completely abandoned, even if anthropometric mental testing appeared to have extreme limitations. On one level, specialized anthropometric tests, designed for specialized uses, proved to be useful. Even one of Titchener's students at Cornell, studying the sense of hearing and techniques for evaluating it, had to admit that they served "practical purposes" when designed carefully. In many ways, the clinical psychology Witmer developed in the late 1890s illustrates the point perfectly. After all, in diagnosing what are today called sensory disorders and learning disabilities, Witmer applied the tests developed by Cattell and others in particularly appropriate ways. Similarly, Scripture's best-known student, Carl E. Seashore, merely developed a set of specialized tests relating to the sense of hearing when he constructed his widely used tests of musical talent.[65] In these ways anthropometric mental tests, which were especially designed to focus on specific sensory problems, played (and continue to play) a major role in bringing order to American society, and especially to American education.

On another level, however, the continued use of anthropometric tests in the early twentieth century was much less successful and set the stage for the tests that followed. Though testing worked when applied narrowly, it yielded essentially useless results when the testers set larger goals. Cattell had continually implied that his tests would prove of great use in education, and though he designed his tests for individual students, teachers for several years followed the results of his work closely. At the same time, Jastrow argued that his own tests demonstrated the proper spheres of activity for each of the sexes. Others used anthropometric tests to justify, and argue for, their own ideas as to the proper relations between the races.[66] More prosaically, though still on a large scale, Frank Parsons in the early 1900s established a vocational guidance bureau in Boston with a goal of helping young men find the profession for which they were best suited. Here he used tests of the "delicacy of touch, nerve, sight and hearing reactions, association time, etc." And as late at 1908, Parsons argued that reaction-time tests had a great value for judging an "individual's probable aptitudes and capacities."[67]

More important for the development of testing was the work of Henry H. Goddard, a Clark University Ph.D., a student of G. Stanley

Hall, and the subject of the next chapter. In 1906, after several years of teaching psychology at a small state college, he became director of the recently founded psychological laboratory at the New Jersey Training School for Feebleminded Boys and Girls at Vineland. There he worked with children who would today be called retarded or developmentally disabled. To obtain some estimate of the children's abilities, he used various anthropometric techniques, more than five years after Wissler's analysis was published. Although he did not find this approach very helpful, he continued to employ it for lack of another. Finally, in the last years of the decade, he traveled to France and there discovered in detail the full range of functional work carried out by Binet and his colleagues. When he brought this knowledge back to America, his English-language version of Binet's tests finally supplanted anthropometric mental testing, at least outside its narrower applications.[68] Thereby, Goddard introduced a new testing movement, which has done much to shape modern America.

NOTES

This essay derives from a paper presented before the History of Science Society in Washington, D.C., in December 1972, and is greatly revised from "James McKeen Cattell and the Failure of Anthropometric Mental Testing, 1890–1901," which appeared in *The Problematic Science: Psychology in Nineteenth-Century Thought*, edited by William R. Woodward and Mitchell G. Ash (New York: Praeger, 1982). It is published here with Praeger's permission and was prepared with the support of grant RH-20616-85 from the Humanities, Science, and Technology Program of the National Endowment for the Humanities, and the assistance of the Reading Room staff of the Manuscript Division of the Library of Congress, Washington, D.C. This version owes much to the example of Raymond E. Fancher, Reese V. Jenkins, James Reed, and Leila Zenderland.

1. On the overwhelming importance of application for the history of American psychology, see John M. O'Donnell, *The Origins of Behaviorism: American Psychology, 1870–1920* (New York: New York University Press, 1985).
2. See C. P. Snow, *The Masters* (New York: Charles Scribner's Sons, 1951), 185.
3. Michael M. Sokal, "*Science* and James McKeen Cattell, 1894 to 1945," *Science* 209 (1980): 43–52.

4. Michael M. Sokal, "The Origins of the Psychological Corporation," *Journal of the History of the Behavioral Sciences* 17 (1981): 54–67.
5. Most of the discussion of Cattell's early education here is paraphrased from the Introduction of Michael M. Sokal, ed., *An Education in Psychology: James McKeen Cattell's Journal and Letters from Germany and England, 1880–1888* (Cambridge, Mass.: MIT Press, 1981), 1–12.
6. David Bishop Skillman, *The Biography of a College: Being a History of the First Century of Lafayette College*, 2 vols. (Easton, Pa.: Lafayette College, 1932). See also Laurence R. Veysey, *The Emergence of the American University* (Chicago: University of Chicago Press, 1965), 21–56.
7. James McKeen Cattell, "The American College," *Science* 26 (1907): 368–373.
8. George H. Daniels, *American Science in the Age of Jackson* (New York: Columbia University Press, 1968); Theodore Dwight Bozeman, *Protestants in an Age of Science: The Baconian Ideal and Antebellum American Religious Thought* (Chapel Hill: University of North Carolina Press, 1977).
9. Francis Andrew March, "The Study of Jurisprudence," *The New Englander* 5 (1848): 543–548; *A Comparative Grammar* (New York: Harper, 1869); James Wilson Bright, "Address in Commemoration of Francis Andrew March, 1825–1911," *Publications of the Modern Language Association* 29 (1914): 1–24.
10. Francis Andrew March, "The Future of Philology," *The Presbyterian Quarterly*, n.s. 33 (1984): 698–714.
11. Seldon J. Coffin, ed., *The Men of Lafayette, 1826–1893: Lafayette College, Its History, Its Men, Their Record* (Easton, Pa.: George W. West, 1891), 63–68.
12. J. C. Robertson, "A Bacon-Facing Generation: Scottish Philosophy in the Early Nineteenth Century," *Journal of the History of Philosophy* 14 (1976): 37–50.
13. Frank M. Albrecht, Jr., "A Reappraisal of Faculty Psychology," *Journal of the History of the Behavioral Sciences* 6 (1970): 36–38.
14. Joseph Haven, *Mental Philosophy: Including the Intellect, Sensibilities and Will* (Boston: Gould and Lincoln, 1857); Mark Hopkins, *An Outline Study of Man: Or the Mind and Body in One System, with Illustrative Diagrams, and a Method for Blackboard Teaching* (New York: Scribner, Armstrong, 1873).
15. James McKeen Cattell, manuscript undergraduate essays, *JMC;* "Extracts from Testimonials of the Faculty of Lafayette College to Accompany the Thesis of James M. Cattell, an Applicant for a Fellowship in Philosophy in Johns Hopkins University, May 1882," *JMC.*
16. See Sokal, *An Education in Psychology*, 16–17.
17. Ibid., 19–46.
18. Ibid., 47–82.
19. James McKeen Cattell, "Über die Zeit der Erkennung und Benennung von Schriftzeichen, Bildern und Farben," *Philosophische Studien* 2 (1885):

635–650; idem, "Über die Tragheit der Netzhaut und des Sehcentrums," *Philosophische Studien* 3 (1886): 94–127.

20. Sokal, *An Education in Psychology,* 83–105, 121–217; idem, "Graduate Study with Wundt: Two Eyewitness Accounts," in *Wundt Studies: A Centennial Collection,* edited by Wolfgang G. Bringmann and Ryan D. Tweney (Toronto: C. J. Hogrefe, 1980), 210–225.
21. Sokal, *An Education in Psychology,* 96–105, 151–152, 156.
22. Ibid., 132–135, 179. See also Franz Samelson, "Cattell: The Beginnings of a Career," *Science* 212 (1981): 777–778.
23. James McKeen Cattell, "Psychometrische Untersuchungen," *Philosophische Studien* 3 (1886): 305–335, 452–492; idem, "The Time Taken up by Cerebral Operations," *Mind* 11 (1886): 220–242, 377–392, 524–538. See also Sokal, *An Education in Psychology,* 202–203, 206.
24. Sokal, *An Education in Psychology,* 218–313.
25. Noel G. Annan, "The Intellectual Aristocracy," in *Studies in Social History: A Tribute to G. M. Trevelyan,* edited by J. H. Plumb (London: Longmans, Green, 1955), 241–287.
26. Raymond E. Fancher is preparing what promises to be an insightful and revealing biography of Galton. Meanwhile, the most complete review of Galton's career is Karl Pearson, *The Life, Letters, and Labours of Francis Galton,* 3 vols. in 4 (Cambridge, Eng.: Cambridge University Press, 1914–1930).
27. Pearson, *Galton,* vol. 1, 70–215; Francis Galton, *Hereditary Genius* (London: Macmillan, 1869); idem, *English Men of Science: Their Nature and Nurture* (London: Macmillan, 1874).
28. Pearson, *Galton,* vol. 2, 357–386; Francis Galton, "The Anthropometric Laboratory," *Fortnightly Review,* n.s. 31 (1882): 332–338; idem, "On the Anthropometric Laboratory of the Late International Health Exhibition," *Journal of the Anthropological Institute* 14 (1885): 205–221; idem, *Inquiries into Human Faculty and Its Development* (London: Macmillan, 1883).
29. Sokal, *An Education in Psychology,* 89–90.
30. Francis Galton, "Notes and Calculations about Reaction Time, 1878–83," unpublished notes, *FG;* see also Galton to John Shaw Billings, November 13, 1884, Billings papers, New York Public Library.
31. Sokal, *An Education in Psychology,* 191–192, 218, 222–223; Francis Galton, "On Recent Designs of Anthropometric Instruments," *Journal of the Anthropological Institute* 16 (1887): 2–11.
32. James McKeen Cattell, "Psychology in America," *Science* 70 (1929): 335–347.
33. See Michael M. Sokal, "Anthropometric Mental Testing in Nineteenth-Century America," unpublished Sigma Xi National Lecture, 1979–1981.
34. Michael M. Sokal, "The Unpublished Autobiography of James McKeen Cattell," *American Psychologist* 26 (1971): 625–635.
35. James McKeen Cattell, "Mental Tests and Measurements," *Mind* 15 (1890): 373–381.
36. Ibid., 373, 379–381.

37. See this volume's Introduction, and Robert H. Wiebe, *The Search for Order* (New York: Hill and Wang, 1967).
38. William T. Porter, "The Physical Basis of Precocity and Dullness," *Transactions of the Academy of Science of St. Louis* 6 (1893): 161–181; Franz Boas, "On Dr. William Townsend Porter's Investigation of the Growth of School Children of St. Louis," *Science* 1 (1895): 225–230.
39. For example, see Arthur MacDonald, "Mental Ability in Relation to Head Circumference, Cephalic Index, Sociological Conditions, Sex, Age, and Nationality," unpublished paper, Arthur MacDonald files, U.S. Office of Education papers, U.S. National Archives, Washington, D.C.; and James B. Gilbert, "Anthropometrics in the U.S. Bureau of Education: The Case of Arthur MacDonald's 'Laboratory,'" *History of Education Quarterly* 17 (1977): 169–195. See also Michael M. Sokal, "Anthropometric Mental Testing in Nineteenth-Century America"; James Allen Young, "Height, Weight, and Health: Anthropometric Study of Human Growth in Nineteenth-Century American Medicine," *Bulletin of the History of Medicine* 53 (1979): 214–243; Elizabeth Lomax, "Late Nineteenth-Century American Growth Studies: Objectives, Methods and Outcomes," paper presented at the Fifteenth International Congress of the History of Science, Edinburgh, Scotland, August 15, 1977.
40. Sokal, "Anthropometric Mental Testing"; Harry K. Wolfe, "Simple Observations and Experiments: Mental Tests and Their Purposes," *North Western Journal of Education* 7 (1896): 36–37; Edward W. Scripture, "Tests of Mental Ability as Exhibited in Fencing," *Studies from the Yale Psychological Laboratory* 2 (1894): 114–119; Michael M. Sokal, "The Psychological Career of Edward Wheeler Scripture," in *Historiography of Modern Psychology: Aims, Resources, Approaches,* edited by Josef Brozek and Ludwig J. Pongratz (Toronto: C. J. Hogrefe, 1980), 255–278.
41. For example, see Joseph Jastrow to Galton, August 19, 1887, *FG;* Joseph Jastrow, "Some Anthropometric and Psychologic Tests on College Students: A Preliminary Survey," *American Journal of Psychology* 4 (1982): 420–428.
42. Joseph Jastrow, "A Study in Mental Statistics," *New Review* 5 (1891): 559–568; Mary Whiton Calkins, "Community of Ideas of Men and Women," *Psychological Review* 3 (1896): 426–430. See also Laurel Furumoto, "Mary Whiton Calkins (1863–1930)," *Psychology of Women Quarterly* 5 (1980): 55–68.
43. World's Columbian Exposition, *Official Catalog, Department M. Ethology: Archaeology, Physical Anthropology, History, Natural History, Isolated and Collective Exhibits* (Chicago: W. B. Conkey, 1893).
44. Jastrow to Galton, July 17, 1892, *FG;* Michael M. Sokal, ed., "APA's First Publication: Proceedings of the American Psychological Association, 1892–1893," *American Psychologist* 28 (1973): 277–292. William Kessen even suggests that psychologists formed their association when they did in large part to provide institutional support for Jastrow's work.
45. James McKeen Cattell and George S. Fullerton, *On the Perception of*

Small Differences, with Special Reference to the Extent, Force and Time of Movement, Publications of the University of Pennsylvania, Philosophical Series, no. 2 (Philadelphia: University of Pennsylvania, 1892); James McKeen Cattell and Charles S. Dolley, "On Reaction-Times and the Velocity of the Nervous Impulse," *Proceedings of the National Academy of Sciences* 7 (1896): 393–415.

46. James McKeen Cattell, "Psychological Literature: Anthropometry," *Psychological Review* 2 (1895): 510–511; idem, "Tests of the Senses and Faculties," *Educational Review* 5 (1893): 257–265.

47. Cattell to Seth Low, January 10, 1893, James McKeen Cattell collection, Columbia University Archives, New York.

48. Sokal, "Anthropometric Mental Testing."

49. James McKeen Cattell and Livingston Farrand, "Physical and Mental Measurements of the Students of Columbia University," *Psychological Review* 3 (1896): 618–648.

50. Edward C. Sanford, "The Philadelphia Meeting of the American Psychological Association," *Science* 3 (1896): 119–121.

51. John O'Donnell, "The Clinical Psychology of Lightner Witmer: A Case Study of Institutional Innovation and Intellectual Change," *Journal of the History of the Behavioral Sciences* 15 (1979): 3–17.

52. James Mark Baldwin, *Mental Development in the Child and the Race: Methods and Processes* (New York: Macmillan, 1895).

53. Sanford to Baldwin, December 7, 1896, *JMC;* James Mark Baldwin, James McKeen Cattell, and Joseph Jastrow, "Physical and Mental Tests," *Psychological Review* 5 (1898): 172–179.

54. Baldwin et al., "Physical and Mental Tests."

55. Hugo Münsterberg, "The Danger from Experimental Psychology," *Atlantic Monthly* 81 (1898): 159–167.

56. Matthew Hale, Jr., *Human Science and Social Order: Hugo Münsterberg and the Origins of Applied Psychology* (Philadelphia: Temple University Press, 1980); Sokal, "The Psychological Career of Edward Wheeler Scripture."

57. Alfred Binet and Victor Henri, "La psychologie individuelle," *L'Année psychologique* 2 (1895): 411–415.

58. Cattell and Farrand, "Physical and Mental Measurements."

59. Stella Emily Sharp, "Individual Psychology: A Study in Psychological Method," *American Journal of Psychology* 10 (1898): 329–391.

60. See Richard J. Herrnstein and Edwin G. Boring, eds., *A Source Book in the History of Psychology* (Cambridge, Mass.: Harvard University Press, 1965), 438–442.

61. Sokal, "The Psychological Career of Edward Wheeler Scripture"; Joseph Jastrow, *A History of Psychology in Autobiography,* vol. 1, edited by Carl Murchison (Worcester, Mass.: Clark University Press, 1930), 135–162. See also correspondence with Frederic Ward Putnam, 1891–1900, Frederic Ward Putnam papers, Harvard University Archives, Cambridge, Mass.

62. Clark Wissler, "The Contribution of James McKeen Cattell to American Anthropology," *Science* 99 (1944): 232–233; James McKeen Cattell, "Memorandum for Miss Helen M. Walker," undated note, *JMC*.
63. Clark Wissler, "The Correlation of Mental and Physical Tests," *Psychological Review Monograph Supplement* 3, no. 6 (1901).
64. Sokal, "The Origins of The Psychological Corporation."
65. Benjamin Richard Andrews, "Auditory Tests," *American Journal of Psychology* 15 (1904): 14–56; O'Donnell, "The Clinical Psychology of Lightner Witmer"; Audrey B. Davis and Uta C. Merzbach, *Early Auditory Studies: Activities in the Psychology Laboratories of American Universities,* Smithsonian Studies in History and Technology, no. 31 (Washington, D.C.: Smithsonian Institution Press, 1975).
66. R. Meade Bache, "Reaction Time with Reference to Race," *Psychological Review* 2 (1895): 475–486; Anna Tolman Smith, "A Study of Race Psychology," *Popular Science Monthly* 50 (1896): 354–360; Arthur MacDonald, "Colored Children—A Psycho-Physical Study," *Journal of the American Medical Association* 32 (1899): 1140–1144. See also Charles S. Johnson and Horace M. Bond, "The Investigation of Racial Differences Prior to 1910," *Journal of Negro History* 3 (1934): 328–339.
67. Frank Parsons, "The Vocation Bureau: First Report to Executive Committee and Trustees, May 1st, 1908," as reprinted in John M. Brewer, *History of Vocational Guidance: Origins and Early Development* (New York: Harper and Brothers, 1942), 303–308.
68. Henry H. Goddard, *The Research Department: What It is, What It is Doing, What It Hopes To Do* (Vineland, N.J.: The Training School, 1914).

3

The Debate over Diagnosis:

Henry Herbert Goddard and the Medical

Acceptance of Intelligence

Testing

In May 1910 the American Association for the Study of the Feeble-minded, the predecessor of the American Association on Mental Deficiency, quietly adopted intelligence testing as its main criterion for diagnosing mental subnormality. Although dominated by physicians, the Association accepted the new measures at the urging of psychologist Henry Herbert Goddard, the first American to appreciate the ideas of Alfred Binet. "It was agreed," these doctors reported, "that the Binet mental tests afforded the most reliable method at present in use for determining the mental status of feeble-minded children."[1]

Their decision marked a stunning victory, not only for Goddard but for applied psychology, for it defined and institutionalized a new diagnostic function for the emerging profession. At the time, few psychologists realized its full import. Lewis Terman soon did. "The view that the diagnosis of mentality is a task for the psychologist," Terman wrote only six years later, "is now so generally accepted that it is hard for us to realize how novel and revolutionary it was a dozen years ago."[2]

In the decades since, the consequences of this revolution have not escaped controversy. Recent scholarship has focused on the debate that ensued concerning the causes of mental subnormality—the

46

"heredity-environment" debate. Goddard's position on this issue is well documented: he became a vocal hereditarian.[3] The older debate, however—the debate over how to diagnose just what it was that one either inherited or acquired—has received much less attention.

Nevertheless, the debate over diagnosis was as significant as the debate over causation. "It cannot be overemphasized," psychologists Seymour Sarason and John Doris have concluded, "that diagnoses give rise to actions, which is but another way of saying that they influence the lives of individuals."[4] In this historical instance, diagnoses influenced not only individuals, but the shape of the psychological profession. In fact, it was through their new roles as diagnosticians that psychologists such as Goddard first reached positions of social power—positions that made their ideas about heredity or environment meaningful.

In order to explain the diagnostic revolution that Goddard initiated in America in 1910, historians need to place the testing movement in a broader context. Intelligence testing forms a controversial chapter not only within the history of psychology and the history of education, but within the social history of medicine as well. In fact, it was American physicians, not educators nor even academic psychologists, who first granted intelligence tests scientific legitimacy.

Within the context of the history of medicine rather than the history of psychology, it is easy to see why it was Henry Herbert Goddard and not mental tester James McKeen Cattell, nor educational psychologist Edward Thorndike, nor even the most prescient of psychological entrepreneurs, G. Stanley Hall, who first saw the significance of Alfred Binet's ideas in 1908, nearly three years after Binet published his first intelligence tests. Goddard, a former schoolteacher who earned his doctorate under Hall in 1899 and taught pedagogy and psychology for the next six years at the Pennsylvania State Normal School at West Chester, was hardly the most intellectually distinguished of the new psychologists. Nonetheless, at the time that Goddard encountered Binet's ideas, he was in an unusual institutional position. Through his involvement with Hall's Child Study movement, he had worked closely with teachers of handicapped children. One of these, Edward Johnstone, superintendent of the New Jersey Training School for Feebleminded Boys and Girls in Vineland, had been especially impressed with the possibilities of a more scientific approach to educational problems. In 1906 Johnstone offered to build Goddard a laboratory on the grounds of his institution if he would begin psychological research into the problems of the "feebleminded"; Goddard accepted and moved to Vineland. By 1908 he had thus spent two years living and working with institutionalized children.[5]

In abandoning academics to accept this new form of psychological employment, Goddard became one of the first Ph.D.'s to devote his full attention to problems of birth defects, brain damage, and learning disabilities that afflicted children like those living at Vineland—the same problems being studied by institutional physicians. His new position brought him into regular contact with the most important medical leaders in the field, including Dr. Walter Fernald of the Waverly institution outside Boston, Dr. A. C. Rogers of the Faribault institution near Minneapolis, and Dr. Martin Barr of the Elwyn institution in suburban Philadelphia, author of the most authoritative American treatise on the subject, *Mental Defectives: Their History, Treatment, and Training.* And so in the years that many of his contemporaries were studying "neurasthenics," those fashionable sufferers from "weak nerves," Goddard dedicated himself to the less glamorous field that called itself "psycho-asthenics," the study of "weak minds."[6]

It was a field with a long popular and a brief scientific history. English common law, for example, had defined this condition as early as the sixteenth century. An "idiote, or a naturall foole" was one who

> notwithstanding he bee of lawful age, yet he is so witlesse that he can not number to twentie, nor can he tell what age he is of, nor knoweth who is his father, or mother, nor is able to answer to any such easie question.[7]

Yet whereas insanity had long captured the medical imagination, idiocy had not. Before the nineteenth century, only a handful of physicians even tried to explain medically the mental conditions long regarded as unalterable consequences of Divine Providence. As one early chronicler recounted, the field's scientific history was a subject for which the "data are scarce, and the study has not many charms." Psychiatrist Leo Kanner, a more contemporary chronicler, confirmed this view in noting that the most complete index of literature relating to psychiatry, neurology, and psychology for the three and a half centuries preceding 1800 records barely a single entry regarding idiocy.[8]

Medical attention to mental deficiency was actually a legacy of the French Enlightenment, when physicians of the Age of Reason accepted the unreasoning mind as a medical problem capable of amelioration and suggested that the state bore responsibility for the humane treatment of even its lowliest subjects. These physicians included Jean Itard, who treated the feral child captured in 1798 known as the Wild Boy of Aveyron, and his student Edouard Seguin, who left France after 1848 and became the intellectual leader of the small American medical community treating idiocy. *"PROGRESS,"* Seguin prophesied, reflecting the new field's empiricism and optimism, *"is in proportion to the thoroughness of observation."*[9]

By the century's end, the creation of large institutions provided physicians with ample opportunity to observe an increasing number of mentally handicapped individuals. Institutional physicians formed their own professional organization, the Association of Medical Officers of American Institutions for Idiotic and Feeble-Minded Persons, in 1876. They met annually, published their proceedings, and began their own professional journal, the *Journal of Psycho-Asthenics,* in 1896.[10]

Yet despite these outward trappings of professional progress, physicians remained confused and frustrated. They could not agree on any of the issues most critical to their field. They floundered over the definition of the condition they were studying. They used different diagnostic criteria, and arrived at inconsistent prognoses. Most frustrating of all, they could not agree on a common classification system. Injunctions to observe thoroughly produced a proliferation of case descriptions; nevertheless, instead of a single system of diagnosis and classification, these descriptions suggested an ever-increasing heterogeneity within the institutionalized population.[11]

According to medical accounts, those living within institutions varied markedly in their physical characteristics, their behavior, and their aptitudes for learning, all of which complicated the question of classification. "To the student of mental defect," Dr. Barr lamented, "the very first requisite is a classification that shall be at once simple and comprehensive, definite and clear." Toward that elusive end, he could only report that "the conditions, incident upon diversity of times and nationalities, as well as the difference of bases constituting premises, has so far prevented the adoption of a standard of comparison resulting in one common order of classification." Instead, Barr's 1904 text cited over a dozen conflicting classification systems.[12]

Perhaps it was their impatience with medical progress, or more positively their curiosity concerning the new ideas emerging from psychology and education, that convinced institutional physicians to open their Association to nonmedical personnel. Whatever their reasoning, in 1906, the Association of Medical Officers changed its name to the American Association for the Study of the Feebleminded, and Goddard became a member. Spending time among physicians, he too came to focus on the problems of diagnosis and classification. "I was early impressed," Goddard later told the doctors, "with the fact that we are not all using the same classification. This results in much confusion."[13]

Goddard also understood, however, the reasons for this confusion, for in significant ways, his institutional position distanced him from academic psychology and made him a part of the medical world. He attended medical meetings and read medical literature. Most important of all, he observed the same patients as physicians. While his psychological contemporaries such as Cattell conducted "mental tests" on Columbia University students, Goddard had a more intractable group of subjects upon which to examine the relationship between mind and body—subjects whose minds and bodies often both seemed seriously misshapen.[14]

Like his medical colleagues, Goddard observed a heterogeneous population with few common traits. Easiest to describe were the children suffering obvious physical as well as mental handicaps. This included about a third of those confined to institutions. Of these, over half were epileptics, while the remainder, in the terminology of the day, were blind, deaf-mute, maimed, crippled, deformed, or paralyzed.[15]

Even children with analogous symptoms, however, often had disparate medical histories. Some had been ill since birth; others, according to parents' accounts, had been healthy children who failed to recover from spinal meningitis, measles, diphtheria, "brain fevers," accidents, or a long list of other traumatic events. For those who still bore forceps marks on their skulls, birth itself seemed harmful. Goddard found twenty Vineland children who gave positive readings on the Wasserman test, indicating that they suffered from congenital syphilis. In fact, by the time a child came to an institution, he often had a complex medical history.[16] "Upton," for example, arrived at Vineland at the age of six with the following history:

> Instruments used at birth; child had convulsions at five weeks; spasms from three years on; measles at six months; meningitis at seventeen months; has had whooping-cough and paralysis.[17]

Physicians could categorize some common physical types. They recognized the "cretins," for example, identifiable by their bodily proportions and growth deficiencies, as well as the "hydrocephalics" and "microcephalics," identifiable by their large or small heads respectively.[18] Some recognized the children with Asiatic eyes that Dr. J. Langdon Down had first described and christened "Mongolians." [19] Many institutionalized children, however, manifested no physical stigmata at all; physicians accordingly described them using other criteria.

Some children could be distinguished by their behavior, even though behavior actually varied as widely as physical appearance. While Goddard described one child brought to Vineland at the age of six as "a cheerful, affectionate little girl, quiet and obedient, very willing, tries, and is making considerable progress," staff members had found another six-year old to be "excitable and nervous, cried and laughed without cause, was gluttonous, destroyed clothing and furniture, was dangerous with fire, not truthful, nor trustworthy; active, obstinate, sly and passionate." How could physicians categorize the boy who enjoyed "stealing even from himself," according to Dr. Barr, since he frequently reported his possessions stolen just to watch the staff search for them? In such children, doctors surmised, the physical senses might be operating, but the "moral sense" was surely damaged. Some children even posed a physical danger to parents, teachers, or physicians. Barr described a child removed from school because he "had a habit of kicking children in the stomach and struck a blow like a sledge-hammer." Others had set homes on fire. Parents brought one child to the Elwyn institution after he shot his younger sister. In such cases, Barr lamented, there was "no moral sense to appeal to." [20]

More puzzling were the children who hurt only themselves. There were, for example, the "rocking" children who frequently beat themselves, such as these institutional cases described in 1898:

> M. W., a girl, 11, rocks constantly back and forth. . . . A different movement . . . is that of F. C., a boy of nine. This boy sits upon the floor or settee with legs crossed Turkish Fashion under him; His arms are crossed and placed in front of the knees. The body is then raised, and the head is brought down like a trip-hammer upon the wrists. The beating is rapid, and if the boy is undisturbed it will continue incessantly for hours.[21]

Goddard saw similar children at Vineland, such as "Mattie," a 10-year-old who "has what seem like insane spells; has pulled out two teeth and pulled out her earrings while in one of them; beats her head; digs herself with her nails, screaming all the time."[22]

Still other children, however, both looked and behaved properly. Nevertheless, they seemed unable to master elementary lessons. Perhaps the most bizarre were "idiot savants"—individuals simultaneously manifesting both idiocy and genius. Seguin, for example, recounted a description of the "historical cook," a man who could both cook and quote entire pages of history, thus offering "an intimate account of the Peloponnesian War, or the history of Tallyrand," but who was in all other ways a "real simpleton, utterly without judgment."[23] Such cases were rare. More common, and more frustrating to institutional personnel, were the children who, despite years of instruction, made no school progress. "Keith," a 16-year-old who had lived at Vineland for six years, was one such case. Goddard described him as "a handsome boy with no marks of his defect on his body; quite active and pleasant spoken, just the kind of boy to tempt any teacher to believe that with a little special training he could be made thoroughly normal; yet every effort put upon him meets with failure." Despite the absence of physical or behavioral abnormalities, Keith had "never been able to do much with his reading, writing and counting" and Goddard found him "one of the most disappointing cases in the whole School."[24]

It is not surprising that institutional physicians were having a hard time classifying cases that in later years would be labeled, among other designations, epileptic, retarded, emotionally disturbed, learning disabled, or autistic. Nevertheless, doctors continued to search for characteristics commonly shared by the institutionalized population. They did not doubt that they were dealing with genuine pathology—pathology somehow connected to feeble "mindedness," or mental weakness. But what exactly did mental weakness mean? Were all these cases variants of a common underlying medical condition? Could mental weakness itself be described? Could it be measured? Most important, could it be consistently diagnosed?

In 1877 the Association of Medical Officers adopted a definition broad enough to cover all contingencies. "Idiocy and imbecility," it stated, are "conditions in which there is a want of natural and harmonious development of the mental, active and moral powers. . . ." They were "usually associated with some visible defect or infirmity of the physical organization, or with functional anomalies. . . ." These could be "expressed in various forms and degrees of disordered vital action"; moreover, there was "frequently defect or absence of one or more of the special senses, always irregular or uncertain volition and dullness or absence of sensibility and perception."[25]

This description did indeed cover all cases. However, while it provided an illusory unity to medical discussions, its vagueness hampered its diagnostic usefulness. Even more significantly, it did not address the crucial question of classification. Administering a residential, educational, and training facility for hundreds of heterogeneous, disabled individuals required physicians to separate their charges into manageable subgroups. Institutionalized children exhibiting different physical, behavioral, and learning characteristics evidently required different amounts of medical care, daily supervision, and educational instruction. Moreover, doctors hoped to be able to distinguish cases that might improve from those that would deteriorate. They longed for a prognostic classification system that would allow them to tell parents what to expect.

By 1908 physicians had yet to find a system that met any, much less all, of these needs. In the absence of consensus, each institution adopted its own system of diagnosing and subdividing its charges. Most called severely impaired cases "idiots," those less impaired "imbeciles," and those only mildly impaired by a variety of other labels.[26] Because there were no common criteria to distinguish between categories, however, a child could be classified as an idiot in one institution and an imbecile in another. Such subjectivity made it especially difficult for institutional specialists to instruct general practitioners on the means of recognizing feeblemindedness in children.

Seguin had realized this problem years earlier. Speaking before the New York Medical Journal Association in 1869, he had tried to summarize "the minimum of *what a general practitioner must know about idiocy.*" Physicians should overlook intellectual deficiencies (for example, lack of comprehension, or incapacity to follow directions), he recommended, unless these were accompanied by apparent physiological disorders. They should watch for a swinging walk, "automatically busy" hands, saliva dripping from a "meaningless mouth," a "lustrous and empty" look, and "limited" or "repetitive" speech. Based on such observations, general practitioners could offer prognoses to anxious parents. They could predict a favorable outcome if the walk was steady, the hand firm, the look "easily called to action," the words connected in meaning, and the child "active without restlessness, is pleased to obey, sensible to eulogy, quite as capable of giving as of receiving caresses." Doctors should offer negative prognoses, however, if serious physiological conditions like epilepsy or paralysis were present, or if parental affection did not bring "corresponding intellectual progress." The "criterion of idiocy," Seguin insisted, "is found more in the physiological than in the psychological symptoms"; nevertheless, his medical admonitions actually conflated physiological and psychological observations. Physicians received no guidance on how to gauge physiologically the meaning of "corresponding intellectual progress."[27]

While general practitioners grew more confused, institutional physicians ironically gained increasing confidence in their own diagnostic abilities, despite their inability to agree on the criteria they were using. By the twentieth century most maintained that, after years of experience with feeblemindedness, they knew it when they saw it. Goddard thus recounted the following incident:

> Dr. Fernald, the famous superintendent of the Inst[itution] for F[eeble]-M[inded] at Waverly a few miles out of Boston, told a group of us that two of his attendants stopped in his office on their return from town, to tell him that a new boy was coming. He asked them how they knew. They replied "We saw him." That is it. They "saw him" and knowing the type, that was enough.[28]

From his own experiences, Goddard soon agreed. Living among nearly four hundred mentally handicapped children, he too came to believe that one could indeed diagnose mental deficiency intuitively.[29] Nevertheless, such subjective, intuitive understandings could not form the foundation for laboratory research, and Goddard soon joined the debate over diagnosis and classification—a debate that had absorbed the energies of institutional doctors for nearly half a century.

In light of the countless systems advocated by physicians, the contours of this debate seem confused and unfocused. Perhaps this is why historians of psychology have paid it so little attention. Nevertheless, by overlooking medical arguments of the day, historians have missed much of what both Binet and Goddard were responding to in their writings. These issues of mental diagnosis and institutional classification deserve closer scrutiny, for in order to understand the "revolutionary" acceptance of intelligence tests, one must know the available alternatives.

Despite their diversity and the absence of a common vocabulary, medical writings of the late nineteenth and early twentieth centuries evidence the emergence of three general approaches toward diagnosing and classifying "feeblemindedness." In order to categorize medical thinking broadly, these can be labeled the pathological, psychiatric, and sociological approaches.

The most important advance in organizing the empirical data acquired by physicians was the pathological classification system developed by Dr. William Ireland in the late nineteenth century. "I found it was necessary to have some arrangement in order to say clearly what I wanted to say," Ireland explained. Since he had "gained some experience in medicine" before becoming chief physician to the Scottish National Institution, he approached idiocy "from the standpoint of pathology." Treating mental handicaps as disease entities like any others, Ireland emphasized somatic causes. By 1877 he had elaborated a classification system based on what he assumed were twelve known causes of idiocy: epilepsy, hydrocephalia, microcephalia, paralysis, inflammation, trauma, cretinism, deprivation, eclampsia, syphilis, sclerosis, and "genetous" or congenital conditions.[30]

While many American physicians lauded Ireland's pathology as a breakthrough, others argued against its adoption. Dr. Isaac Kerlin voiced a common objection: Ireland's categories were not mutually exclusive. "The faultiness of this classification," he noted, "is evident in the facts, that an individual in any single class may be found in two or more of the other classes. . . ." Even more serious were children who fit no class. Ireland had grouped these together in his largest single category, "genetous idiocy," his classification for cases that "cannot be traced back to any known disease" and whose cause was "shrouded in the obscurity of intra-uterine existence. . . ."[31] He hoped to reclassify these cases when more might be known; his contemporaries, however, pointed out the impracticality of classifying by cause when, in the majority of cases, cause could not be determined reliably.[32]

Besides impracticality, physicians raised a more theoretical objection: Ireland's classification failed to distinguish the mental abilities of each type. His system "omits from consideration entirely," Kerlin remarked, "the essential features of idiocy—the mental deficiency. There is nothing in the mental incompetency of a hydrocephalic idiot, or a paralytic idiot, that is peculiar, one from the other."[33] Dr. Hervey Wilbur of the State Institution of New York at Syracuse was equally critical. Such systems, he claimed, "regard the mental manifestations as mere symptoms of abnormal and pathological physical condition. . . ." Before adopting it, Wilbur insisted that its proponents prove first that there was "a measurably constant relation (of cause and effect) between certain physiological and pathological conditions and corresponding manifestations of defective intelligence, sensibility, and will," and secondly, that such conditions could be "detected, located, measured, and clearly defined."[34]

Physicians emphasizing the mental rather than the physical handicaps of their patients often looked instead to the examples of their colleagues classifying insanity. Although most psychiatrists were only peripherally interested in idiocy, a few had defined and classified the condition to distinguish amentia, the "absence of mind," from dementia, the "loss of mind." Idiocy is not a disease, the French psychiatrist Jean Esquirol had maintained, but a condition in which the intellectual faculties "have never developed sufficiently for the idiot to acquire the knowledge which other individuals of his age receive when placed in the same environment." "The insane man," he explained, ". . . is a rich man become poor; the idiot has always been in misery." Classifiers, these psychiatrists argued, ought to be less concerned with cause than with degree of such impoverishment. In one brief but suggestive paragraph, Esquirol proposed classifying idiots and imbeciles into five groups based on their language skills.[35]

The idea intrigued Wilbur. "Even the number of words used," he maintained, ". . . is a tolerably fair test of the intelligence of a people, or an individual, under the same or similar conditions of life." Expanding Esquirol's five categories into eight and omitting only the deaf-mutes, in 1878 he classified 225 cases in his institution by language abilities. His classes ranged from those who neither spoke nor comprehended language to those with a "fair command of language."[36]

Wilbur's classification system, however, also had its shortcomings. With no "specific distinctions to stand as metes and bounds between the different categories," his classes "shade into each other," he conceded. Moreover, he was proposing that physicians adopt a "strictly mental test." Nevertheless, his system attempted to parallel, he maintained, the "growth of intelligence from infancy to manhood."[37]

Other psychiatrists, while agreeing with the need to classify cases by degree rather than cause, were less impressed with systems based on language. "The parrot can be taught to articulate," Daniel Hack Tuke concluded, "but in intelligence is far below the elephant, which cannot." Reflexes, Tuke suggested, were more reliable indicators of mental impairment than speech. He proposed a classification system based upon the quality of motor control. The lowest group were those exhibiting "nothing beyond the reflex movements known as the excito-motor." Those in the second group were capable of "consensual or sensori-motor" reflexes, including "those of an ideo-motor and emotional character." The highest group included "those who manifest volition—whose ideas produce some intellectual operations and consequent will." Tuke's psychiatric ideas sound closest to the psychophysical assumptions of nineteenth-century academic psychologists.[38]

By the first decade of the twentieth century a third approach toward classification was gaining medical acceptance. The new theory broadened the concept of "education" to incorporate a range of social and vocational skills. Of course, "education" for feebleminded children throughout the nineteenth century usually meant something more than intellectual pursuits. Seguin's theories of "physiological education," for example, stressed manual dexterity and sensory training. The newer theories, however, widened "education" even further to encompass the individual's ability to function socially in the outside world. Thus, in his 1904 text, Barr proposed an "Educational Classification" system conflating intellectual, vocational, and social skills. The lowest of his four educational groups included those who would need perpetual asylum care, while the highest group could be "trained for a place in the world." [39]

The introduction of sociological criteria into medical systems was even more apparent in the classification adopted by the Royal College of Physicians in London in 1908. In starkly Spencerian language, British doctors defined mental deficiency in terms of fitness for surviving. Idiots, the lowest group, were those "so deeply defective . . . as to be unable to guard themselves against common physical dangers." The imbecile was "incapable of earning his own living, but is capable of guarding himself against common physical dangers." The highest grade was "capable of earning a living under favorable circumstances, but is incapable . . . of competing on equal terms with his normal fellows . . . or managing himself and his affairs with ordinary prudence." [40] While the British medical establishment had reached consensus by adopting the language of evolutionary sociology, however, American physicians remained divided. At their meetings and in their writings, they continued to debate the merits and shortcomings of systems stressing pathological causes, mental assessments, or social educability.

This was the confusing situation that Goddard inherited when he began his "psychological work among the feebleminded." But would psychological methods be any more successful than those of pathologists, psychiatrists, or sociologists in developing a common system for classifying the heterogeneous feebleminded population? After two years of laboratory work, Goddard's answer seemed to be no, for he soon faced the same problems that had undermined the work of his medical predecessors.

Of the approaches then available, Goddard's psychological training oriented him most closely toward psychiatry. In fact, he greatly admired the work of Adolf Meyer, the psychiatrist whom he had met as a student at Clark University. "I shall never forget the impression made upon me," he told physicians, "when Dr. Adolf Meyer took us into this laboratory at Worcester and taking a brain from a jar said, 'this is the brain of the patient you saw last spring. You recall the symptoms. We shall now examine this, and probably shall find such and such conditions'—describing very minutely hemorrhage, degenerate fibres and cells. His prediction was verified at every point!"[41]

Goddard, too, hoped to correlate brain and behavior; such correlations, however, were impossible without a precise language to describe the actions of "feeble" minds. In this regard, he concurred with Cattell's student, Shepard Franz, another psychologist working closely with physicians. "From a psychological standpoint," Franz argued, "what is lacking in all the accounts is a careful analysis of the mental condition." Franz attacked the imprecision of medical descriptions. "Apathetic, dull, stolid, irritable, restless, nervous, deficient memory, slow comprehension," he argued, "are general terms for conditions which for scientific purposes and in the present state of psychology, the observer could and should try to describe more carefully."[42]

Goddard's notes from his first year at Vineland show him trying to do just that. Within a week of his arrival, he began buying and building the psychophysical equipment commonly found in university laboratories—equipment with which to measure correlations between motor and mental abilities. "Worked on ergograph," he noted in his journal. "As soon as I get an electro-magnet shall have the ergograph complete[;] also apparatus for testing the rapidity of tapping. This is used to test will power."[43]

Yet psychophysical examinations proved difficult to administer to children suffering from both physical and mental handicaps. He described one attempt to test a child on the automatograph, a machine designed to measure involuntary motions. "He would not try to hold it still," Goddard noted.

> I explained and illustrated, held his hand, and threatened him when he moved. No use. He could not be made to do it. I put my hand on his and held it still for five long minutes. At last a gleam came into his eyes. I removed my hand and he held his still for a minute, making a good tracing. He had at last comprehended what was wanted, found he could do it, and immediately rose in my estimation and in his own.[44]

While Goddard could overcome these problems in test administration, he had more difficulty assessing the meaning of his results.

The problem is apparent in his Vineland notes. "Put him through all the tests," he recorded about one child. "He did them well and in the absence of standards cannot attach any significance. My *impression* is he ranks rather high." [45] Undermining his attempts to describe subnormal mental development was the absence of a commonly accepted language to describe *normal* mental development in children. Without such a language, neither the degree of "feebleness" nor the amount of individual progress could be measured.

This problem had been apparent even to Seguin. It was "paramount," he had warned, that "any investigation made on idiocy upon idiots be conducted . . . upon normal subjects with the strictest similarity . . . everywhere, near the abnormal, the normal; next to the shadow, the light." [46] Seguin had hoped that physicians would soon be able to time mental responses. "The improvement in these processes is capable of positive measurement," he explained.

> since, at the beginning an idiot requires several seconds to transmit an impression from without within, or a volition or order from within without, whereas the normal time for these operations is only 1/25th of a second for the former operation, and 1/28th for the latter. Thus the progress of sensation, perception, volition, and even self-control, may become susceptible of mathematical measurement. [47]

Dr. Hervey Wilbur had hoped for similar measurements. "Do we not need some mile-posts along the educational path to the same end?" he had inquired of his colleagues in 1877. What he wanted were "some generally recognized tests of physical and mental condition" to show "the starting-point in the pupil's career, to which reference can be made from time to time to test their absolute or relative progress. . . ." [48]

By 1908, however, no such "mile-posts" existed, and Goddard was no closer than his predecessors to developing any. Even when he did standardize some of his tests, such as needle threading or line drawing, the results failed to match the best evidence available for determining the mental status of institutionalized children—the staff's intuitive assessments based on years of living with them. [49]

Searching for new ideas, Goddard toured Europe in the spring of 1908, visiting nineteen institutions and ninety-three special classes for the feebleminded in eight countries. Through his Child Study contacts in Belgium, he first came across the "intelligence tests" developed by French psychologist Alfred Binet and his assistant Theodore Simon three years earlier. Beginning with Binet's 1905 article entitled, "Upon the Necessity of Establishing a Scientific Diagnosis of Inferior States of Intelligence," Goddard finally found his answer to a fundamental institutional problem.[50]

To Goddard this discovery was merely serendipitous. Nevertheless, two years studying institutionalized children had undoubtedly put him in a position to appreciate and understand what others aware of Binet's work (like Cattell) had not seen.[51] In fact, while Henry Herbert Goddard can in no sense be compared to Alfred Binet in terms of either intellectual power or originality of ideas, by 1908 the careers of these two psychologists did exhibit some striking parallels.

For different reasons, both Goddard and Binet had become alienated from academic psychology—Goddard because he had abandoned his teaching position, and Binet because he had been unable to secure a university appointment in France. More significantly, Binet, like Goddard, had spent several years actively involved with the European equivalent of Hall's Child Study movement. While Goddard had presided over the Pennsylvania Child Study Association, Binet had been president of La Société libre pour l'étude psychologique de l'enfant. In these contexts, both men had worked closely with teachers of the handicapped. Most important of all, Binet was no stranger to medical ideas. He descended from a distinguished family of physicians and had himself begun and then abandoned the study of medicine. In addition, his co-author, Theodore Simon, was a physician who had interned at an institution for mental defectives at Perray-Vaucluse, thus giving Binet access to a patient population analogous to Goddard's at Vineland.[52]

Although Binet designed his "tests of intelligence" for a Paris education commission interested in establishing admission standards for special classes, his articles suggest he had a medical audience in mind as well. Before presenting his own classification system, he reviewed systems advocated by Seguin, Esquirol, Ireland, and many other physicians. In fact, Binet's articles actually contain a blistering attack on medical authorities. One had to guard, he warned, "against intuition, subjectivism, gross empiricism, decorated by the name of medical tact, and behind which ignorance, carelessness, and presumption, hide themselves."[53]

Binet mocked the writings of his medical contemporaries such as Dr. P. Bourneville, the most prominent French physician treating the feebleminded, who had distinguished a "fugitive" from a "fleeting" attention in separating idiots from imbeciles. "The vagueness of their formulas reveals the vagueness of their ideas," he noted contemptuously. "They cling to characteristics which are by 'more or less,' and they permit themselves to be guided by a subjective impression which they do not seem to think necessary to analyze. . . ."[54]

Physicians, Binet bluntly suggested, did not know what they were talking about. "[T]hey deceive themselves who think that at bottom this is only a question of terminology," he insisted in criticizing medical confusion. "It is very much more serious." Going further, he emphatically dismissed both pathological and psychiatric criteria. If a child is diagnosed as an idiot, he argued, "it is not because the child does not walk, nor talk, has no control over secretions, is microcephalic, has the ears badly formed, or the palate keeled." By stressing such criteria, doctors had missed the point.

> The child is judged to be an idiot because he is affected in his intellectual development. This is so strikingly true that if we suppose a case presented to us where speech, locomotion, prehension were all nil, but which gave evidence of an intact intelligence, no one would consider that patient an idiot.[55]

Mental deficiency, Binet concluded, must be classified by purely psychological criteria—criteria that assessed only comparative intellectual development. Moreover, such criteria must be measurable, for differences in degree, he insisted, are of no value unless they can be measured, even if measured only crudely. What had to be measured, however, was something more than motor or language skills.

Although Binet's tests were eclectic, the majority assessed judgment skills. Such skills could be quantified, he demonstrated, not by counting seconds or centimeters but by counting the number of correct answers to a series of questions of increasing degrees of difficulty—questions designed to be graded with as little subjectivity as possible. Binet's real breakthrough came in 1908, when he added the idea of establishing numerical norms for every level of a child's mental growth, based on samples of children's responses. By comparing an individual child's test results with norms established for children of his age, one could determine the child's relative "mental level." [56] Ironically, by emphasizing intellectual capacity over physiology or pathology, Binet had brought the definition of idiocy full circle: his psychological definition harkened back to the common-law conception, for once again, an idiot was one who, age notwithstanding, could not answer easy questions.

Returning from Europe, Goddard translated and administered Binet's questions to the Vineland children. To his surprise, he found that the mental levels ascribed to the children by the Binet scale correlated well with the staff's intuitive assessments. "It met our needs," he stated simply. "A classification of our children based on the Scale agreed with the Institution experience." Thereafer, he quickly became a convert to Binet's new psychological method of diagnosing mental deficiency. [57]

By 1909 Goddard was ready to present Binet's ideas to American physicians. Using less provocative language, he too challenged medical methods. First, he attacked the pathology of his day. "We have our medical classification such as microcephalic, hydrocephalic, Mongolian, etc.," he remarked, but "what is the value of this classification? How closely can we classify? . . . How small must a head be before it is microcephalic? It is a convenient way to shelve these cases, perhaps, but does it help us in our dealing with them? Is a microcephalic defective limited definitely in his powers?" Goddard then criticized sociological systems. Barr's "educational classification," he noted, while valuable, was "of no use until we have had the child in the institution long enough to find out how trainable he is." Doctors needed a faster means of diagnosis. [58]

Abandoning psychiatric models stressing reflexes, however, proved more difficult. Admitting that psychophysical tests had been unsuccessful would have posed problems, since such tests provided the rationale for the existence of Goddard's psychological laboratory, with its expensive equipment. Even after he began using Binet's tests, Goddard still hoped that psychophysical measurements might prove useful indicators of mental abilities. "I have a feeling," he told the Association in 1909, "that motor control—how the child handles its muscles—may be ultimately a stronger basis of classification than the mental process,—the more purely psychological." After all, he explained, psychologists no longer considered mind an entity in itself; instead it was the sum of processes, including movements that "we certainly can and do measure."[59] Nevertheless, recognizing the superiority of Binet's approach, he informed physicians that Binet had developed a "tentative set of mental tests which might serve as a basis for classification."[60]

In the discussion that followed, physicians too expressed their dissatisfaction with available medical methods and their interest in psychological alternatives. "In connection with the so-called pathological classification," one physician remarked, "I think we have no right to consider it of any worth at present."[61]

> Here is a case of microcephalis or hydrocephalis—what does it mean? I do not consider these terms indicative of any definite pathological condition; they refer to size. Mongolian does not mean anything definite pathologically, it does not suggest any underlying condition. We have no intelligent pathological classification at present.[62]

The discussion ended with a call for consensus. "It seems to me we ought to get together," one doctor remarked, "the institutions, anyhow—and have a basis of classification." Toward this goal, the Association designated a Committee on Classification to study all available methods. Goddard was made a member.[63]

The committee got off to a sluggish start. "I beg to call attention," Chairman Fernald wrote members less than a month before their report was due, "that we are on a committee on classification." Fernald recommended that the committee avoid pathology in favor of a system "based entirely upon the degree of intelligence present. . . ." Classes should be "so descriptive that they are obvious and intelligible to the well-educated general practitioner who studies the scheme." "The non-institution man," he went on, "has never been able to gather from textbooks or the literature of the subject the fact that . . . pathological types may present any degree of mental defect. . . ."[64]

Most members responded vaguely; Goddard, however, now had his own agenda. "I have felt just exactly as you express it in regard to classification for sometime," he tactfully reported to his physician colleague, "but I feared that I was a heretic and that no one would agree with me." He told Fernald that since trying Binet's tests, he had been "constantly amazed" at the agreement between "the mental age of these children as shown by these tests and what we know of them from experience." At least temporarily, he suggested, the Association ought to consider using Binet testing, a purely psychological criterion, to diagnose and classify mental subnormality. "The difficulty now," he concluded, "is that we are hardly any two of us agreed. The old classifications . . . are so illogical, based as they almost all are on more than one basis of classification, and consequently leading to confusion throughout." [65]

The classification committee took no action. In fact, Goddard was the only committee member who even attended the Association's 1910 meeting. Since no report had been submitted, Goddard was invited to speak for his committee. He decided to present his own classification system based on Binet testing "and let the Association decide." [66]

By 1910, however, Goddard was certainly not a "heretic," for there were now several psychologists working in institutions who had tried Binet's tests and found them useful. [67] Goddard presented the strongest evidence himself. His paper on "Four Hundred Feebleminded Children Classified by the Binet Method" showed how institutions could adopt a precise language to describe and classify all their cases. "I believe it is true," he reported, "that no one can use the tests on any fair number of children without becoming convinced that whatever defects or faults they may have, and no one can claim that they are perfect, the tests do come amazingly near what we feel to be the truth in regard to the mental status of any child tested." [68]

The following day, the Association unanimously adopted Goddard's "New Classification (Tentative) of the Feeble-Minded," along with his recommendation that mental subnormality be diagnosed by Binet-Simon tests. An idiot was now defined as one testing between 0 and 2 years of mental age on the Binet scale; an imbecile as one testing between 3 and 7; and a "moron," Goddard's new term for the highest group, as one testing between 8 and 12. [69] The concept of "mental age," moreover, appealed to physicians, for it objectified their intuitive understanding of the differences between normal and subnormal child development. "Who is there that does not have a mental picture, always in view, of the activities and capacities of normal children at different ages?" the Association's journal noted in explaining the new system. "What is more natural and rational than to compare the mind, backward in development, with a normal one?" Pathological terms, such as hydrocephalic, paralytic, or Mongolian, would still be used as descriptive adjectives (for example, Mongolian imbecile). "As to the matter of emphasizing a psychological basis for classification rather than a pathological one," the journal noted, "we can see no serious objection to it if thereby we can secure a means of determining quickly even an approximate estimate of the child's mental ability by some system . . . that presents to all . . . the same mental picture to be referred to a common mental standard." [70] For the first time, American institutional physicians shared a common diagnostic vocabulary.

Goddard's success in establishing a classification system for American physicians based on Binet testing received little attention, both in his day and in ours. Nevertheless, this quiet victory for applied psychology helped shape professional behavior for at least a decade. Not only did medical acceptance legitimate intelligence testing scientifically, but, of equal importance, medicine provided psychologists like Goddard with a new model of social intervention. In fact, in an era when physicians were expanding their profession's social powers, intelligence testers often followed their wake.

Goddard's attempts to place psychological testers in schools, for example, were modeled after the school doctor and school nurse movements; after physicians tested eyes and ears, psychologists would diagnose equivalent mental defects. A far more dubious example of this medical logic was Goddard's short-lived attempt to place psychological testers on Ellis Island. Despite the fact that Binet-Simon testing was useless on millions of non-English-speaking immigrants, the rationale for such intervention again suggested that psychological inspection paralleled medical inspection. Even the most famous episode in early testing history, the mass examination of nearly two million World War I army recruits, was initially justified as a health measure designed to diagnose the mentally unsound. [71] Medicine, moreover, supplied many of the metaphors of the early intelligence-testing movement. Goddard spoke not only of diagnosis but also of prevention, treatment, and hygiene. [72]

Of course, the working relationship between physicians and psychologists did not remain for long as friendly as it appeared to be in 1910. The debate over diagnosis and classification soon resumed, with psychological criteria raising as many questions as they settled. Moreover, the increasing popularity of testing quickly exacerbated a bitter professional rivalry. World War I psychological testers were not included in the Medical Corps; instead they were relegated to the less prestigious Sanitary Corps. Nevertheless, testing retained its medical affiliation, for while other psychologists serving the war effort reported to the Adjutant General, intelligence testers reported to the Surgeon General.[73]

Perhaps the most serious effects of this rapid medical acceptance were more subtle. The institutional usefulness of intelligence testing sustained Goddard's confidence in his methods and allowed him to ignore critics from psychological and educational circles. Criticisms that did "from time to time appear," he calmly announced in 1914, a year in which psychological and educational battles were already raging, "only arouse a smile and a feeling akin to that which the physician would have for one who might launch a tirade against the value of the clinical thermometer."[74]

Yet if historians ever since have wondered why the early tests gained such sudden support, physicians at the time had their own answer. "If it had been easy to advise a classification of general application," an editorial in the *Journal of Psycho-Asthenics* stated, "it would have been done long ago. . . ." Many students "familiar with medical and pathological studies" with "plenty of material on which to work" had tried to solve the problem, and had failed.[75] Psychologists, it seemed in 1910, had succeeded.

NOTES

This article could not have been written without access to the resources of the College of Physicians of Philadelphia and the Archives of the History of American Psychology in Akron, and I am indebted to the staffs of both institutions. In addition, John Popplestone and Marion White McPherson, directors of the Archives, have consistently offered me their insights, guidance, and support. I also want to thank Charles Rosenberg, Wayne Hobson, Karen Lystra, Deborah Forczek, and above all Richard Flaten for their helpful readings and criticisms of this essay.

1. "Report of Committee on Classification of Feeble-Minded," *Journal of Psycho-Asthenics* 15 (1910–1911): 61.
2. Lewis Terman, "Review of the Vineland Translation of Articles by Binet and Simon," *Journal of Delinquency* 1 (November 1916): 258.
3. On Goddard's hereditarian ideas, see, for example, Nicholas Pastore, *The Nature-Nurture Controversy* (New York: Columbia University Press, 1949), 77–84; Mark H. Haller, *Eugenics: Hereditarian Attitudes in American Thought* (New Brunswick, N.J.: Rutgers University Press, 1963), 95–123; Leon J. Kamin, *The Science and Politics of IQ* (Potomac, Md.: Erlbaum, 1974), 5–13; Hamilton Cravens, *The Triumph of Evolution: American Scientists and the Heredity-Environment Controversy, 1900–1941* (Philadelphia: University of Pennsylvania Press, 1978), 48–49, 81–84, 242–245; Stephen Jay Gould, *The Mismeasure of Man* (New York: Norton, 1981), 158–174; Raymond E. Fancher, *The Intelligence Men: Makers of the IQ Controversy* (New York: Norton, 1985), 105–116; J. David Smith, *Minds Made Feeble: The Myth and Legacy of the Kallikaks* (Rockville, Md.: Aspen Systems, 1985).
4. Seymour Sarason and John Doris, *Psychological Problems in Mental Deficiency* (New York: Harper and Row, 1969), 27.
5. For the founding of the Vineland laboratory, see Edward Johnstone, "The Institution as a Laboratory," in *Twenty-Five Years: A Memorial Volume in Commemoration of the Twenty-Fifth Anniversary of the Vineland Laboratory, 1906–1931*, edited by Edgar Doll (Vineland, N.J.: The Training School, 1932), 3–15. For a description of Goddard and other psychologists working in new laboratory environments, see John A. Popplestone and Marion White McPherson, "Pioneer Psychology Laboratories in Clinical Settings," in *Explorations in the History of Psychology in the United States,* edited by Josef Brozek (Lewisburg, Pa.: Bucknell University Press, 1984), 196–272.
6. Institutional physicians invented the term "psychoasthenics," probably to parallel "neurasthenics," since there was at the time "no universal, or even very general use that implies a knowledge of that condition which is termed idiocy or feeble-mindedness. . . ." See "Announcement," *Journal of Psycho-Asthenics* 1 (1896–1897): 34.
7. Henry Swinburne, *A briefe treatise of testaments and last willes* . . . (London: John Windet, 1590), vol. 2, 39, as cited in Albert Deutsch, *The Mentally Ill in America: A History of Their Care and Treatment from Colonial Times* (New York: Columbia University Press, 1937, 1949), 333.
8. P. M. Duncan and W. Millard, *A Manual for the Classification, Training, and Education of the Feeble-Minded, Imbecile, and Idiotic* (London: Longmans, Green, and Co., 1866), viii, as cited in Leo Kanner, *A History of the Care and Study of the Mentally Retarded* (Springfield, Ill.: Charles C. Thomas, 1964, 1974), vii. The index to which Kanner referred is Heinrich Laehr, *Die Literatur der Psychiatrie, Neurologie und Psychologie von 1459 bis 1799* (Berlin: Georg Reimer, 1899). Kanner states that in

"this magnificent collection, which comprises two huge volumes and a separate index of authors and subjects, there is among the many thousands of recorded and sometimes annotated items not one, however faint, allusion to mental deficiency, except for the evidence of sporadic interest in cretinism toward the end of the Middle Ages." Kanner, *Care and Study,* 7–8.

9. See Kanner, *Care and Study,* 9–44; Edouard Seguin, *Idiocy, and Its Treatment by the Physiological Method* (New York: Wood, 1866), 457 (emphasis in original).

10. For the history of the Association of Medical Officers, which became the American Association for the Study of the Feeble-Minded in 1906 and the American Association on Mental Deficiency in 1933, see G. E. Milligan, "History of the American Association on Mental Deficiency," *American Journal of Mental Deficiency* 66 (1961–1962): 357–369; see also Kanner, *Care and Study,* 78–82. For a more complete discussion of the social history of American institutions, see Peter Tyor, "Segregation or Surgery: The Mentally Retarded in America, 1850–1920" (Ph.D. diss., Northwestern University, 1972).

11. Edouard Seguin collected sixty-five case descriptions from his own records in France and America as well as from published sources in his appendix to *Idiocy,* although later reprinted editions dropped the appendix. Isaac Kerlin described twenty-two cases in *The Mind Unveiled* (Philadelphia: Hunt, 1858). Many other case descriptions can be found in William Ireland, *On Idiocy and Imbecility* (London: Churchill, 1877); J. Langdon Down, *On Some of the Mental Affections of Childhood and Youth* (London: Churchill, 1887); Martin Barr, *Mental Defectives: Their History, Treatment, and Training* (Philadelphia: Blakiston, 1904); and in medical articles of the period. Goddard described over three hundred Vineland cases in *Feeble-Mindedness: Its Causes and Consequences* (New York: Macmillan, 1914).

12. Martin Barr, *Mental Defectives: Their History, Treatment, and Training,* 78–90; quotation on p. 78.

13. Henry H. Goddard, "Suggestions for a Prognostical Classification of Mental Defectives," *Journal of Psycho-Asthenics* 14 (1909–1910): 48.

14. Cattell's tests were tried out on Columbia students, while Joseph Jastrow tested visitors to the Columbian Exposition in Chicago in 1893. See Michael M. Sokal, "James McKeen Cattell and Mental Anthropometry: Nineteenth-Century Science and Reform and the Origins of Psychological Testing," chapter 2 of this volume.

15. Department of Commerce and Labor, *Bureau of the Census Special Reports: Insane and Feeble-Minded in Hospitals and Institutions, 1904* (Washington, D.C.: Government Printing Office, 1906), 212.

16. For a discussion of parental reports of the causes of feeblemindedness, see Frederick Wines, "Report on the Defective, Dependent, and Delinquent Classes of the Population of the United States, as returned at the

Tenth Census (June 1880)," in *House Miscellaneous Documents,* 47th Cong., 2d sess. (1882–1883), 13, pt. 21: 240–241. The cases of syphilis are cited in Goddard, *Feeble-Mindedness,* 518–521.

17. Goddard describes "Upton" in *Feeble-Mindedness,* 271.
18. Kanner cites the specific conditions that were beginning to be recognized before 1900, including tuberosclerosis and amaurotic family idiocy (Tay-Sachs disease), in *Care and Study,* 87–109.
19. Down's description of "Mongolians" is part of his larger "physiognomical" or "ethnological" classification system. He also suggested that one would find Ethiopians, Malays, Americans (native Americans) and Caucasians; however, most superintendents only reported seeing the Mongolians. This condition is now called Down's Syndrome. J. Langdon Down, "Observations on an Ethnic Classification of Idiots," *London Clinical Lectures and Hospital Reports* 3 (1866): 259–262.
20. The Vineland cases are described in Goddard, *Feeble-Mindedness,* 428, 52. For these and other "moral imbeciles," see Barr, *Mental Defectives,* 264–281.
21. G. E. Johnson, "Contribution to the Psychology and Pedagogy of Feeble-Minded Children," *Journal of Psycho-Asthenics* 2 (1897–1898): 70–71.
22. Goddard, *Feeble-Mindedness,* 385–386.
23. The "historical cook" is first cited by Dr. Sidney in the *Edinburgh Review* (July 1865) and collected by Seguin in the appendix to *Idiocy,* 444.
24. Goddard, *Feeble-Mindedness,* 124.
25. Isaac Kerlin, "The Organization of Establishments for the Idiotic and Imbecile Classes," *Proceedings of the Association of Medical Officers of American Institutions for Idiotic and Feeble-Minded Persons* (1877), 20.
26. Among the names suggested for the mildly impaired were fools or simpletons, the "backwards," the "almosts," the "morally imbecile," the "moral paranoids," and the "juvenile insane." The British called this group the "feeble-minded," but Americans eventually adopted this as a generic term that included idiots and imbeciles.
27. Seguin, *New Facts and Remarks Concerning Idiocy,* Lecture before the New York Medical Journal Association, October 15, 1869 (New York: Wood, 1870), 8–9 (emphasis in original).
28. Draft of letter from Goddard to Nicholas Pastore, n.d. [1948], folder 4, box M32, *HHG.*
29. In fact, it was his insistence on the ability of those who lived within institutions to identify intuitively the condition when they saw it that caused Goddard trouble in later disputes over *The Kallikak Family.* For Goddard's defense of this position, see "In Defense of the Kallikak Study," *Science* 95 (1942): 574–576.
30. See W. W. Ireland, *On Idiocy, especially in its Physical Aspects* (Edinburgh: Oliver and Boyd, Tweeddale Court, 1874), a pamphlet reprinted from the *Edinburgh Medical Journal,* January and February 1874, 1–34; quotation on p. 6. See also idem, *The Mental Affections of Children: Idiocy, Imbecility, and Insanity* (Philadelphia: Blakiston, 1900), 39.

31. Isaac Kerlin, "A Clinical Lecture on Idiocy and Imbecility," *Medical and Surgical Reporter* 46 (May 27, 1882): 534; Ireland, *On Idiocy, especially in its Physical Aspects,* 28.

32. For problems in determining medical histories, see A. C. Rogers, "On the *Ascribed* Causation of Idiocy As Illustrated in Reports to the Iowa Institution for Feeble Minded Children," *Proceedings of the Association of Medical Officers . . .* (1884): 296–301.

33. Kerlin, "A Clinical Lecture," 534.

34. Hervey Wilbur, "The Relation of Speech or Language to Idiocy," *Proceedings of the Association of Medical Officers . . .* (1878): 66–80; quotation on p. 74.

35. Jean Esquirol, *Des Maladies Mentales,* vol. 2, 340, as cited in Alfred Binet and Theodore Simon, *The Development of Intelligence in Children,* translated by Elizabeth Kite (Baltimore: Williams and Wilkins, 1916), 15–17. See also G. E. Johnson, "Contribution to the Psychology and Pedagogy of Feeble-Minded Children," *Journal of Psycho-Asthenics* 1 (1896–1897): 91. Another version is cited in Barr, *Mental Defectives,* 79.

36. Wilbur, "The Relation of Speech," 67, 76–79.

37. Ibid., 75.

38. J. C. Bucknell and D. H. Tuke, *A Manual of Psychological Medicine,* 4th ed. (Philadelphia: Lindsay, Blakiston, 1879), 152; Barr, *Mental Defectives,* 80.

39. Barr, *Mental Defectives,* 90.

40. This system is described in A. F. Tredgold, *Mental Deficiency* (New York: Wood, 1908, 1922), 92–96. A version of this definition is cited by Dr. Murdoch in the "Discussion" following Goddard's paper, "Suggestions for a Prognostical Classification," 53. See also Tyor, "Segregation or Surgery," 1–16.

41. Henry H. Goddard, "Psychological Work Among the Feeble-Minded," *Journal of Psycho-Asthenics* 12 (1907): 29–30.

42. Shepard Ivory Franz, "On the Function of the Cerebrum: The Frontal Lobes," *Archives of Psychology,* March 2, 1907, 24, as cited in Goddard, "Psychological Work," 29. For a description of Franz's work, see Popplestone and McPherson, "Pioneer Psychology Laboratories," 216–222.

43. Goddard, entry for Monday, September 17, 1906, in "1906–1907 First Year at Vineland" [hereafter Vineland Diary], folder 1, box M43, *HHG.*

44. Goddard, "Psychological Work Among the Feeble-Minded," 26.

45. Goddard, entry for Tuesday, November 27, 1906, in Vineland Diary, *HHG.*

46. Seguin, "New Facts and Remarks," 25.

47. Ibid., 18–19.

48. Hervey Wilbur, "The Classifications of Idiocy," *Proceedings of the Association of Medical Officers . . .* (1877): 29–35; quotation on p. 34.

49. Goddard describes various attempts to standardize these tests in Vineland Diary, *HHG.*

50. Goddard, European Diary, 1908, folder AA4(1), box M33.1, *HHG;* Goddard, "In the Beginning," *Understanding the Child* 3, no. 2 (April 1933): 2–6.

51. James McKeen Cattell, the most prominent American "mental tester," was aware of Binet's work since the 1890s. However, since he had a different test population and different goals, he never saw the institutional applications of Binet testing that Goddard saw. See Sokal, "James McKeen Cattell and Mental Anthropometry," chapter 2 of this volume.

52. Binet was passed over for several French university appointments, largely because he failed to meet the proper social and academic prerequisites of his day. Simon interned at the colony for retarded children and adolescents at Perray-Vaucluse, thus giving Binet access to two hundred subjects analogous to the more than three hundred subjects that Goddard was studying at Vineland. For a brief biography of Binet, see Fancher, *Intelligence Men*, 49–83; for a more complete biography, see Theta H. Wolf, *Alfred Binet* (Chicago: University of Chicago Press, 1973).

53. Alfred Binet and Theodore Simon, "Upon the Necessity of Establishing a Scientific Diagnosis of Inferior States of Intelligence" and "New Methods for the Diagnosis of the Intellectual Level of Subnormals," *L'Année Psychologique* (1905), 163–191 and 191–244, reprinted in Binet and Simon, *The Development of Intelligence in Children*, 9–91, quotation on p. 89.

54. Binet and Simon, *The Development of Intelligence in Children*, 20–24.

55. Ibid., 22.

56. Alfred Binet and Theodore Simon, "The Development of Intelligence in the Child," *L'Année Psychologique* (1908): 1–90, reprinted in Binet and Simon, *The Development of Intelligence in Children*, 182–273. For a concise explanation of Binet's tests, see Fancher, *Intelligence Men*, 69–78.

57. Henry H. Goddard, "Four Hundred Feeble-Minded Children Classified by the Binet Method," *Journal of Psycho-Asthenics* 15 (1910): 17–30; Goddard, "Introduction" to Binet and Simon, *The Development of Intelligence in Children*, 5.

58. Goddard, "Suggestions for a Prognostical Classification," 48.

59. Ibid., 49.

60. Ibid., 52.

61. Dr. Bernstein in "Discussion," following Goddard, "Suggestions for a Prognostical Classification," 53.

62. Ibid.

63. Dr. Keating in "Discussion," following Goddard, "Suggestions for a Prognostical Classification," 54.

64. Circular Letter from Dr. Walter Fernald to the Committee on Classification, April 23, 1910, published with "Report of Committee on Classification," 63.

65. Reply from Goddard to Fernald, April 29, 1910, published with "Report of the Committee on Classification," 64–67.

66. Goddard, "In the Beginning," 5.

67. Another psychologist, A.R.T. Wylie, who did research at the Faribault institution, had also served on the classification committee. The psychologists present and active at the 1910 meeting included Frederick Kuhl-

mann, also of Faribault, and E. B. Huey of the Lincoln, Illinois, institution.

68. Goddard, "Four Hundred Feeble-Minded Children," 19.

69. For descriptions of this committee's work, see "Report of the Committee on Classification," 61–67; see also "Minutes of the Association," *Journal of Psycho-Asthenics* 15 (1910–1911): 130–135; for another account, see Goddard, "In the Beginning," 2–6. Goddard derived the word "moron" from the Greek root meaning "foolish" and intended it to be a technical term that as yet had no disparaging connotations.

70. Goddard, "In the Beginning," 61; "Editorial: The New Classification (Tentative) of the Feeble-Minded," *Journal of Psycho-Asthenics* 15 (1910–1911): 68–71; quotations on pp. 69–70.

71. On school testing, see, for example, Henry H. Goddard, "The Hygiene of the Backward Child," *The Training School Bulletin* 9 (1912): 114–116; on Ellis Island testing, see idem, "The Feeble Minded Immigrant," *The Training School Bulletin* 9 (1912): 109–113. On the army tests, see Daniel J. Kevles, "Testing the Army's Intelligence: Psychologists and the Military in World War I," *Journal of American History* 55 (1968): 565–581; Franz Samelson, "World War I Intelligence Testing and the Development of Psychology," *Journal of the History of the Behavioral Sciences* 13 (1977), 274–282; and Richard T. von Mayrhauser, "The Manager, the Medic, and the Mediator: The Clash of Professional Styles and the Origins of Group Mental Testing," chapter 7 of this volume.

72. For an example of Goddard's work making extensive use of medical metaphors, see "The Possibilities of Mental Hygiene in Cases of Arrested Mental Development," presented at the Tenth Congress of the American School Hygiene Association, Albany, N.Y., *The Training School Bulletin* 15 (1918): 67–72.

73. Applied psychologists Walter Dill Scott and Walter Bingham, both academics from the Carnegie Institute of Technology, worked for the Committee on Classification of Personnel in the Office of the Adjutant General. See Kevles, "Testing the Army's Intelligence," 569–571, and von Mayrhauser, "The Manager, the Medic, and the Mediator," chapter 7 of this volume. For an example of the reemergence of the debate over the nature of mental deficiency, see John Clausen, "Mental Deficiency—Development of a Concept," *American Journal of Mental Deficiency* 71 (1966–1967): 727–745. For a discussion of some aspects of the changing relationship between psychiatry and psychology in relation to mental deficiency, see Robert Haskell, "Mental Deficiency Over a Hundred Years," *American Journal of Psychiatry* 100 (1944): 107–118. For an example of later controversies between Goddard and physicians, see Hamilton Cravens, "Applied Science and Public Policy: The Ohio Bureau of Juvenile Research and the Problem of Juvenile Delinquency, 1913–1930," chapter 8 of this volume.

74. Henry H. Goddard, "The Binet Measuring Scale of Intelligence: What It Is and How It Is To Be Used," *The Training School Bulletin* 11 (1914): 88.

For evidence of some of the controversies surrounding intelligence testing by 1914, see, for example, Lewis M. Terman, "A Report of the Buffalo
Conference on the Binet-Simon Tests of Intelligence," *Pedagogical Seminary* 20 (1913): 549–554.

75. "Editorial: The New Classification," 68–69.

4

Robert M. Yerkes and

the Mental Testing

Movement

Cultural historians have often asserted that World War I marked a profound shift in intellectual tone—from the confident expectation of material and moral progress characteristic of Victorians and positivists, to the "Waste Land" of hollow men and despair portrayed by T. S. Eliot and a generation of alienated intellectuals for whom the carnage of war epitomized the absurdity of human endeavor.[1] Some American intellectuals drew pessimistic conclusions from war experience, but to a remarkable extent the United States avoided the costs of the Great War in terms of lost lives, lost business, or even lost hopes. The war advanced America's status as a political and economic power and left stronger most of the national conceits concerning our particular virtues and destiny. The United States had not served as the "Arsenal of Democracy," but Americans believe otherwise. General "Blackjack" Pershing and his Yank army enjoyed very modest success on the battlefield, but their legend thrived. President Woodrow Wilson delivered on few of his promises for a just peace, and his ideals prevented neither the vicious suppression of dissent at home nor social calamity abroad, but the American public continued to believe in the unique righteousness of their institutions and values.[2]

The history of American psychologists in World War I mirrors this larger national theme of modest and self-serving achievement cloaked in wishful myths of heroic success. For Robert M. Yerkes

(1876–1956), the leader of the team of psychologists who tested 1.7 million United States army recruits, the Great War was a fabulous opportunity to show the value of psychology in the management of human resources. Yerkes regarded his leadership of the army testing as "vastly more than an episode in my life. In endless ways it transformed me . . .," and he regretted that the armistice cut short the opportunity to practice his discipline on an unprecedented scale.[3] Yerkes's account of the army testing program provided one of the longest "memoirs" published by the National Academy of Sciences; his monographs and popular articles on the contributions of psychology to the war effort helped to create an aura of practical success and of immense potential, if only policy makers would utilize the powerful technologies of social diagnosis and control that Yerkes claimed behavioral scientists would quickly deliver, given adequate support.[4]

Historians have generally agreed that the army testing program "put psychology on the map." The war changed the image of testers and of the tested. Intelligence tests were no longer things given by college professors and resident examiners like Henry H. Goddard to crazy people and imbeciles in psychopathic institutes and homes for the feebleminded, but legitimate means of making decisions about the aptitudes and achievements of normal people—an essential means of making objective judgments about individuals in a mass society. For academics in need of research funds, one of the most important indicators of their enhanced status after the war was the willingness of the large corporate philanthropic foundations to finance their projects. Before the war Yerkes had been competing with Lewis Terman of Stanford University for funds to standardize their rival intelligence tests, and neither got what he sought. The war provided both of them with unprecedented numbers of human subjects for experiment and with the experience of cooperating for mutual gain. After the war, Yerkes and Terman successfully lobbied the Rockefeller-funded General Education Board for the funds that made possible their successful effort to promote the differentiated school curriculum based on intelligence tests.[5]

Perhaps this "reform" would have been institutionalized without the encouragement of Rockefeller money or the entrepreneurship of academic psychologists. The development of school testing paralleled the growth of mass public-education systems and was an appropriate, if not essential, response to the needs of the new bureaucracies of education and social welfare that characterize a mature industrial society. Testing helped Progressive educators to finesse a fundamental and potentially threatening contradiction. American society needed public schools as a means of imposing some semblance of common identity in a society that was no longer Protestant nor even Christian—an urban society of great cities in which a majority of the people were foreign-born or the children of the foreign-born. The school's mission to acculturate the new folk of urban mass society was potentially at odds, however, with the structure of a society that needed different kinds of people in different quantities—a few managers and professionals, many semiskilled white-collar and blue-collar workers, many common laborers. Mental testing flourished because it helped the American school to be both a comprehensive and a differentiated institution; the tests squared American ideals of equality of opportunity with a social structure that resembled a pyramid.

Yerkes and Terman regarded their tests as a means of liberating gifted individuals from the tyrannies of ascribed status based on class or race or ethnicity. They did not expect, however, to find much gold among the masses. They believed in equality of opportunity, not equality, and they shared with other American Galtonians the assumption that "civic worth" or "mental ability" or "IQ" were inherited biological capacities distributed unevenly among classes and ethnic groups. They translated Galtonian ideology into harsh judgments that fit all too well with the nativism and xenophobia of their culture. Thus, the efforts of Yerkes and Terman to promote their discipline were greatly eased by the fact that their technology of mental measurement reconciled equality of opportunity with inequality; they provided numbers that seemed to confirm the "naturalness" of social class and racial caste.[6]

Although it seems in retrospect that the psychological entrepreneurs were favored by social changes that created a market for their services, before the war Yerkes had enjoyed only modest support and recognition during his fifteen years as an instructor and assistant professor of comparative psychology at Harvard. His failure to gain promotion to higher rank in part reflected administrative lack of appreciation for Yerkes's biological orientation. He called himself a "psychobiologist" at a time when psychology at Harvard was still an orientation within the Department of Philosophy. Yerkes was convinced, however, that evolutionary naturalism was *the* model that provided means for understanding human experience in both its biological and social aspects. While the precise date of his conversion to the Darwinian faith is not clear, he was certainly on his way when he arrived in Cambridge in the fall of 1897.[7]

In his origins he was typical of his generation of professional academicians—a farm boy from Bucks County, Pennsylvania, in rebellion against his father and the narrow provincialism of rural and Protestant America. He got from the farm to Ursinus College by claiming that he wanted to be a doctor but, after graduation, decided to put off medical school to get a better scientific background through study at Harvard. After one year in Cambridge, he was no longer hesitant to declare his intent to be a professional researcher, but vestiges of his Protestant background continued to shape his life in many forms, including his vision of science as a form of service to others. His was a secular altruism, however—superior, he believed, to that of the preacher. He would search for root causes and radical solutions.

Two biology professors, Charles B. Davenport and William Castle, both prominent figures in the Mendelian revival that seemed to offer the key to understanding the hereditary factor in evolution, were sponsors and models for the scientific novice. His immediate problem was to find a place for himself in the scientific division of labor that was emerging among exponents of evolutionary naturalism. His mentors in zoology had already taken for themselves the task of explaining variation or the mechanisms of heredity. A second major gap in understanding the history of life was the lack of a satisfactory account of the significance of behavior in evolution—that is, an analysis of the role of intelligence or effective response to environment in the evolutionary process. The role of consciousness, mind, or behavior in the evolution of life was a live topic in an intellectual community that included William James and Josiah Royce, and remembered Chauncey Wright. In 1896 Lloyd Morgan, the great British pioneer in comparative psychology, visited Boston and soon afterward James's student Edward Lee Thorndike started experimenting with chicks in James's basement. Thorndike moved on to Columbia University and James McKeen Cattell, who had more support available for animal work, leaving intellectual space for someone like Yerkes who could bring rigorous experimental methods to the study of the evolution of consciousness.[8]

On the advice of Josiah Royce, Yerkes defined his intellectual mission as the mapping of the uncharted regions between mind and body.[9] He would delineate the relationship between "material" and "mental" evolutionary processes. The study of mind needed a methodology and subjects for study equivalent to the fossils of paleontologists. Yerkes believed that simpler forms of life might be viewed as living fossils and began the task of tracing the phylogenetic development of human intellectual capacity back through lower forms of life to its origins with studies of the behavior and "mental life" of frogs, jelly fish, crustaceans, worms, mice, crows, pigs, racoons—and eventually insane persons, schoolchildren, soldiers, orangutans, chimpanzees, and gorillas.

Yerkes never forgot his original scientific mission, despite his prominence as a scientific bureaucrat and applied psychologist. One of Yerkes's great strengths as a builder of behavioral science was his eclecticism and aversion to extreme forms of reductionism. This trait becomes more salient in examining his remarkable relationships with Lewis M. Terman and John B. Watson. Like Terman, Yerkes was a key exponent of intelligence testing, but testing was never his primary goal or interest. Like Watson, Yerkes was a prime mover in the development of animal behavior studies, but he was always simply an "objectivist," or one who wanted to bring a more rigorous experimental methodology to psychology, and never a "behaviorist" in the Watsonian mode.[10] Psychometricians and Watsonians shared a willingness to define their subjects operationally; they dealt with empty organisms in the sense that the test taker, whether school boy or white rat, was known solely by response to stimulus—whether the stimulus was a maze to be run or a written question that required the selection of one out of five possible answers.

Yerkes, in contrast, was never content to limit himself to observation of behavior. Just like Jean Piaget turned *from* the business of estimating the mental age of children on the basis of right or wrong answer *to* the more fruitful question of determining why the child got a wrong answer, or what went on inside its head—Yerkes repeatedly sought empathy with his subjects and speculated about their internal states, much to the dismay of his friend John Watson.[11] He operated in the approved Galtonian or Watsonian mode only when the expectations of others forced him to do so. Crudely put, Yerkes honored Terman's scientific godfather, Francis Galton, and he honored Watson's scientific godfather, Jacques Loeb; he was a hereditarian and a eugenicist à la Galton-Terman, and an objectivist, who wanted to be able to control behavior à la Loeb-Watson, but Yerkes looked first and last to Darwin and the tradition of evolutionary naturalism that his Galtonian and Loebian colleagues mistrusted.[12] In pursuit of the Darwinian paradigm, he could not afford to reject any source of insight that might advance knowledge. In contrast to Jacques Loeb or John Watson, Yerkes retained respect for the arts of "naive" collection and description. Much of his 1911 textbook, *Introduction to Psychology*, was devoted to structuralist or Titchenerian accounts of perception, association, and consciousness, or the by then traditional art of introspection.[13] Thus, in matters of method Yerkes was a Jamesian pluralist despite, or perhaps because of, his Darwinian fundamentalism. As a leader of his profession he maintained good relations with warring factions of structuralists, functionalists, behaviorists, and psychometricians.[14] Their various insights and social contacts might be needed in the pursuit of his largest ambition—to develop a natural history of behavior that would provide the basis for a science of man—a behavioral science that would be as useful as physics or chemistry because one could use it to predict and to control human behavior, and to redesign human nature along more satisfactory lines.

By 1915, when John Watson's election as president of the American Psychological Association symbolized the coming of age of Yerkes's generation of biologically oriented psychologists, Yerkes had gone a long way toward his goal of charting natural hierarchies of intelligence or adaptive behavior. He was ready to move from dancing mice and racoons to primates, but the resources for acquiring such expensive subjects had not materialized. In fact, even his position at Harvard was shaky. His colleagues in the philosophy department resisted awarding their Ph.D. to those who studied only animals, and philosophers whom Yerkes considered dilettantes were promoted, while Yerkes remained a junior colleague. President A. L. Lowell, guided by the counsel of Professor Hugo Münsterberg, the man picked by William James to lead the development of psychology at Harvard, saw no future in Yerkes's brand of comparative psychology. It was smelly and expensive and seemed to have no relation to practical public service. Word came to Yerkes that the way to promotion might lie through educational psychology. Yerkes told his Harvard superiors that he would not concentrate on educational psychology because he was not interested in nurture but in nature. Yerkes's prospects for promotion at Harvard seemed bleak.[15]

An acceptable opportunity to demonstrate the social relevance of psychology came through Yerkes's friend and fellow eugenicist Ernest Southard, M.D., who was in charge of the new psychopathic service at the Boston State Hospital, which was an attempt to provide short-term diagnosis and treatment for the mentally ill, some of whom would be treated on an outpatient basis while others faced long-term hospitalization. Southard asked Yerkes to develop methods for assessing the intellectual abilities of his patients and provided him with a means of joining "service" with research that added *homo sapiens* to his collection of species for comparison. For four years Yerkes combined teaching and unsurpassed production as an experimental animal behaviorist, while he was paid as a half-time consultant by Southard. He later reflected that it was "fortunate for my health" that this divided existence was ended by World War I.[16]

Despite competing interests, Yerkes's work in developing diagnostic mental tests attracted national attention. He attempted to improve on the techniques of Alfred Binet by developing a more sophisticated scoring system, one in which subjects were rated according to how closely their answers came to being correct rather than on a simple right-or-wrong basis. Ironically, in view of the claims that would soon be made for the hereditability of intelligence based on the army tests, Yerkes was extremely critical of Terman's revision of Binet's tests while he was still trying to develop his alternative Point Scale. He complained that many items in the Stanford Revision were "highly dependent on education," and that chronological age was given too much emphasis in assessing performance because "sex, language, race, and social and economic status are quite as important as are norms for age. It is, for example, not adequate for us in the school system of the American city to treat all individuals as though born to the English language. . . ." Yerkes recommended a universal rather than age-graded scale of performance, one that could be evaluated by comparison with a series of norms based on both social and biological differences.[17]

Thus, Yerkes's work in the army testing program in many respects contradicted his own earlier work as a mental tester. His Point Scale was a test administered to individuals. After it became apparent that the best opportunity to demonstrate the usefulness of mental testing lay in mass screening rather than evaluation of exceptional individuals, a test was needed that could be administered to groups in a single session. During the hectic period of May-June 1917, when the army Alpha examination was written, Terman's Stanford Revision provided the working model of a group test because he had brought with him improved tests developed by protégé Arthur Otis, and these were used "practically in the form in which Otis had used them in his own scale." [18]

By 1922, when he wrote a glowing foreword for Carl Brigham's *A Study of American Intelligence,* a benchmark in the history of scientific racism, Yerkes was praising methods and interpretations that might seem incompatible with his own work conducted both before and after the army program.[19] What happened? The war and the opportunities it provided for promoting psychology made it apparent that there was relatively little to be gained through *intradisciplinary* competition.[20] The big prizes would go to those who could present a united front to the power brokers of the emerging American research establishment, and, in order to pursue his agenda as a comparative psycholgist, Yerkes needed resources that had never before been available to psychologists.

By 1916 Yerkes was involved in two lines of research that were limited by their capital requirements. From February to August 1915, he had studied the "mental life of monkeys and apes," thanks to a former student at Harvard, G. V. Hamilton, who bought an orangutan for Yerkes's use and made his personal collection of monkeys available. The site of the research was a California estate where Hamilton served as the personal psychiatrist to a mad millionaire, and thus had the time and resources to help his former professor realize a long-frustrated ambition to extend his natural history of intelligence to primates. Despite Yerkes's exciting discovery that the five-year-old orangutan Julius engaged in "ideational" behavior that seemed to call for revision of the mechanistic interpretations of animal learning that had flourished since the publication of Thorndike's 1898 Ph.D. dissertation "Animal Intelligence," Yerkes lacked the means to continue his primate research.[21] Meanwhile, his attempts to develop better scales for measuring human intelligence also had reached a point where large funds seemed necessary to proceed with the process of standardization. Yerkes's efforts to tap Rockefeller interests proved frustrating, however, and he found himself in competition with Terman for philanthropic dollars.[22]

Yerkes's solution to the lack of capital proved to be the development of close ties with a small group of scientists and philanthropists who shared his vision that the days of the lone entrepreneur or craftsman in science were numbered. In the future, science would be capital-intensive and bureaucratically organized, like the major productive sectors of the American economy. The chief exponent of this "ideology of national science" was the astronomer George Ellery Hale, the prime mover in the creation of the National Research Council, whose grant-making committees proved to be the single most important source of research funds between the world wars.[23]

In his accounts of the origins of the army testing program, Yerkes claimed that his efforts to involve psychologists in the war effort began in April 1917, when Congress declared war. As president of the American Psychological Association, he was "compelled by duty" to lead his profession into national service despite personal modesty and lack of social skills.[24] In fact, Yerkes began his efforts to win a place for psychology in the National Research Council, and in the preparedness campaign, much earlier than he later remembered. These promotional efforts were part of a general search for institutional support that sprang from the capital-intensive nature of his research, his ambitions as a social engineer, and his sensitivity to the need to sell his discipline to any potential sponsors—whether politicians, rich patrician nativists, government bureaucrats, or corporate philanthropists.

In February 1916, while Congress debated the issue of military preparedness, Yerkes wrote to the War Department to suggest that psychological testing ought to be part of military recruiting. Rebuffed by U.S. officials, he responded to a letter from a colleague in Canada concerning the possible employment of mental tests in evaluating incapacitated soldiers by offering to travel north at his own expense. He reacted to the April 6 Congressional declaration of war by turning a meeting of experimental psychologists in Cambridge into a pro-war rally that ended with Yerkes in charge of a committee to investigate possible contributions of psychology to mobilization. He made his trip to Canada to inspect the work of its Military Hospitals Commission and wrote to Hale, now chairman of the National Research Council, asking that psychologists be drafted into government service. The problem was to convince Hale that they had something to offer. It helped that Yerkes could confide that he had been "summoned" to Ottawa, where "their psychology workers desire my advice concerning methods of dealing with the returned soldiers. . . ."[25]

Yerkes got an audience with Hale, and happily Hale sought a reference from Harvard physiologist Walter B. Cannon, a close Yerkes friend since their apprenticeships in biological science under Davenport.[26] In short, when Yerkes emerged as a protégé of Hale, as chairman of the National Research Council Psychology Committee, leader of the army testing program, and an officer of the National Research Council in various capacities during the rest of his career, it was the result of aggressive and skillful lobbying campaigns that succeeded despite the indifference of many fellow psychologists and the skepticism of physical scientists about the ability of behavioral scientists to deliver on their promises.

In retrospect, Yerkes's greatest coup as a scientific bureaucrat and promoter was not in getting the Surgeon General to find a place for psychologists in the army, although that was a notable accomplishment, nor in writing tests, recruiting several hundred officers and technicians, and administering examinations to over 1.7 million individuals, despite fierce competition for resources and status from army officers and psychiatrists, although that too was a notable accomplishment. His most remarkable achievement was the myth that the army testing program had been a great practical success and that it provided a "goldmine" of data on the heritability of intelligence.

Beginning with the work of Daniel J. Kevles and Thomas M. Camfield in 1968–1969, historians have provided detailed critical accounts of the army testing program. It is now clear that the program contributed little to the war effort.[27] Test scores were never used consistently in the assignment or rating of recruits, and the program was probably saved from separate termination by the armistice and general demobilization. The fact that the data gathered from the examinations has been cited so often and for so long in support of the Galtonian paradigm is a commentary on the will to believe among psychometricians and others who ought to know better. The tests may have predicted "practical soldier value," with a bit less precision than traditional army procedures, but there was and is no way to separate the influence of learning, acculturation, class, racial caste, or motivation from native ability in evaluation of performance on the army examinations.

Perhaps the most troubling point raised by historians is not that the army psychologists misinterpreted their data but that they repeatedly violated their own protocols—for example, by failing to retest men who scored zero on one or more parts of an examination. The scores of these men were included in the invidious group comparisons that received so much attention, and they account in part for the differences in ratings that eugenicists and nativists found so meaningful. The testers could hardly have excluded and/or retested the thousands of individuals who were not willing or able to participate in the examination, and thus got zero or suspiciously low scores, because there were so many of them. To discard them from the army or from the data base would have been to risk the legitimacy of the whole program. Despite all of this, Yerkes not only saved face, but he also emerged as an Influential in the affairs of the National Research Council.

Hale had large plans to reorganize the National Research Council as an instrument for promoting and integrating postwar American scientific research and recruited Yerkes for the key position of chairman of the Research Information Service. This division was eventually downgraded, but originally Hale and Yerkes saw it as a kind of master intelligence unit that would point the way for philanthropists and researchers. In a sense Yerkes "failed" again, since he was never able to find the large funds needed to realize the original plan for the Research Information Service, but five years with the NRC made it possible for him to publicize his version of the army testing program and to assume the chairmanship of two grant-making committees— the Committee for Research in Problems of Sex and the Committee on Problems of Human Migration—that were working models of the ideology of national science.[28]

Despite his prominence as a scientific bureaucrat, in the early 1920s Yerkes was a would-be experimental scientist without a laboratory or a prestigious university post. His salience as a good organization man who had an unsurpassed knowledge of the network of foundations that subsidized research, an insider's knowledge of the latest developments in biosocial science, and imaginative plans that might attract large funds finally paid off after James R. Angell assumed the presidency of Yale in 1921. Angell had gone from acting president of the University of Chicago, to chairman of the National Research Council, to president of the Carnegie Corporation of New York, to president of Yale in less than four years. His mission at Yale was to increase the endowment, revive graduate education and research, and establish the nontraditional disciplines. A key part of this strategy lay in developing the human sciences and using them to attract big money, distinguished scholars, and top graduate students.

Yerkes had not missed many opportunities over the preceding decade to brief potential patrons about his large plans for an institute of psychobiological research, with emphasis on primate studies. Angell and Yerkes—as fellow Harvard men, champions of a functional psychology, and eugenically minded advocates of a coordinated national research effort—had usually gotten along well, although Angell was often in the position of trying to restrain his junior colleague without destroying his enthusiasm. Apparently Angell went to Yale having promised to keep Yerkes in mind. Angell's personal agenda came first, of course, but after he had seen to the most pressing problems of his new office, Angell and Yerkes began a campaign to find resources for a psychobiological institute. An initial effort in 1922 to secure funds from the Rockefeller-funded General Education Board failed and put a strain on the Angell-Yerkes connection. Yerkes persisted, however, and Angell appreciated Yerkes's success as chair of NRC committees in raising funds and generating attractive research agendas. Yerkes, in turn, made it clear that his NRC committees would not object if their most prestigious recipients moved to Yale.[29]

Finally, the support they needed was supplied by Beardsley Ruml, a Chicago Ph.D. in psychology and Angell's former assistant at the Carnegie Corporation. In 1922 Ruml became head of the Laura Spellman Rockefeller Memorial. John D. Rockefeller, Sr., had established this foundation as a minor tribute to his late wife, but Ruml proceeded to redefine its mission and to expand its objectives, changing its program from ameliorative direct aid to women and children to basic research in the social sciences. In 1924 the LSRM promised Yale $200,000 over five years for an Institute of Psychology, with Yerkes as the first big name committed to the institution. In 1925 Yerkes obtained an additional Rockefeller Foundation grant of $40,000 for anthropoid research, and he had found the institutional base he needed to become the founder of American primatology.[30]

Yerkes's career as a mental tester was not over, of course, since human beings were but one of the species whose "intelligence" he set out to study early in his career. In resuming full-time pursuit of his agenda as a Darwinian comparative psychologist, Yerkes once again displayed the methodological eclecticism and common sense that marked his best work before the war. While evaluation of his work on the mental ability of primates cannot be attempted here, Yerkes the primatologist stands in stark contrast to the popular image of the intelligence tester that has emerged from contemporary criticism of the Galtonian paradigm. For example, Stephen Jay Gould, in *The Mismeasure of Man,* has pointed to *reification* and *ranking* as the two fundamental errors or abuses of scientific method characteristic of Galtonians.[31] I have already noted Yerkes's prewar criticism of Terman's Stanford Revision. As late as March 19, 1917, Yerkes attacked Terman's work in G. Stanley Hall's Clark University seminar. In the Binet-Terman scales, Yerkes complained,

> . . . the process of selecting tests according to percentage of passes and of grouping them according to age constitutes standardization. The result of this method of selecting and standardizing tests is an inflexible scale, which however accurate it may be for the race, social stratum, or sex for which it is constructed, cannot possibly yield reliable results when applied to widely differing groups of individuals.[32]

Yerkes was apparently sensitive to the dangers of making group comparisons or ranking individuals by standards inappropriate to their background and experience.

Yerkes the primatologist also exhibited considerable caution when comparing the test scores of individuals of different species. In his work with primates, Yerkes administered individual tests instead of the group examinations that the army program demanded. He was interested in developing methods that would generate good statistics, usually in the form of learning curves that represented the number of trials that a subject required to master a particular problem. He understood, however, that the numbers generated by his tests were simply indicators that required careful assessment—only one of a series of signs generated by a good experiment.

Yerkes's famous multiple choice apparatus was the first successful attempt as a method for studying learning in different kinds of animals, where performance would not depend on the subject's perceptual or motor abilities or on its level of activity. Having tried the method on crows, pigs, and humans at the Boston State Hospital, Yerkes was ready in 1915 for his long-anticipated attempt to demonstrate that Thorndike had been wrong in asserting that no animal could think.[33] Julius, a five-year old orangutan, provided Yerkes with the first "hard" evidence that there were qualitative differences in learning patterns between species. Julius did not achieve a higher score, however, that other creatures—in this case pigs and monkeys—who were presented with the same problem. Rather, he took many more trials to learn that the "right answer" was always the door or compartment on the extreme left. But Julius did provide Yerkes with a different kind of learning curve. He *abruptly* stopped making errors, in contrast to the pigs and monkeys who *gradually* learned the correct response.[34] Julius's learning curve was only the first of many efforts by Yerkes to document "ideation" in the ape.

As a primatologist Yerkes did not reify statistical indexes, and he was careful to avoid making inappropriate comparisons between individuals or groups, despite the mighty demands on the patience of experimenter and reader alike imposed by such subjects as Congo the gorilla or a pair of chimpanzees that never learned to talk. I conclude that Yerkes's career as a mental tester and comparative psychologist provides some contradictions that require explanation. The man who tolerated and rationalized questionable methods and interpretations in the army testing program—and who participated in harsh judgments about the native capacity of human beings—was in other situations a more self-conscious methodologist and an eager defender of the "intelligence" of other creatures.

Part of the explanation for the contradictions in Yerkes's career may lie in his deeply felt need to prove that psychologists had technologies analogous to those of physical scientists, and thus deserved higher status and support. By claiming that an inherited capacity accounted for the correlations between social status, ethnicity, and test scores, psychologists seemed to demonstrate that they were the equals of other natural scientists in their capacity to identify a fundamental law of nature and to predict its influence on human affairs.

For Robert Yerkes, ambition for his discipline and personal success were so closely intertwined as to be indistinguishable. As Franz Samelson has shown, Yerkes's enthusiastic, and brief, promotion of Carl Brigham's *A Study of American Intelligence* required the suppression of his own critical insights. One of Yerkes's motives for supporting Brigham was a desire to cultivate support among influential men of affairs who might become patrons of psychobiological research.[35]

In an autobiographical manuscript, Yerkes declared, "I shall view myself as an experimental animal whose solution of daily problems ultimately spells out a way of life."[36] This statement, probably intended as a rhetorical device, may tell us more than its author intended. Yerkes was a pioneer in an ill-defined area of research that held immense promise as well as dead ends. He was guided by some large and abstract assumptions—faith in Darwin, faith in scientific method, faith in the promise of human engineering, but the specifics of his research—the subjects, the methods, the interpretations—often reflected pragmatic responses to a complex range of stimuli, including professional mentors, institutional situations, and perceived social needs or opportunities.

In many respects Yerkes was a much more successful investigator in dealing with animals than with human beings. His involvement with human subjects resulted from his efforts to meet the criticisms of Harvard superiors who felt that his work as a comparative psychologist had limited value and from his own desire, as a committed eugenicist, to find social relevance in his research. Yerkes's work at the Boston State Hospital provided the credentials he needed to win a prominent role in the academic mobilization during World War I. And war-related experience, both as a mental tester and as a scientific bureaucrat with the National Research Council, paid off in that it allowed Yerkes to realize his chief ambition, the creation of a major center for primate research. Yerkes was both the beneficiary and the victim of the culture he sought to serve. The price he paid for professional opportunity was occasional betrayal of his own best instincts as an investigator. The patient friend of Julius the Orangutan and of Congo the Gorilla would be most often cited thirty years after his death as an exponent of scientific racism.

NOTES

Research for this essay was supported by a Beveridge Grant from the American Historical Association. Thanks to James H. Capshew, Richard T. von Mayrhauser, and Franz Samelson for their critical readings of the first version of this essay.

1. For a recent prize-winning and best-selling recapitulation of this theme, see Paul Fussell, *The Great War and Modern Memory* (New York: Oxford University Press, 1977).
2. David Kennedy develops the theme that American contributions to the defeat of Germany were exaggerated and misinterpreted in *Over Here: The First World War and American Society* (New York: Oxford University Press, 1980), 194 note 5, 202–205, 216–218, 344–349, 351, 357–359, 366.
3. "The Scientific Way," autobiographical manuscript, *RMY,* 166; this document consists of 425 typewritten pages. For succinct published descriptions of Yerkes's career, see his contribution to *A History of Psychology in Autobiography,* vol. 2, edited by Carl Murchison (Worcester, Mass.: Clark University Press, 1932), 381–407, hereafter cited as "Psychobiologist"; Ernest R. Hilgard, "Robert Mearns Yerkes," in National Academy of Sciences, *Biographical Memoirs,* vol. 38 (New York: Columbia University Press, 1965), 385–411 (this essay includes a good bibliography of Yerkes's work).
4. The official account of the mobilization and contribution of psychologists is Robert M. Yerkes, *Psychological Examining in the United States Army,* vol. 15, Memoirs of the National Academy of Sciences (Washington, D.C.: Government Printing Office, 1921). In addition to this massive monograph, Yerkes published a number of influential articles that helped to shape the legend of achievement among professional and lay audiences. They include "Psychology in Relation to the War," *Psychological Review* 25 (1918): 85–115; "The Measurement and Utilization of Brain Power in the Army," *Science* 44 (1919): 221–226, 251–259; "Report of the Psychology Committee of the National Research Council," *Psychological Review* 26 (1919): 83–149; "The Role of Psychology in the War," chaps. 20 and 21 in *The New World of Science: Its Development During the War,* edited by Yerkes (New York: The Century Company, 1920); *Army Mental Tests,* with C. S. Yoakum (New York: Henry Holt and Co., 1920); "Eugenic Bearing of

Measurements of Intelligence in the U.S. Army," *Eugenics Review* 14 (1923): 223–245; "Testing the Human Mind," *Atlantic Monthly* (March 1923): 358–370; "Man-power and Military Effectiveness: The Case for Human Engineering," *Journal of Consulting Psychology* 5 (1941): 205– 209; "Psychology and Defense," *Proceedings of the American Philosophical Society* 84 (1941): 527–542.

5. Thomas M. Camfield, "Psychologists at War: The History of American Psychologists and the First World War" (Ph.D. diss., University of Texas at Austin, 1969), 268–288; Franz Samelson, "Putting Psychology on the Map: Ideology and Intelligence Testing," in *Psychology in Social Context,* edited by Allan Buss (New York: Irvington Publishers, 1979), 104–107; Paul D. Chapman, "Schools as Sorters: Lewis M. Terman and the Intelligence Testing Movement, 1890–1930" (Ph.D. diss., Stanford University, 1980), 90–96; John M. O'Donnell, *The Origins of Behaviorism: American Psychology, 1870–1920* (New York: New York University Press, 1985), 238–240.

6. For an understanding of the Galtonian paradigm, I have drawn heavily upon Donald A. Mackenzie, *Statistics in Great Britain* (Edinburgh: Edinburgh University Press, 1981), and Ruth Schwartz Cowan, "Nature and Nurture: The Interplay of Biology and Politics in the Work of Francis Galton," in *Studies in the History of Biology,* vol. 1, edited by W. Coleman and C. Limoges (Baltimore: Johns Hopkins University Press, 1977), 133–208. On the use of Galtonian ideas in the United States, see Chapman, "Schools as Sorters"; Mark Haller, *Eugenics: Hereditarian Attitudes in American Thought* (New Brunswick, N.J.: Rutgers University Press, 1963); Clarence Karier, Paul Violas, and Joel Spring, eds., *Roots of Crisis: American Education in the Twentieth Century* (Chicago: Rand McNally, 1973); Henry L. Minton, "Lewis M. Terman and Mental Testing: In Search of the Democratic Ideal," chapter 5 of this volume.

7. Yerkes's valedictory address at Ursinus College, "The Spirit of Modern Science," was revised at the request of the college president. See Yerkes, "The Scientific Way," 79.

8. Yerkes, "The Scientific Way," 92–98; idem, "Psychobiologist," 395. On Thorndike's career at Harvard, See Geraldine Joncich, *The Sane Positivist: A Biography of Edward L. Thorndike* (Middletown, Conn.: Wesleyan University Press, 1968), 79–103. Hamilton Cravens, *The Triumph of Evolution: American Scientists and the Heredity-Environment Controversy, 1900–1941* (Philadelphia: University of Pennsylvania Press, 1978); Matthew Hale, Jr., *Human Science and Social Order: Hugo Münsterberg and the Origins of Applied Psychology* (Philadelphia: Temple University Press, 1980), and Bruce Kuklick, *The Rise of American Philosophy: Cambridge, Massachusetts, 1860–1930* (New Haven, Conn.: Yale University Press, 1977), also describe the academic environment in which Yerkes worked.

9. Yerkes, "The Scientific Way," 89.

10. As Robert Boakes has observed, few of Watson's students or colleagues supported his more extreme reductionist views. See Boakes, *From Darwin to Behaviorism: Psychology and the Minds of Animals* (Cambridge, Eng.: Cambridge University Press, 1984), 172–173, 235.

11. There is a rich correspondence between Yerkes and Watson in *RMY* that happily is most detailed during the years when their separate views on the study of behavior developed. Hamilton Cravens analyzes their relationship in *The Triumph of Evolution,* 204–210.

12. On Loeb and his relationship to Watson, see Philip J. Pauly, "Jacques Loeb and the Control of Life: Experimental Biology in Germany and America, 1890–1920" (Ph.D. diss., Johns Hopkins University, 1980), and Boakes, *From Darwin to Behaviorism,* 145, 172.

13. Yerkes, "Psychobiologist," 392; *Introduction to Psychology* (New York: Henry Holt and Company, 1911).

14. The best account of the relationship between the various psychological persuasions is provided by John O'Donnell, *The Origins of Behaviorism: American Psychology, 1870–1920.* Hamilton Cravens provides an overview of the relationship between psychology and other disciplines in *The Triumph of Evolution.*

15. Yerkes, "The Scientific Way," 129–133; Hugo Münsterberg to A. Lawrence Lowell, January 30, 1911, December 22, 1911, *HM.* There was little room at Harvard for a second full professor of psychology, regardless of special field of research, as long as Münsterberg was there and intent on protecting his status as the principal person in psychology.

16. Ibid., 140–155; Yerkes, "Psychobiologist," 393.

17. Robert M. Yerkes, "The Binet versus the Point Scale Method of Measuring Intelligence," *Journal of Applied Psychology* 1 (1917): 118; Yerkes and Helen M. Anderson, "The Importance of Social Status as Indicated by the Results of the Point Scale Method of Measuring Mental Capacity," *Journal of Educational Psychology* 6 (March 1915): 150. See also Yerkes, James W. Bridges, and Rose S. Hardwick, *A Point Scale for Measuring Mental Ability* (Baltimore: Warwick & York, 1915), 82 and passim.

18. Lewis M. Terman to O. S. Reimbold, May 18, 1920, *LMT,* quoted in Chapman, "Schools as Sorters: Lewis M. Terman and the Intelligence Testing Movement," 77. I do not mean to imply that Otis and Terman supplied all of the test items. Materials were contributed by all members of the committee, who freely borrowed from many sources. For example, some sections of the Alpha were written by Walter Bingham and Guy Whipple, who adapted items that they had developed in collaborative research with Walter D. Scott on salesmanship. Thus, even though Scott "walked out at the Walton" (see Richard T. von Mayrhauser, "The Manager, the Medic, and the Mediator: The Clash of Professional Psychological Styles and the Wartime Origins of Group Mental Testing," chapter 7 of this volume), and did not participate actively in Yerkes's Committee on Psychological Examining of Recruits, the practice-oriented group of mental testers that he represented did influence the content of the army tests.

19. Robert M. Yerkes, "A Foreword" in Carl C. Brigham, *A Study of American Intelligence* (Princeton, N.J.: Princeton University Press, 1923), v–viii. For a perceptive analysis of how Yerkes was drawn into close association with Brigham and with avid lay advocates of immigration restriction, see Franz Samelson, "Putting Psychology on the Map," 131–135.

20. Samelson provides a good example of how differences between Terman and Yerkes were resolved in response to the need to present a united front to the General Education Board. See "Putting Psychology on the Map," 112–114.

21. Robert M. Yerkes, *The Mental Life of Monkeys and Apes: A Study of Ideational Behavior* (Cambridge, Mass.: Henry Holt and Company, 1916); Edward Thorndike, *Animal Intelligence: An Experimental Study of the Associative Processes in Animals,* Monograph Supplement No. 8, *Psychological Review* (1898).

22. Chapman, "Schools as Sorters," 91–93.

23. Ronald C. Tobey, *The American Ideology of National Science, 1919–1930* (Pittsburgh: University of Pittsburgh Press, 1971), chap. 2; National Research Council, *A History of the National Research Council, 1919–1923* (Washington, D.C.: National Research Council, 1933).

24. Yerkes, "The Scientific Way," 167–168; idem, "Psychobiologist," 397.

25. Edwin G. Boring, "The Society of Experimental Psychologists," *American Journal of Psychology* 51 (1938): 414–415; Yerkes to Hale, April 9, 1917, quoted in Camfield, "Psychologists at War," 89; see also pp. 79–80, 83–89. Richard T. von Mayrhauser provides a detailed study of one aspect of Yerkes's activities during this period in "The Manager, the Medic, and the Mediator," chapter 7 of this volume.

26. Camfield, "Psychologists at War," 89–91.

27. Daniel J. Kevles, "Testing the Army's Intelligence: Psychologists and the Military in World War I," *Journal of American History* 55 (1968): 565–581; Franz Samelson, "Putting Psychology on the Map," 142–158; Stephen Jay Gould, *The Mismeasure of Man* (New York: Norton, 1981), 192–233.

Yerkes's Committee on the Psychological Examination of Recruits was not the only group of psychologists active in the mobilization effort. In contrast to their criticism of Yerkes, recent scholars have argued that Walter Dill Scott's Committee on the Classification of Personnel in the army made significant contributions to the war effort. See Richard T. von Mayrhauser, "The Triumph of Utility: The Forgotten Clash of American Psychologies During World War I" (Ph.D. diss., University of Chicago, 1985), for a vigorous defense of Scott's work.

28. Yerkes, "The Scientific Way," 215–235.

29. This story may be followed in the Yerkes-Angell correspondence, *RMY.*

30. James H. Capshew, "Psychology, Yale University, and the Rockefeller Foundation: A Case Study in the Patronage of Science, 1920–1940," paper presented at the Fourteenth Meeting of Cheiron, The International Society for the History of the Behavioral and Social Sciences, Newport,

Rhode Island, June 12, 1982; Martin Bulmer and Joan Bulmer, "Philanthropy and Social Science in the 1920s: Beardsley Ruml and the Laura Spellman Rockefeller Memorial, 1922–29," *Minerva* 19 (1981): 347–407; Franz Samelson, "Organizing for the Kingdom of Behavior: Academic Battles and Organizational Policies in the Twenties," *Journal of the History of Behavioral Sciences* 21 (January 1985): 33–47.

31. Gould, *Mismeasure,* 24, 30–31, 151, 158–159, 238–239, 250–252, 268–269, 273–274, 288–292.

32. Yerkes, "The Binet versus the Point Scale," 114.

33. Robert M. Yerkes and C. A. Coburn, "A Study of the Behavior of the Crow, *Corvus americanus* Aud. by the Multiple Choice Method," *Journal of Animal Behavior* 5 (1915): 75–114; idem, "A Study of the Behavior of the Pig *Sus scrofa* by the Multiple Choice Method," ibid.: 185–225; Robert M. Yerkes, "A New Method for Studying Ideational and Allied Forms of Behavior in Man and Other Animals," *Proceedings of the National Academy of Sciences* 2 (1916): 231–233.

34. Yerkes, *The Mental Life of Monkeys and Apes,* 68, 87, 131–132.

35. Samelson, "Putting Psychology on the Map," 128–135.

36. Yerkes, "The Scientific Way," 2.

5

Lewis M. Terman and Mental

Testing: In Search of the Democratic

Ideal

There is nothing about an individual as important as his IQ, except possibly his morals . . . the great test problem of democracy is how to adjust itself to the large IQ differences which can be demonstrated to exist among the members of any race or nationality group. . . . All the available facts that science has to offer support the Galtonian theory that mental abilities are chiefly a matter of original endowment. . . . It is to the highest 25 per cent. of our population, and more especially to the top 5 per cent., that we must look for the production of leaders who will advance science, art, government, education, and social welfare generally. . . . The least intelligent 15 or 20 per cent. of our population . . . are democracy's ballast, not always useless but always a potential liability. How to make the most of their limited abilities, both for their own welfare and that of society; how to lead them without making them helpless victims of oppression; are perennial questions in any democracy.[1]

So stated Lewis M. Terman in 1922 with respect to the implications of intelligence testing for American democracy. According to Terman, who in 1916 had produced the most successful American revision of the Binet-Simon intelligence tests, the American democratic ideal with its traditional assumption that there were no inborn differences in mental functions had to be reconciled with the scientific facts that clearly demonstrated otherwise. The purpose here is to explore the roots of Terman's views about democratic society and to understand why such pronouncements played a prominent role in his career as one of the leaders in the American mental testing movement.

Terman was born in 1877, the twelfth of fourteen children of a farm family in central Indiana.[2] He went to a one-room school, completing the eighth grade when he was twelve. He had already started to work on the farm a year earlier, and although he found the work pleasant, he had other aspirations. He had recalled that when he was nine or ten a book peddler, who visited the farm, was selling a book on phrenology. Each of the family members was given a phrenological examination, and based on the "bumps" of young Lewis's head, great things were predicted. This incident, apparently, stimulated ambitions beyond the farm. For an Indiana farm boy in the 1890s, to pursue an education beyond the eighth grade meant preparing to teach school. At fifteen, with his parents' support, Terman left the farm to attend Central Normal College in Danville, Indiana. Over the course of the next six years he completed three undergraduate degrees at the normal college, and at seventeen had already begun to teach in a rural school.

In 1901, after three years as a township high school principal, Terman entered the junior year at Indiana University. His immediate goal was to obtain an A.B. degree from a university so that he might eventually be able to pursue work toward a Master's degree. Terman had been married in 1899, and the arrival of his first child a year later seemed to kindle an interest in psychology. Indeed, Indiana University was a fertile ground for anyone interested in the study of children. Several of the professors offering courses in psychology had studied with G. Stanley Hall of Clark University, who was a pioneer in the Child Study movement. Within two years, Terman completed both his Bachelor's and Master's degrees. One of Hall's students, E. H. Lindley, served as Terman's mentor. In a senior seminar with Lindley, Terman was asked to prepare two reports, one on mental deficiency and one on genius. The reading for these two reports introduced him to the writings of Frances Galton and Alfred Binet on mental tests. The following year, in his Master's thesis on leadership among children, Terman included some of Binet's measures of suggestibility.[3] In his Master's research, he reported that intelligence was one of the most important qualities contributing to leadership.[4]

Toward the end of his second year at Indiana, concerned about paying off financial debts and supporting his family, Terman began to look for a teaching position in the public schools. At Lindley's suggestion, he had also applied for a fellowship at Clark. To his surprise, he was offered the fellowship, and with the urging of Lindley and Indiana's other Clark alumni (W. L. Bryan and J. A. Bergström) he seriously considered accepting it. With further financial support from his father and one of his brothers, Terman decided to accept the Clark offer.

For Terman in 1903, entering Clark fulfilled his highest aspirations. In describing Clark, Terman noted its uniqueness from other American universities. It was primarily a graduate-level institution with a small student body. Its informality was unusual, as exemplified by the absence of grades and course requirements for graduation. The guiding spirit at Clark was its president, G. Stanley Hall. Hall had received his doctorate in psychology under William James, taught psychology at Johns Hopkins, and became the first president of Clark.[5] He was an ardent evolutionist who believed that heredity was a more significant determining factor than environment. By 1903 he was acknowledged as a leader of the child-centered philosophy of education, a point of view that emphasized the need for schools to adjust their curricula to the needs and inherent nature of children. According to Hall, the traditional nineteenth-century emphasis on academic subjects with regimented drill was inappropriate. Instead, he championed industrial training, moral education, physical training, and health. He also favored individualized instruction and believed that gifted children, who he assumed came primarily from the middle class, should be singled out for academic training by the time they reached adolescence.

The highlight of the Clark years for Terman was Hall's Monday-evening seminar. In these sessions, which started at 7:15 P.M. and often lasted until eleven or twelve, two students would report about their work to about thirty students in psychology, philosophy, and education. According to Terman, after the student presentations and ensuing discussion,

Hall would sum things up with an erudition and fertility of imagination that always amazed us and made us feel that his offhand insight into the problem went immeasurably beyond that of the student who had devoted months of slavish drudgery to it. . . . [At the end of each session] I always went home dazed and intoxicated, took a hot bath to quiet my nerves, then lay awake for hours rehearsing the drama and formulating the clever things I should have said and did not.[6]

Hall was such an inspiring figure for Terman that it was a disappointment to learn that Hall disapproved of mental tests. Following up on his Master's research, Terman wanted to carry out an experimental study of mental tests, and had to turn to Edmund C. Sanford, Clark's experimental psychologist, as his dissertation advisor.[7] In his research, Terman was interested in the types of mental processes involved in intelligence, and he therefore selected two groups of children of about the same age—a "bright" group and a "dull" group—and proceeded to determine which tests would best differentiate the two groups.[8] Terman completed his doctoral work in 1905, and as he was to comment later, all of his subsequent career interests were shaped by his years at Clark.[9]

During his stay at Clark, Terman had become ill with tuberculosis. While he made a successful recovery, it was decided that once he was finished with his studies it would be best to choose a warm climate. He therefore accepted a position as a high school principal in San Bernardino, California. A year later, he obtained a position more in line with his graduate training—teaching child study and pedagogy at the Los Angeles State Normal School, the forerunner of the University of California at Los Angeles. He remained at the normal school until 1910, when he received an appointment in the education department at Stanford University. He spent the rest of his career at Stanford, becoming head of the psychology department in 1922, a position he held until his retirement in 1942.

The move to Stanford in 1910 coincided with Terman's physical ability to pursue a more active academic schedule. He therefore was able to return to the research interests that he had developed in his graduate work. One of these areas was school hygiene, an area to which he was first exposed by Lindley and Bergström at Indiana, and then by William H. Burnham at Clark. His own personal health problem acted as a further stimulant. His work in school hygiene involved literature reviews and school surveys on such diverse problems as malnutrition, dental defects, adenoids, tuberculosis, childhood neuroses, and juvenile suicide. Hall's evolutionary perspective and its implications for education and society pervaded Terman's writings on these topics. Hall had stressed physical development and health as prerequisites for mental development. Disease and pathology were wasteful and therefore detrimental to the educational goals of training students to become efficient workers and contribute to the industrial development of the nation.[10] Terman echoed these sentiments by pointing to the school health movement as a means of preventing waste, and consequently harnessing the biological and social forces that would produce a happier, healthier, and better race.[11]

The other major area of research that Terman returned to was mental testing. In 1910, with the encouragement of E. B. Huey, a fellow Clark graduate, Terman began to work with the Binet 1908 scale. As already discussed in chapter 3, Henry H. Goddard, another of Hall's students, who had preceded Terman by a few years, had published translations of Binet's original 1905 scale and the subsequent 1908 revision.[12] Terman's first tentative revision of the Binet appeared in 1912,[13] and the finished product—the so-called "Stanford-Binet"—was published in 1916.[14] An innovative feature of the Stanford-Binet was the inclusion of the "Intelligence Quotient" or IQ—that is, the ratio between mental and chronological ages—a concept first introduced by William Stern but not previously used in mental tests.

As in the case of his work in school hygiene, Terman's views about testing were guided by an evolutionary biological perspective. Assuming the physical health of the child, the intelligence tests could be used to assess the child's inherent ability as well as potential for educational progress and level of vocational competence. In his 1916 handbook on the Stanford-Binet, Terman outlined the application and significance of intelligence tests.[15] First of all, the tests would identify individual differences in native intelligence and thus enable the schools to develop specialized programs. Such programs would allow each child to progress at his or her own rate, whether that rate was rapid or slow.

With respect to mental retardation, intelligence tests were already being effectively used to identify and grade the feebleminded. It was therefore possible to ascertain the degree of defect and then decide upon the type of instruction suited to the training of the backward child. Intelligence tests would also make it possible to detect milder degrees of mental defect, and thus correct the tendency of older methods of diagnosis to overlook the majority of higher-grade defectives. This group of defectives posed a particular threat to society because of their potential for crime, pauperism, and industrial inefficiency.

At the other end of the distribution of intelligence, Terman pointed to the benefits to be derived from identifying superior children through the use of mental tests. He noted that the future welfare of the country was dependent upon thle right education of superior children. The progress of civilization would be based on the advances made by those who were at the upper end of the continuum of native ability.

Terman also believed that through the use of intelligence tests it would be possible to study the effects of heredity and environment on mental development. For example, he posed the following question: "Is the place of so-called lower classes in the social and industrial scale the result of their inferior native endowment, or is their apparent inferiority merely a result of their inferior home and school training.?"[16] Based on a sample of about five hundred schoolchildren who were given IQ tests and classified by their teachers into five social-class groups, Terman concluded that children of higher social classes make a better showing on the tests primarily because of their superiority in original endowment. Although he had some reservations about this conclusion, apparently because of the correlational nature of the data, he went on to suggest that from what was already known about heredity it should be expected that the children of higher-social-class parents would be better endowed than those children reared in slums and poverty.

Regarding heredity and environment in relation to racial differences in intelligence, Terman posed the following question: "Are the inferior races really inferior, or are they merely unfortunate in their lack of opportunity to learn?"[17] Consistent with his biological orientation to differences in intelligence, he offered the following response, given in the context of discussing the low IQ scores of two boys of Portuguese extraction:

It is interesting to note that . . . [these cases] represent the level of intelligence which is very, very common among Spanish-Indian and Mexican families of the Southwest and also among negroes. Their dullness seems to be racial, or at least inherent in the family stocks from which they come. The fact that one meets this type with such extraordinary frequency among Indians, Mexicans, and negroes suggests quite forcibly that the whole question of racial differences in mental traits will have to be taken up anew and by experimental methods. The writer predicts that when this is done there will be discovered enormously significant racial differences in general intelligence, differences which cannot be wiped out by any scheme of mental culture.[18]

With the publication of his 1916 test, Terman had become a highly visible figure in the mental testing movement. It was therefore not surprising that he was called to serve on a committee that had been assembled at Vineland, New Jersey, in the spring of 1917 to devise mental tests for the army. The United States had entered World War I and Robert M. Yerkes, as shown in an earlier chapter, spearheaded the American Psychological Association in contributing to the war effort.[19] Yerkes chaired the test committee and among the members were Goddard and Guy M. Whipple. In his test development, Terman had corresponded with Yerkes, Goddard, and Whipple.[20] Terman brought with him a new group test of intelligence that had been developed by his doctoral student, Arthur S. Otis.[21] The Otis test served as a basis for the development of the army group tests. While serious questions have been raised about the significance of the psychologists' contributions to the war, there is no doubt that the war provided an enormous boost for the mental testing movement.[22] Approximately 1.75 million men were tested, and on this basis recommendations were made with respect to job placements or immediate discharge from the army.[23]

After the war, Terman seized upon the contribution of the army tests to military efficiency and predicted that they would soon be universally used in the schools.[24] To this end, in collaboration with Yerkes, he was able to secure a grant from the General Education Board of the Rockefeller Foundation to adapt the army tests for school use.[25] Working with a National Research Council committee, which included Yerkes and Edward L. Thorndike, the "National Intelligence Tests" for grades three to eight were developed and ready for use in 1920.[26] In 1922 Terman, as chairman of a National Education Association committee on the use of intelligence tests in revising elementary education, published a book with the committee that extolled the use of testing for reorganizing schools so that students could be classified into homogeneous ability groups—in other words, a tracking system.[27] As an example of this, he referred to the five-track plan in Oakland, California, developed by his former student, Virgil E. Dickson.[28]

A year later, Dickson published a monograph about his ability-grouping system.[29] In introducing this work, Terman commented that one of the author's most important contributions was to show that the differentiation of curricula and the ability classification of school-children were not undemocratic measures. On the contrary, they were absolutely essential if the public school was to be made a real instrument of democracy. As he stated, "True democracy does not rest upon equality of endowment, but upon equality of opportunity. . . . Reclassification of children and differentiation of courses of study . . . will go far toward insuring that every pupil, whether mentally superior, average, or inferior, shall have a chance to make the most of whatever abilities nature has given him."[30] Terman's prescription for a democratic society was not to go unchallenged.

The results of the army testing had been disseminated in various technical sources in the early 1920s.[31] In 1922 the testing results became widely known because of the appearance of several reports and discussions in popular periodicals.[32] Walter Lippmann, in his series in the *New Republic,* was highly critical of the test interpretation, and singled out Terman because of his development of the Stanford-Binet. Lippmann asserted that the claim made by Terman and the other army psychologists that the tests measured innate ability had no scientific foundation. He voiced his conern that "Intelligence testing in the hands of men who hold this dogma could but lead to an intellectual caste system in which the task of education had given way to the doctrine of predestination and infant damnation."[33] It should be noted that Lippmann did not simply rely on persuasive argument in challenging Terman. He specifically homed in on what he felt were faulty interpretations of the data. For example, Terman had argued that the correlation between IQ and social class among schoolchildren pointed to a hereditarian interpretation because the correlation co-efficient declined with increasing age, thereby indicating the de-creasing effect of the home environment.[34] Lippmann contended that as the child grows up he or she spends less time in the home and more time in the school and playground. He therefore concluded that Terman's data were "a rather strong argument . . . for the traditional American theory that the public school is an agency for equalizing the opportunities of the privileged and the unprivileged."[35] Despite the fact that Lippmann was quite technically sophisticated in many of his criticisms, Terman in his published reply recommended that Lippmann, as a layman, should stay out of issues he was not informed about.[36] Terman, in fact, was quite evasive in responding to such spe-cific criticisms as the assumption of innate intelligence and the issue of the average mental age of adults.[37]

In 1922, some months prior to his exchange with Lippmann, Terman engaged in a debate with psychologist William C. Bagley of Teachers College.[38] This marked the beginning of a controversy with fellow psychologists about intelligence testing that would last inter-mittently through 1940. Bagley, like Lippmann, challenged Terman's assumption that intelligence tests measure native intelligence, and branded Terman a "Determinist" because of his fatalistic conclusions regarding the influence of education on intellectual performance. Bagley was especially critical of Terman's contention that through IQ tests the limits of a child's educability could be determined by the fifth or sixth school year, and consequently differentiated vocational training could begin at that time. For Bagley, who was committed to a social evolutionary perspective in which mass education could im-prove the intellectual functioning of children generally and better prepare them to participate in a democratic society, Terman's pre-scription of equality of opportunity for each child to develop his or her original nature was tantamount to a system of intellectual aris-tocracy. Bagley, like Lippmann, acknowledged the existence of differ-ences in native ability, but he professed that it was the similarities in ideas, ideals, aspirations, and standards that were more significant for social progress. As he stated, "A little more light for the common man this year, next year, a hundred years from now, and the battle for humanity, for democracy, and for brotherhood is won."[39] According to Bagley, in order to achieve a "pervasive common culture," which was the prime function of democratic education, the significant goal should not be rate of school progress, but the ultimate product—in other words, schools should afford equality of results.

In his responses to both Lippmann and Bagley, Terman dismissed his critics as being unscientific. Terman was convinced that the facts of science pointed to a hereditarian explanation of IQ differences. But, in fact, did the data unequivocally point to such an interpretation, and was it empirically established that the schools could do little to raise the level of pupils' intellectual functioning? These were the questions raised by Lippmann and Bagley. Furthermore, a more basic question alluded to by these critics concerned the assumption that intelligence could be defined by a common factor, such as "abstract thinking."[40] Could it not be argued that such a criterion as reflected in intelligence tests was a socially constructed one—that is, used as a scheme of social ranking by those who had already achieved the standard of comparison? This line of attack was heralded by John Dewey.[41]

While Dewey did not make any further forays into the public arena of testing controversy, the Terman-Bagley debate generated considerable discussion in the professional literature.[42] In an effort to resolve matters, Terman took on the task of chairing a committee to organize a yearbook on "The Possibilities and Limitations of Training," under the auspices of the National Society for the Study of Education.[43] The yearbook, which appeared in 1928, included a series of empirical studies relevant to hereditarian and environmental influences on mental development.[44] Terman in his assessment of the yearbook was less dogmatic than he had been in previous exchanges, but still held that environmental factors contributed little to IQ scores.[45] Among those arguing for the significance of environmental influences were Bagley, Charles H. Judd, and Bird T. Baldwin. Judd, an educational psychologist from the University of Chicago, emphasized, as Bagley had, a social evolutionary perspective, pointing to the broad historical movements that account for modern advances in intelligence.[46] Along similar lines, Baldwin, the director of the University of Iowa's Child Welfare Research Station, referred to the relevance of child development and the role of environmental factors in accelerating developmental progress.[47]

As in the previous exchanges, both sides often seemed to talk past one another. This is because they were each operating from opposing frameworks. Terman, Whipple, and the other army testers—Yerkes, Goddard, and Thorndike—were committed to a biologically rooted democratic model of meritocracy. Bagley, Dewey, Judd, and Baldwin held to a contextual, sociohistorical model of democratic egalitarianism. It appeared as though an impasse had been reached—but Terman was to be dragged, one more time, over the coals for his hereditarian position. Baldwin, who died prematurely in 1928, had begun to study developmental changes in IQ scores. His successor at Iowa, George D. Stoddard, guided a cadre of Iowa researchers who looked at the effects of various environmental enrichment programs. Influenced by New Deal social reconstruction, Stoddard and his group challenged Terman, in 1940, to a yearbook rematch that was to prove far more acrimonious than any of Terman's previous exchanges.[48] Stoddard campaigned for the limited use of IQ tests. He maintained that such tests should be used only for diagnostic and research purposes. Furthermore, Stoddard argued that environmental enrichment could raise IQ scores. The 1940 debate, as in the past, led to an impasse. However, Terman worried that Stoddard's determined effort to disseminate recommendations against mass testing would be successful. If that happened, Terman's democratic ideal of a meritocracy could, indeed, be threatened.[49] In fact, no great changes took place in the use of IQ tests in the schools. It would not be until the 1960s, in the context of the civil rights movement, that mass testing would be seriously challenged.[50] Terman did modify his position somewhat after World War II. He still held to his democratic ideal of a meritocracy, but he no longer held to a hereditarian explanation of race differences, and he acknowledged that among the gifted, home environment was related to degree of success.[51]

Terman, in his role as a social scientist, was dedicated to the values of a democratic society. In an unpublished paper written in 1948 and entitled "My Faith," he declared his lifelong support for the promotion of social justice, mutual understanding, racial tolerance, and equalization of opportunity.[52] With respect to social, economic, and political issues, Terman consistently identified himself as a liberal.[53] Indeed, the roots of his career are situated within the liberal reform movement of the Progressive Era.[54] As part of the spirit of reform, Terman was committed to advancing psychology as a science that could contribute to the social progress of American society. He, like so many of the psychologists of his generation, was swept up by the promise of applied psychology as demonstrated by the army testing program of World War I. His advocacy of a meritocratic society based on the "democratic" principle that all people have an equal opportunity to make the most of their potential provided the basis for an efficient and ordered society. "Prediction and control," "human engineering," and "social efficiency" were the catch phrases for postwar American psychology. Moreover, American society was receptive. Efficiency and order had already become the established themes of the Progressive movement.

Social science during the Progressive Era was dominated by Darwinian evolutionary thought. There were, however, two interpretations: (1) "Social Darwinism," which was committed to a biologically deterministic point of view regarding social phenomena, and (2) "Reform Darwinism," which emphasized the role of social forces in shaping society.[55] It was out of these two schools of thought that the debate on mental testing arose: the meritocratic view of Terman and the other testing advocates reflecting Social Darwinism, and the egalitarian view of the testing critics, such as Bagley and Dewey, reflecting Reform Darwinism. It was the Social Darwinists who were the more influential group, at least through the early 1920s.[56] In general, it seemed that biological determinism and a hereditarian explanation of human differences were very compatible with the vertical division of labor necessary for an industrialized society. More specifically, the use of mental tests provided an efficient means of classifying individuals in terms of their potential contribution to the social order of the corporate state. Within the context of public education, mental tests were welcomed as an expedient tool for classifying a burgeoning population of schoolchildren, swelled by large numbers of recent immigrants.[57] To bring order out of chaos, the leaders of the educational establishment, by 1918, had clearly opted for a differentiated curriculum.[58] Vocational education was emphasized at the secondary level—mass education did not mean mass academic education. Thus, there was agreement among psychologists and educators that mental tests had great potential in the schools for appropriately sorting students.[59] Only the students toward the upper end of the IQ distribution would be sorted into academic tracks.

Terman, in the context of his times, was a liberal social scientist. His vision of a democratic society, to be led by those at the highest levels of native ability, was shared by many in the scientific and educational community. Such a biological determinist view would eventually be seen as anathema to liberalism, but during the Progressive Era liberals often viewed hereditarian explanations as scientific tools that could be used for social progress. While Terman received considerable support from his peers, he was, by the 1920s, also criticized. The debate that emerged from these criticisms reveals weaknesses in Terman's scientific credibility. First of all, his adherence to a hereditarian explanation of IQ differences was not explicitly supported by the data. Critics, such as Lippmann, had demonstrated that the data could just as easily be interpreted by an environmentalist hypothesis. Furthermore, as Dewey had contended, the definition of intelligence was based on a social standard. Those who were already at the top of the social order, by virtue of their occupational status, were chosen as the standard of success. IQ distributions of schoolchildren reflected, for the most part, the existing ranking system of opportunities provided by the social position of their parents. Terman made the false assumption that American society contained no significant class and race barriers against social advancement. In the guise of "objective science," he was, in fact, defining intelligence from his own middle-class position.[60] Based on his background and experience, as well as his uncritical acceptance of social reality (or his failure to perceive it), he was unable to realize that the black child or the child of recent immigrants did not have the same opportunities he had had as a white Protestant farm boy who could choose a school-teaching career as a vehicle for social mobility.

Terman's democratic ideal of a meritocracy based on innate ability was not, in the context of his own times, a bona fide democratic ideal. His legacy of mass intelligence testing served to perpetuate an unjust social order. This is not to say that Terman's class bias was intentional—rather, it seems to have been the product of the natural-science model that he and the majority of psychologists of his generation were wedded to. Within this model, which still dominates much of contemporary psychology, data are treated in a sociohistorical vacuum.[61] What Terman failed to see, working within the confines of such a framework, was that individual differences in intelligence are influenced by such sociocultural factors as historical conditions and class structure. This failure to take sociocultural context into account has been a particular problem in the area of intelligence testing from Terman's time to the more recent controversies of the 1960s and 1970s about race and class differences in IQ.[62]

NOTES

Research for this chapter was carried out while I was on sabbatical leave at the Stanford University Archives with the generous support of a Leave Fellowship from the Social Sciences and Humanities Research Council of Canada. I would like to thank Roxanne L. Nilan and Linda Long of the Stanford University Archives, and Maxine B. Clapp of the University of Minnesota Archives for their help in obtaining archival materials.

1. Lewis M. Terman, "Were We Born that Way?" *World's Work* 44 (1922): 657–659.
2. Lewis M. Terman, "Trails to Psychology," in *A History of Psychology in Autobiography,* vol. 2, edited by Carl Murchison (Worcester, Mass.: Clark University Press, 1932), 297–331.
3. Lewis M. Terman, "A Preliminary Study in the Psychology and Pedagogy of Leadership," *Pedagogical Seminary* 11 (1904): 413–451.
4. Ibid., 433.
5. See Dorothy Ross, *G. Stanley Hall: The Psychologist as Prophet* (Chicago: University of Chicago Press, 1972); Merle Curti, *The Social Ideas of American Educators* (Paterson, N.J.: Littlefield, Adams, 1959), 396–428.
6. Terman, "Trails to Psychology," 316. Terman continued the Clark tradition of weekly evening seminars when he was at Stanford.
7. Hall nevertheless accepted Terman's choice (Terman, "Trails to Psychology," 318), and Terman never held Hall's position on mental tests against him. See Joseph Peterson, *Early Conceptions and Tests of Intelligence* (Yonkers, N.Y.: World Book Company, 1925), 225–226.
8. Lewis M. Terman, "Genius and Stupidity: A Study of Some of the Intellectual Processes of Seven 'Bright' and Seven 'Stupid' Boys," *Pedagogical Seminary* 13 (1906): 307–373.
9. Terman, "Trails to Psychology," 321.
10. See G. Stanley Hall, "The Ideal School as Based on Child Study." *Forum* 32 (1901): 24–39; idem, *Educational Problems,* vol. 1 (New York: Appleton, 1911), 627, 634, 639. See also Ross, *G. Stanley Hall,* 417–419.
11. Lewis M. Terman, *The Hygiene of the School Child* (Boston: Houghton Mifflin, 1914), 1–2.
12. Henry H. Goddard, "The Binet and Simon Tests of Intellectual Capacity,"

The Training School 5 (1908): 3–9; idem, "A Measuring Scale for Intelligence," *The Training School* 6 (1910): 146–155. Although Hall did not approve of mental tests, his perspective of child psychology apparently served as a catalyst for the development of these tests. During the 1910s Goddard, Huey, Terman, Fredrick Kuhlmann, and J. E. W. Wallin, all of whom studied with Hall at Clark, produced revisions of the Binet scales. For a discussion of Goddard's work in testing, see Leila Zenderland, "The Debate over Diagnosis: Henry Herbert Goddard and the Medical Acceptance of Intelligence Testing," chapter 3 of this volume.

13. Lewis M. Terman and H. G. Childs, "A Tentative Revision and Extension of the Binet-Simon Measuring Scale of Intelligence," *Journal of Educational Psychology* 3 (1912): 61–74, 133–143, 198–208, 277–289.

14. Lewis M. Terman, *The Measurement of Intelligence* (Boston: Houghton Mifflin, 1916).

15. Ibid., 3–21, 65–104.

16. Ibid., 19.

17. Ibid., 20.

18. Ibid., 91–92.

19. See Robert M. Yerkes, "Psychology in Relation to the War," *Psychological Review* 25 (1918): 85–115. For Yerkes's contribution to army testing, see also James Reed, "Robert Yerkes and the Mental Testing Movement," and Richard T. von Mayrhauser, "The Manager, the Medic, and the Mediator: The Clash of Professional Psychological Styles and the Wartime Origins of Group Mental Testing," chapters 4 and 7 of this volume.

20. Terman, "Trails to Psychology," 324.

21. Clarence S. Yoakum and Robert M. Yerkes, *Army Mental Tests* (New York: Holt, 1920), 2.

22. See Daniel J. Kevles, "Testing the Army's Intelligence: Psychologists and the Military in World War I," *Journal of American History* 55 (1968): 565–581; Franz Samelson, "Putting Psychology on the Map: Ideology and Intelligence Testing," in *Psychology in Social Context,* edited by Allan R. Buss (New York: Irvington, 1979), 103–168.

23. Yoakum and Yerkes, *Army Mental Tests,* 12.

24. Lewis M. Terman, *The Intelligence of School Children* (Boston: Houghton Mifflin, 1919), xiv.

25. Lewis M. Terman, Virgil E. Dickson, A. H. Sutherland, Raymond H. Franzen, C. R. Tupper, and Grace Fernald, *Intelligence Tests and School Reorganization* (Yonkers, N.Y.: World Book Company, 1922), 2.

26. Terman also developed a comparable test at the high-school level: the "Terman Group Test of Mental Ability."

27. Terman et al., *School Reorganization,* 2–3.

28. Ibid., 18–19. In the 1920s Terman and his students fostered several tracking systems in school districts near Stanford. See Paul D. Chapman, "Schools as Sorters: Lewis M. Terman and the Intelligence Testing Movement, 1890–1930" (Ph.D. diss., Stanford University, 1980).

29. Virgil E. Dickson, *Mental Tests and the Classroom Teacher* (Yonkers, N.Y.: World Book Company, 1923). This book was in the "Measurement and Adjustment Series," a series edited by Terman and initiated in 1923.

30. Ibid., xiv–xv.

31. See Carl C. Brigham, *A Study of American Intelligence* (Princeton, N.J.: Princeton University Press, 1923); Robert M. Yerkes, ed., *Psychological Examining in the United States Army,* vol. 15, Memoirs of the National Academy of Sciences (Washington, D.C.: Government Printing Office, 1921); Yoakum and Yerkes, *Army Mental Tests.*

32. See Cornelia J. Cannon, "American Misgivings," *Atlantic Monthly* 129 (1922): 145–157. See also the series by Walter Lippman: "The Mental Age of Americans," *New Republic* 32 (1922): 213–215, "The Mystery of the 'A' Men," ibid., 246–248; "The Reliability of Intelligence Tests," ibid., 275–277; "The Abuse of the Tests," ibid., 297–298; "Tests of Hereditary Intelligence," ibid., 328–330; and "A Future for the Tests," ibid., 33 (1922): 9–10.

33. Lippmann, "The Abuse of the Tests," 298.

34. Terman had categorized the data into three age levels: 5–8 years, 9–11 years, and 12–15 years. See Terman, *The Stanford Revision,* 97.

35. Lippman, "Tests of Hereditary Intelligence," 329.

36. Lewis M. Terman, "The Great Conspiracy, or the Impulse Imperious of Intelligence Testers, Psychoanalyzed and Exposed by Mr. Lippmann," *New Republic* 33 (1922): 116–120. See also Walter Lippmann, "The Great Confusion: A Reply to Mr. Terman," *New Republic* 33 (1923): 145–146.

37. Lippmann had raised the issue of the discrepancy of the average mental age of adults. Yerkes's 1921 army report had indicated a 13-year mental age, based on the army testing. However, on the Stanford-Binet the age norm for adults was 16. See Nicholas Pastore, "The Army Intelligence Tests and Walter Lippmann," *Journal of the History of the Behavioral Sciences* 14 (1978): 316–327.

38. William C. Bagley, "Educational Determinism; or Democracy and the I.Q.," *School and Society* 15 (1922): 373–384; Lewis M. Terman, "The Psychological Determinist; or Democracy and the I.Q.," *Journal of Educational Research* 6 (1922): 57–62; William C. Bagley, "Professor Terman's Determinism: A Rejoinder," *Journal of Educational Research* 6 (1922): 371–385. Bagley's articles were reprinted, in large part, with a series of related papers in William C. Bagley, *Determinism in Education* (Baltimore: Warwick and York, 1925).

39. Bagley, *Determinism in Education,* 32.

40. For discussions about defining intelligence, see Beardsley Ruml, "Intelligence and its Measurement," *Journal of Educational Psychology* 12 (1921): 143–144; Lewis M. Terman, "Intelligence and Its Measurement," *Journal of Educational Psychology* 12 (1921): 127–133.

41. John Dewey, "Individuality Equality and Superiority," *New Republic* 33 (1922): 61–62.

42. See John C. Almack, James F. Bursch, and James C. DeVoss, "Democracy,

Determinism and the I.Q.," *School and Society* 18 (1923): 292–295; Truman L. Kelley, "Again: Educational Determinism," *Journal of Educational Research* 8 (1923): 10–19; Guy M. Whipple, "The Intelligence Testing Program and Its Objectors—Conscientious and Otherwise," *School and Society* 17 (1923): 561–568, 596–604.

43. See Lewis M. Terman, "The Possibilities and Limitations of Training," *Journal of Educational Research* 10 (1924): 335–343.

44. See Guy M. Whipple, ed., *The Twenty-Seventh Yearbook of the National Society for the Study of Education—Nature and Nurture,* parts 1 and 2 (Bloomington, Ill.: Public School Publishing, 1928).

45. Lewis M. Terman, "The Influence of Nature and Nurture upon Intelligence Scores: An Evaluation of the Evidence in Part I of the 1928 Yearbook of the National Society for the Study of Education," *Journal of Educational Psychology* 19 (1928): 362–373.

46. Charles H. Judd, "Intelligence as Method of Adaptation," *Journal of Educational Psychology* 19 (1928): 397–404.

47. Bird T. Baldwin, "Heredity and Environment—or Capacity and Training?" *Journal of Educational Psychology* 19 (1928): 405–409.

48. See Henry L. Minton, "The Iowa Child Welfare Research Station and the 1940 Debate on Intelligence: Carrying on the Legacy of a Concerned Mother," *Journal of the History of the Behavioral Sciences* 20 (1984): 160–176.

49. Terman's concerns about Stoddard's attack on mass testing can be determined from the following correspondence: Terman to Benjamin R. Simpson, April 7, 1939, folder 1, box 1, *LMT;* Terman to Simpson, March 12, 1940, folder 35, box 15, *LMT;* William C. Ferguson to Terman, April 26, 1940, and Terman to Ferguson, May 1, 1940, folder 20, box 20, *LMT;* and Terman to Florence L. Goodenough, May 1, 1940, Correspondence files, *FLG.*

50. Chapman, "Schools as Sorters," 190–191.

51. See Ernest R. Hilgard, "Lewis Madison Terman: 1877–1956," *American Journal of Psychology* 70 (1957): 472–479; Lewis M. Terman, "The Discovery and Encouragement of Exceptional Talent," *American Psychologist* 9 (1954): 221–230.

52. Lewis M. Terman, "My Faith," typescript (1948), 6, *LMT.*

53. Terman, "Trails to Psychology," 330; Terman to Nicholas Pastore, March 4, 1948, folder 18, box 15, *LMT.* For an analysis of Terman's liberal ideology, see Russell Marks, "Lewis M. Terman: Individual Differences and the Construction of Social Reality," *Educational Theory* 24 (1974): 336–355.

54. See Arthur A. Ekrich, Jr., *Progressivism in America: A Study of the Era from Theodore Roosevelt to Woodrow Wilson* (New York: Franklin Watts, 1974), 19–33; Robert H. Wiebe, *The Search for Order: 1877–1920* (New York: Hill and Wang, 1967), 111–132.

55. See Ekrich, *Progressivism in America,* 19–33; for a more extended discussion, see Richard Hofstadter, *Social Darwinism in American Thought,* rev. ed. (Boston: Beacon, 1955).

56. See Hamilton Cravens, *The Triumph of Evolution: American Scientists and the Heredity-Environment Controversy, 1900–1941* (Philadelphia: University of Pennsylvania Press, 1978), for an analysis of the intellectual shift that occurred in the 1920s.

57. See Lawrence A. Cremin, *The Transformation of the School: Progressivism in American Education, 1876–1957* (New York: Knopf, 1961); David B. Tyack, *The One Best System: A History of American Urban Education* (Cambridge, Mass.: Harvard University Press, 1974).

58. Richard Hofstadter, *Anti-intellectualism in American Life* (New York: Knopf, 1962), 323–358.

59. See Chapman, "Schools as Sorters"; Tyack, *The One Best System*, 198–216. As in the case of the psychological community, there were, by the 1920s, differing opinions among educators about the value of testing.

60. For similar analyses of the class bias on the part of the leaders of the mental testing movement, see Seymour B. Sarason, *Psychology Misdirected* (New York: Free Press, 1981), 83–91; Samelson, "Putting Psychology on the Map," 152–156. For discussions of the class bias inherent in the use of intelligence tests, see Samuel Bowles and Herbert Gintis, *Schooling in Capitalist America: Educational Reform and the Contradictions of Economic Life* (New York: Basic Books, 1976), 114–124; Clarence J. Karier, "Testing for Order and Control in the Corporate Liberal State," *Educational Theory* 22 (1972): 154–180.

61. See Kenneth J. Gergen, *Toward Transformation in Social Knowledge* (New York: Springer-Verlag, 1982); Henry L. Minton, "Emancipatory Social Psychology as a Paradigm for the Study of Minority Groups," in *Dialectics and Ideology in Psychology,* edited by Knud S. Larsen (Norwood, N.J.: Ablex, 1986), 257–277.

62. See Richard J. Herrnstein, *I.Q. in the Meritocracy* (Boston: Little, Brown, 1973); Arthur A. Jensen, "How Much Can We Boost I.Q. and Scholastic Achievement?" *Harvard Educational Review* 39 (1969): 1–123; Ashley Montague, ed., *Race and I.Q.* (London: Oxford University Press, 1975).

6

Was Early Mental Testing

(a) Racist Inspired,

(b) Objective Science,

(c) A Technology for Democracy,

(d) The Origin of Multiple-Choice Exams,

(e) None of the Above?

(Mark the RIGHT Answer)

"The general mental test," Stanford psychologist Lee Cronbach wrote in the 1960s, " . . . stands today as the most important single contribution of psychology to the practical guidance of human affairs."[1] Nevertheless, or perhaps for that very reason, "psychological testing has been a controversial area from its beginnings, perhaps never more so than in the past decade."[2] This description still seems to fit today, even if the decade in question is long gone. Yet when we ask how carefully and soberly the effects of this major contribution to society have been evaluated, we do not find very comforting answers. Only selected aspects of the question have been dealt with, and those largely in polemical fashion.

The major argument in the public controversy over mental testing revolved around the initial claims of the fixed, genetic nature of the IQ, and with it the innate basis of individual and group differences found with this measure. The quarrel began in the 1910s with the agitation over the "Menace of the Feebleminded."[3] In the 1920s the debate initially focused on the "average American's 13-year-old mentality,"[4] but was displaced quickly by the alleged genetic differences between the "Nordic" and the southeastern European "races." After the passage of the Immigration Restriction Act of 1924—with some, but no crucial, assistance from intelligence tests[5]—the focus shifted once more, to differences between white and nonwhite groups.[6] But while questions about the testing pioneers' "racist" attitudes and about the institutional racism built into testing continue to remain in the spotlight—on a backdrop of more diffuse arguments about the oppressive effects of "standardized" selection tests on individuals[7]—other issues related to the testing movement have been largely ignored.

One of these issues concerns the global impact of testing on the organization of social institutions, above all the educational system, followed by the labor market and its system of work-force selection. The massive introduction of testing into these settings was largely justified by two claims. The first, seemingly pragmatic one concerned the improvement in *efficiency* that would be achieved by the scientific selection and differential assignment of individuals to particular slots in the system. But just as the army testers of World War I had loudly proclaimed their large contribution to the efficiency of the U.S. Army with little hard evidence to back it up (in their more cautious moments the testers spoke only of the *potential* contribution to efficiency, *if* the army had used the test information appropriately),[8] so have the beneficial effects on education and industry been more often assumed than systematically investigated. Recently, some researchers have produced calculations claiming impressive results for the economy by use of selection tests;[9] however, their procedures involve large extrapolations in a hypothetical model rather than actual, observed outcomes. They also neglect any unanticipated consequences so typical of large-scale social interventions.

Neither do we have solid evidence, beyond testimonials, for the second type of claim: that testing made an important contribution to the *democratic character* of the system through the objectivity and universalism of its procedures. Actually, at its beginning, mental testing was justified by some eugenicist meritocrats as leading to the "rule of . . . the real and total aristocracy," which would supplant the "delusion" of an unworkable democratic ideal and do away with universal adult suffrage in the process.[10] But the elimination of bias and privilege by objective tests was the more usual theme. The counterargument, that testing functioned largely as a technique to maintain social *inequality,* and as its ideological justification to boot,[11] is not all that easy to disprove—although test scores did, unquestionably, assist the upward mobility of an unknown number of individuals.[12] One large-scale attempt to investigate the "social consequences" of testing for its subjects ended in some rather ambiguous conclusions. It did find that among both students and adults positive opinions about the personal consequences of test taking and about the general fairness of the use of tests were more frequent than negative opinions. But the study even failed to present clear summary data of the frequency of the negative opinions, not to mention a fuller investigation of possible negative consequences.[13] And a forty-page literature survey of studies of the effects of testing devoted only a final half page to the effects on society.[14]

In the new spirit of accountability, these questions deserve more sustained exploration than they have received. But the present essay will not pursue such complex and affect-laden issues. Neither will it address the other interesting issue, concerning the rather ambivalent attitudes of academic psychologists toward testing. After it had first provided enormous publicity for the young and struggling science of psychology, testing soon found itself segregated, as the "other psychology," from the prestige-carrying experimental mainstream of the discipline. Since then it has been invoked mainly by Introductory Psychology lecturers as an example of the objective, quantitative nature of psychology, or (more recently) defended against claims of ideological bias in our science.[15]

I will focus instead on a more specific technological detail of the testing movement, which is taken for granted today but which was nonetheless of major importance, both as a precondition for the massive use of testing and subsequently through its impact on the whole educational process. I am referring to the humble yet all-pervasive multiple choice question and its variants—an invention ingenious in its simplicity—which was the indispensable vehicle for the dramatic growth of mass testing in this country in the span of a few years. It had not existed before 1914; by 1921 it had spawned a dozen group intelligence tests and provided close to two million soldiers and over three million schoolchildren with a numerical index of their intelligence; it was also about to transform achievement testing in the classroom.

Challenged by the enormous expansion of mass education and its ensuing bureaucratization, psychologists and educators had worked on the improvement and standardization of school tests since the turn of the century. But by the 1910s much evidence of the unreliability and subjectivity of grades and scores even in "standardized" achievement examinations, such as the New York Regents Examination, had accumulated.[16] The mental testing movement, on the other hand, had developed "objective" measurement procedures; but it had been saddled with "a distinct prejudice . . . against the group test" and was struggling with what Terman called "Binet's *'methode de luxe'*"[17]: the laborious one-on-one technique of individual testing, rather unwieldy for really large-scale applications needed for the establishment of population norms. The resolution of this dilemma was triggered by America's entry into World War I, which quickly involved the academic psychologists through the formation of the American Psychological Association's Committee on Methods of Psychological Examining of Recruits, under the leadership of Robert M. Yerkes.[18] When the committee members met at Vineland, New Jersey, in May 1917 to plan their strategy, they soon realized that a different and new technique for group testing was needed, if they wanted to carry out their quickly escalating, ambitious schemes, which eventually included the screening of literally the whole U.S. draft army. Within less than two weeks, the committee produced a new format for its tests that combined the mass administration of school examinations and the standardization of individual intelligence tests: they had found a way to transform the testees' answers from highly variable, often idiosyncratic, and always time-consuming oral or written responses into easily marked choices among fixed alternatives, quickly scorable by clerical workers with the aid of superimposed stencils.

Whose flash of genius had produced this powerful invention? The official history of the army testing informs us that "the contribution made by Arthur S. Otis, in devising a system of group tests, deserves special mention." Otis had generously placed all his methods, including "certain ingenious devices which permitted responses to be given without writing . . . [and allowing] objectivity in scoring . . . , in the hands of Terman, who brought them to the committee." The scale subsequently produced by the committee, and which eventually became the famous army Alpha, "bears a close resemblance to the Otis scale."[19]

Arthur S. Otis (1886–1963), then a graduate student at Stanford, had been caught up in Terman's efforts to develop the Stanford-Binet intelligence test.[20] Realizing the need for group testing, Otis constructed a "Scale for the Group Measurements of Intelligence" in the years before the war. Half of its component tests used a response format requiring categorical answers, a procedure recognizable as a precursor of what later became the standard multiple-choice item or its lowly cousin, the true-false item. Obviously, this must have been the scale Terman took to Vineland, even though Otis did not publish it until the following year.[21] In the meantime, Otis had joined the army in 1917 to work for Yerkes's Psychology Division in the Surgeon General's Office. After the war, he became the test editor for the World Book Company, whose publisher, Caspar Hodgson, had earlier recognized the importance as well as the market potential of intelligence and educational tests. In addition to producing a series of his own highly popular group intelligence tests, Otis supervised the publication of a number of other intelligence and achievement tests and test-related books.

Even though the texts of the twenties usually mentioned Otis's contribution to the army group tests,[22] his name gradually disappeared from the history books.[23] But how and when had he hit on the felicitous idea to simplify the test format? The published record is not explicit on this question. It appears that in earlier work Otis had also been involved with educational tests, among them tests of reading. In a 1916 article, he discussed various existing tests of "reading ability" and the confusion among their implicit definitions of the skills involved. Proceeding to strip away what he considered nonessentials, such as pronunciation, his analysis eventually terminated in a definition of the "essence of reading ability" as best measured by the rate of "categorization of words." Otis proposed to determine this rate by asking pupils to find and then underline all words that fitted a particular concept (such as "object") presented in the instruction. Besides providing a purer measure, this technique would permit the administration of the reading test "*en masse*" and its scoring by "unskilled labor" in a very short time.[24]

Although Otis did not present any examples of his own, he illustrated his ideas with an item borrowed from a recently published test of reading skills. In this item, pupils were presented with several words and had to choose the one that fitted a concept defined in the item stem. Here we have the kernel of the multiple-choice idea (even if the item was intended as a measure of reading skill—which, on second thought, may in fact be an appropriate description of many of the billions of multiple-choice items that were to come). But Otis did not follow this lead. Earlier in the article he had discussed, among several other reading tests, Thorndike's Visual Vocabulary Scale A, which included the principle of repeated "checking by classes" of longer lists of single words.[25] Yet Otis thought the particular procedure too complicated. Attempting to simplify it, he ended his 1916 article in a blind alley. He suggested the technique, probably taken from the older "letter cancellation" tests, of presenting a long string of some fifty or more unrelated words and asking the pupil to underline all the nouns signifying "objects." The resulting score of correct marks would be a measure of the rate of silent reading. By the time Otis constructed his group intelligence test, he had dropped this approach and returned to the other item format, which was more concise as well as more widely applicable.

The item cited by Otis was actually only one of a set of similar items that, mixed with others requiring written answers, made up the Kansas Silent Reading Test. This test was produced in 1914–1915 by Frederick J. Kelly (1880–1959), whose Ph.D. dissertation at Teachers College had documented, a few years earlier, the unreliability of teachers' marks.[26] In 1914 he was the director of the Training School at the State Normal School at Emporia, Kansas; a year later he became Dean of Education at the University of Kansas. Kelly set out to purify and improve on existing reading tests, including Thorndike's recently published reading scales. But he was explicit about adding another important goal to his objectives: the reduction of time and effort in the test's administration and scoring.[27]

In his instructions to Kansas school superintendents, whom he asked to cooperate by suggesting additional items, he provided the following specifications: The new test items should "(1) . . . be subject to only one interpretation (2) . . . call for but one thing . . . wholly right or wholly wrong, and not partly right and partly wrong." The first (sample) item in his test read (see Figure 1):

> Below are given the names of four animals. Draw a line around the name of each animal that is useful on the farm: cow tiger rat wolf.[28]

As far as I have been able to determine, this was the first published multiple-choice item—an invention that soon found its way, with Otis's modifications including the true-false question, from reading tests to intelligence tests. In view of the high frequency of multiple inventions and discoveries, it would not be surprising if similar devices had been constructed independently by other educators or testers. Indeed, the use of stencils to simplify test scoring was presented by Yerkes as a double invention by Thorndike and Otis.[29] Actually, however, Thorndike had described the use of stencils already in his 1914 article, when Otis was just getting involved in test construction. Concerning the item format, on the other hand, Thorndike and his students had developed since 1900 a number of variations on the letter cancellation test and administered them to school classes; and in the context of psychophysics rather than psychometrics, a multiple-choice response format labeled "selection from a variety" had been used even earlier, at least on one occasion.[30] Such leads, especially Thorndike's categorization task in his Vocabulary Scale, may well have affected Kelly's ideas about item construction. Still, the historical line of influence in the development of the multiple-choice format does proceed from Kelly to Otis, and on to Terman and the Vineland group preparing to test the U.S. Army.

The enormous publicity given to the army intelligence tests soon led to what Stephen Leacock satirized as the "testing craze." The early twenties spawned more than a dozen group intelligence tests, fulfilling Terman's dream of "a mental test for every child."[31] The second step in the development was the rapid and extensive spreading

---

Test II.

State Normal School,
EMPORIA, KAN.
Bureau of Educational Measurements
and Standards.

Put
Pupil's
Score
Here.

THE KANSAS SILENT READING TEST.

Devised by F. J. Kelly

FOR

Grades 6, 7 and 8.

City.................................... State.................. Date....................

Pupil's Name.. Age.......... Grade..............

School.. Teacher..............................

Directions for Giving the Tests.

After telling the children not to open the papers ask those on the front seats to distribute the papers, placing one upon the desk of each pupil in the class. Have each child fill in the blank spaces at the top of this page. Then make clear the following:

Instructions to be Read by Teacher and Pupils Together.

This little five-minute game is given to see how quickly and accurately pupils can read silently. To show what sort of game it is, let us read this:

> Below are given the names of four animals. Draw a line around the name of each animal that is useful on the farm:
>
> cow   tiger   rat   wolf

This exercise tells us to draw a line around the word cow. No other answer is right. Even if a line is drawn *under* the word cow, the exercise is wrong, and counts nothing. The game consists of a lot of just such exercises, so it is wise to study each exercise carefully enough to be sure that you know exactly what you are asked to do. The number of exercises which you can finish thus in five minutes will make your score, so do them as fast as you can, being sure to do them right. Stop at once when time is called. Do not open the papers until told, so that all may begin at the same time.

The teacher should then be sure that each pupil has a good pencil or pen. Note the minute and second by the watch, and say, BEGIN.

Allow exactly five minutes.

Answer no questions of the pupils which arise from not understanding what to do with any given exercise.

When time is up say STOP and then collect the papers at once.

FIGURE 1. Frederick J. Kelly's first Multiple-Choice Item. Front page of the *Kansas Silent Reading Test*, 1915.

of the alternative-response format from intelligence tests back to achievement tests, not only for reading but for various subject matters, in the schools and colleges. Standard histories of educational measurement credit a 1920 article by W. A. McCall on true-false tests with arousing interest in the "new examination."[32] However, McCall, a colleague of Thorndike at Teachers College, was only trying to extend one of the "new technics" to school examinations (although he did not mention Otis nor cite any other specific tests). His article may have helped to spread knowledge of the true-false format; but familiarity with the army psychologists' new group testing methods had already grown fairly wide by then. Adaptation to the classroom proceeded apace. "Most of the tests now on the market, unless measuring handwriting, do not call for written answers,"[33] observed one member of the quickly emerging class of technical experts in educational measurement: in addition to new products, the new technology was also creating another professional specialty eager and ready to instruct the classroom teacher.

Not surprisingly, this revolution in testing included a debate about the desirability of the "new methods." They were accused of emphasizing memorization of unrelated facts, of encouraging guessing and "dependent" rather than independent achievement; they also represented "reactionary ideals" of instruction.[34] Although defenders conceded some merit to such criticisms, they found it impossible to remove completely the effects of guessing by the introduction of special scoring formulae, and the new technology won out quickly in an education system enamored of, or overpowered by, new "scientific" methods and practicing the "cult of efficiency."[35] By 1930 another textbook author could write that "to be a modern teacher to-day one must have mastered the new methods in written examinations."[36]

Throughout the following decades, sporadic protests against the "new methods" erupted in the literature. Allegedly, students prepared for them by memorizing small details, while essay tests would direct their focus on relationships, trends, organization, and major points; the unreliability of essay examinations had been exaggerated; objective tests did not measure creativity.[37] But backed by, at best, rather limited data, even if they found support in the extensive informal criticism among classroom teachers, such attacks made little headway against a technology that was by then firmly entrenched and supported by and supporting a large establishment of experts in educational measurement and an even larger growth industry of test publishers. In 1926 the College Entrance Examination Board added the multiple-choice Scholastic Aptitude Tests (SATs) to its battery of essay examinations for the selection of college students. By 1942, under the pressure of the war exigency, objective achievement tests had also displaced the CEEB's subject matter examinations, for the duration in intent but permanently in fact.[38] Publishers tried to increase textbook sales by supplying their customers with booklets (and currently with floppy disks) containing files of multiple-choice items, many of them atrocious in quality. And in the classroom, teachers produced home-made objective items for use from first grade, if not kindergarten, on. The multiple-choice test—efficient, quantitative, objective, capable of sampling wide areas of subject matter and easily generating data for complicated statistical analyses—had become the symbol or synonym of American education.

The original prototype, Kelly's Reading Test, seems to have been quite popular at least in the Midwest for a few years, and even became known on the other side of the Atlantic;[39] it was also criticized for measuring reasoning and puzzle solving more than reading ability. F. J. Kelly moved up to a deanship at Minnesota in the twenties and became chief of the Higher Education Division in the U.S. Office of Education by 1931.

He had dreamed up a small and not particularly complicated modification. But its impact, one might argue, was enormous, as pervasive and formative for the American education system as any of the more eye-catching substantive results of intelligence tests. The technology it unleashed transformed the content and style of teaching, learning, and grading, contributing powerfully to the peculiarly fragmented form of American mass education. No matter what the educational rhetoric proclaimed, at the operative level this technology did not place the emphasis on the production of coherent ideas, nor on their reproduction, but on the "multiple-guess" recognition of small pieces of mostly factual, and often trivial information. Intolerant of idiosyncrasy and individuality, it carried the latent message that the goal of learning was the identification of the one "wholly right" answer as defined by a seemingly impersonal, "objective," yet often quite arbi-

oup Mental Testing," chaps. 4

mining in the United States
emy of Sciences (Washington,
9.

Mental Testing: In Search of
e.

or the Group Measurements
tional Psychology 9 (1918):

lla C. Pressey, Introduction to
rld Book Company, 1922), 1.

J Psychology (New York: Cen-
on p. 648, an obscure German
in 1914. Presumably Boring's
zprüfungen auf Grund von
z, 1914). It is very doubtful,
the developments described
ed this reference and, though
ay tests (p. 575).

ag the Making of a Scale for
agogical Seminary 23 (1916):

of Ability in Reading," Teach-
, 226.

ling Tests," Journal of Educa-

ng Test. Studies by the Bureau
rds, no. 3 (1915), 1–38, esp.

atal Fatigue, I," Psychological
Naomi Norsworthy, "The Psy-
Archives of Psychology 1, no. 1
"Studies from the Princeton
sychological Review 2 (1895):
ite McPherson for calling the

nt in High School (New York:
New Kind of School Examina-
920): 33–46.

ests Requiring Alternative Re-

trary authority. Not until the 1970s was the Educational Testing Service forced to supply its clients with information about the correct
answers to its SAT questions, and to admit publicly that on occasion a
response officially scored as wrong might actually be reasonable
and, indeed, correct.

This development must have had enormous consequences, even
though it is difficult to demonstrate the effects of such all-pervasive
changes. In the words of one reviewer, "one would expect to find a
great deal of empirical research in this area. However, a review of the
literature revealed only a few small-scale and somewhat peripheral
empirical studies." [40] And just recently, an article brought out by ETS
reported that multiple-choice tests "tend not to measure the more
complex cognitive abilities"; yet the author could find only a limited
number of studies on this issue, and none exploring the effects of
such tests on the educational process. [41] Indeed, another educational
specialist, concerned about the powerful impact of standardized
achievement and competency tests on instruction and school curricula, focused entirely on their content; the shape of such tests was
half-jokingly attributed to prehistorical origins: in effect this test
critic, too, accepted the multiple-choice format as pre-ordained. [42]

But lest anyone think that the development of this mass production
method was inevitable in any large education system, a comparative
perspective proves instructive. European systems have not utilized
such methods at all, at least not until long after the culture of Camels
and Coke had conquered the world; when, as in Norway, a system
eventually attempted to introduce them, a heated public debate over
such testing procedures ensued. This piece of educational technology is as American as the assembly line, and perhaps as alienating.

Half aware of the arbitrariness behind the "objective" format, some
students in the classroom fight a guerrilla war against the authority
hidden in the key for the "right" answers. But overall, recent student
generations have accepted multiple-choice examinations as a routine, taken-for-granted part of their movement through the educational system and often of their move into the job market. Teachers,
many of whom are uneasy about the use of such testing methods,
continue to employ them under the pressure of their workload and in

the absence of better alternatives. Kelly's attem
and effort required for the administration of test:
liantly. His invention had spread as quickly as a
cal breakthrough, legitimized by major societal
by a rapidly developing establishment of exper
the furor of the polemics about the nature-nurtur
the effects of his invention failed to attract syst
though some of the substantive results of test
from groups willing to do ideological battle, the
consequences of the technological innovation r
sence of a constituency willing and able to ask s;
largely invisible.

A recent analysis of historical trends in in
claimed that the average Stanford-Binet IQ of
creased by fourteen points over the last half cent
age SAT score showed a real drop by half a standa
the 1960s and 1970s.[43] Even the study's author
what to make of his startling finding. In the prese
it is striking to note that the IQ data came fro
answer tests, while the SAT scores were obtai
choice group examinations. Would F. J. Kelly, we
happy to see the permanent institutionalization
would he be horrified to find that seventy years of
ysis techniques, computerization, and research
any new breakthroughs or even significant im
rather primitive, if ingenious, pre-World War I t
still the basic vehicle for many important decision

NOTES

I would like to express my gratitude for help beyond
Mary Bogan and Steve Hanschu at the William Allen Wh
State University, Emporia, Kansas.

1. Lee Cronbach, quoted in Orville G. Brim, Jr., Richar
Wayne H. Holtzman, *Intelligence: Perspectives 1965*.
morial Lectures (New York: Harcourt, Brace and Wo
2. Ibid., ix.

logical Styles and the Wartime Origins of G
and 7 of this volume.
19. Robert M. Yerkes, ed., *Psychological Ex*
Army, vol. 15, Memoirs of the National Acac
D.C.: Government Printing Office, 1921), 2
20. See Henry L. Minton, "Lewis M. Terman ar
the Democratic Ideal," chap. 5 of this volu
21. Arthur S. Otis, "An Absolute Point Scale
of Intelligence. Part I," *Journal of Educ*
239–260.
22. For example, see Sidney L. Pressey and Lu
the Use of Standard Tests (Yonkers, N.Y.: W
23. Edwin G. Boring's *A History of Experimen*
tury, 1929) did not mention Otis and cited,
author, M. Lobsien, as inventing group test
reference was to M. Lobsien, *Intellige*
Gruppenbeobachtungen (Langensalza: B
however, that this work is at all related t
here. In the second edition, Boring elimin
he mentioned Otis, gave priority to the ar
24. Arthur S. Otis, "Considerations Concern
the Measurement of Reading Ability," *Pe*
528–549, esp. 543, 544.
25. Edward L. Thorndike, "The Measuremer
ers College Record 15 (1914): 207–277, es
26. Kelly, *Teachers' Marks.*
27. Frederick J. Kelly, "The Kansas Silent Re
tional Psychology 7 (1916): 63–80.
28. Frederick J. Kelly, *The Kansas Silent Rea*
of Educational Measurement and Stand
10, 28.
29. Yerkes, *Psychological Examining,* 300.
30. For instance, Edward L. Thorndike, "M
Review 7 (1900): 466–488 and 547–549;
chology of Mentally Deficient Children,"
(1906); J. Mark Baldwin and W. J. Shav
Laboratory. I. Memory for Square Size,"
236–239. (Thanks are due to Marion W
last items to my attention.)
31. Terman, "Use of Intelligence Tests," 20.
32. Charles W. Odell, *Educational Measurer*
Century, 1930), 41; William A. McCall, "
tion," *Journal of Educational Research* 1
33. Pressey and Pressey, *Introduction,* 186.
34. Charles W. Odell, "Another Criticism of

trary authority. Not until the 1970s was the Educational Testing Service forced to supply its clients with information about the correct answers to its SAT questions, and to admit publicly that on occasion a response officially scored as wrong might actually be reasonable and, indeed, correct.

This development must have had enormous consequences, even though it is difficult to demonstrate the effects of such all-pervasive changes. In the words of one reviewer, "one would expect to find a great deal of empirical research in this area. However, a review of the literature revealed only a few small-scale and somewhat peripheral empirical studies."[40] And just recently, an article brought out by ETS reported that multiple-choice tests "tend not to measure the more complex cognitive abilities"; yet the author could find only a limited number of studies on this issue, and none exploring the effects of such tests on the educational process.[41] Indeed, another educational specialist, concerned about the powerful impact of standardized achievement and competency tests on instruction and school curricula, focused entirely on their content; the shape of such tests was half-jokingly attributed to prehistorical origins: in effect this test critic, too, accepted the multiple-choice format as pre-ordained.[42]

But lest anyone think that the development of this mass production method was inevitable in any large education system, a comparative perspective proves instructive. European systems have not utilized such methods at all, at least not until long after the culture of Camels and Coke had conquered the world; when, as in Norway, a system eventually attempted to introduce them, a heated public debate over such testing procedures ensued. This piece of educational technology is as American as the assembly line, and perhaps as alienating.

Half aware of the arbitrariness behind the "objective" format, some students in the classroom fight a guerrilla war against the authority hidden in the key for the "right" answers. But overall, recent student generations have accepted multiple-choice examinations as a routine, taken-for-granted part of their movement through the educational system and often of their move into the job market. Teachers, many of whom are uneasy about the use of such testing methods, continue to employ them under the pressure of their workload and in the absence of better alternatives. Kelly's attempt to reduce the time and effort required for the administration of tests had succeeded brilliantly. His invention had spread as quickly as any other technological breakthrough, legitimized by major societal values and supported by a rapidly developing establishment of experts and producers. In the furor of the polemics about the nature-nurture problem, however, the effects of his invention failed to attract systematic attention. Although some of the substantive results of testing evoked protests from groups willing to do ideological battle, the wider unanticipated consequences of the technological innovation remained, in the absence of a constituency willing and able to ask systematic questions, largely invisible.

A recent analysis of historical trends in intelligence test data claimed that the average Stanford-Binet IQ of Americans has increased by fourteen points over the last half century, while the average SAT score showed a real drop by half a standard deviation during the 1960s and 1970s.[45] Even the study's author did not quite know what to make of his startling finding. In the present context, however, it is striking to note that the IQ data came from individual, free-answer tests, while the SAT scores were obtained from multiple-choice group examinations. Would F. J. Kelly, were he still alive, be happy to see the permanent institutionalization of his invention? Or would he be horrified to find that seventy years of sophisticated analysis techniques, computerization, and research have not produced any new breakthroughs or even significant improvements of this rather primitive, if ingenious, pre-World War I technique, which is still the basic vehicle for many important decisions about individuals?

NOTES

I would like to express my gratitude for help beyond the call of duty from Mary Bogan and Steve Hanschu at the William Allen White Library, Emporia State University, Emporia, Kansas.

1. Lee Cronbach, quoted in Orville G. Brim, Jr., Richard S. Crutchfield, and Wayne H. Holtzman, *Intelligence: Perspectives 1965. The Terman-Otis Memorial Lectures* (New York: Harcourt, Brace and World, 1966), vii.
2. Ibid., ix.

3. Franz Samelson, "On the Science and Politics of the IQ," *Social Research* 42 (1975): 467–488. See also Leila Zenderland, "The Debate Over Diagnosis: Henry Herbert Goddard and the Medical Acceptance of Intelligence Testing," chapter 3 of this volume.

4. Nicholas Pastore, "The Army Intelligence Tests and Walter Lippmann," *Journal of the History of the Behavioral Sciences* 14 (1978): 316–327.

5. Franz Samelson, "Putting Psychology on the Map: Ideology and Intelligence Testing," in *Psychology in Social Context,* edited by Allan R. Buss (New York: Irvington, 1979), 103–168.

6. Franz Samelson, "From 'Race Psychology' to 'Studies in Prejudice'," *Journal of the History of the Behavioral Sciences* 14 (1978): 265–278.

7. Andrew J. Strenio, *The Testing Trap* (New York: Rawson, Wade, 1981).

8. Franz Samelson, "World War I Intelligence Testing and the Development of Psychology," *Journal of the History of the Behavioral Sciences* 13 (1977): 274–282, esp. 279.

9. John E. Hunter and Ronda F. Hunter, "Validity and Utility of Alternative Predictors of Job Performance," *Psychological Bulletin* 96 (1984): 72–98.

10. George B. Cutten, "The Reconstruction of Democracy," *School and Society* 16 (1922): 477–489, esp. 481, 477.

11. Benjamin Beit-Hallahmi, "Ideology in Psychology: How Psychologists Explain Inequality," in *Value Judgment and Income Distribution,* edited by Robert A. Solo and Charles W. Anderson (New York: Praeger, 1981), 70–106.

12. See Thomas Kellaghan, George F. Madaus, and Peter W. Airasian, *The Effects of Standardized Testing* (Boston: Kluwer-Nijhoff Publishing, 1982).

13. Orville G. Brim, Jr., David C. Glass, John Neulinger, and Ira J. Firestone, *American Beliefs and Attitudes about Intelligence* (New York: Russell Sage Foundation, 1969), 265. See also David A. Goslin, *The Search for Ability* (New York: Russell Sage Foundation, 1963).

14. Marjorie C. Kirkland, "The Effects of Tests on Students and Schools," *Review of Educational Research* 41 (1971): 303–350.

15. For example, see Mark Snyderman and Richard J. Herrnstein, "Intelligence Tests and the Immigration Act of 1924," *American Psychologist* 38 (1983): 986–995. But see also several replies in "Comment," *American Psychologist* 40 (1985): 241–245.

16. For example, see Daniel Starch and E. C. Elliott, "Reliability of Grading High School Work in English," *School Review* 20 (1912): 442–457; Frederick J. Kelly, *Teachers' Marks, Their Variability and Standardization,* Teachers College Contributions to Education, vol. 66 (1914).

17. Rudolf Pintner, *Intelligence Testing* (New York: Holt, 1923), 49; Lewis M. Terman, "The Use of Intelligence Tests in the Grading of School Children," *Journal of Educational Research* 1 (1920): 20–32, esp. 20.

18. Samelson, "Putting Psychology." See also James Reed, "Robert M. Yerkes and the Mental Testing Movement," and Richard T. von Mayrhauser, "The Manager, the Medic, and the Mediator: The Clash of Professional Psycho-

logical Styles and the Wartime Origins of Group Mental Testing," chaps. 4 and 7 of this volume.

19. Robert M. Yerkes, ed., *Psychological Examining in the United States Army,* vol. 15, Memoirs of the National Academy of Sciences (Washington, D.C.: Government Printing Office, 1921), 299.

20. See Henry L. Minton, "Lewis M. Terman and Mental Testing: In Search of the Democratic Ideal," chap. 5 of this volume.

21. Arthur S. Otis, "An Absolute Point Scale for the Group Measurements of Intelligence. Part I," *Journal of Educational Psychology* 9 (1918): 239–260.

22. For example, see Sidney L. Pressey and Luella C. Pressey, *Introduction to the Use of Standard Tests* (Yonkers, N.Y.: World Book Company, 1922), 1.

23. Edwin G. Boring's *A History of Experimental Psychology* (New York: Century, 1929) did not mention Otis and cited, on p. 648, an obscure German author, M. Lobsien, as inventing group tests in 1914. Presumably Boring's reference was to M. Lobsien, *Intelligenzprüfungen auf Grund von Gruppenbeobachtungen* (Langensalza: Belz, 1914). It is very doubtful, however, that this work is at all related to the developments described here. In the second edition, Boring eliminated this reference and, though he mentioned Otis, gave priority to the army tests (p. 575).

24. Arthur S. Otis, "Considerations Concerning the Making of a Scale for the Measurement of Reading Ability," *Pedagogical Seminary* 23 (1916): 528–549, esp. 543, 544.

25. Edward L. Thorndike, "The Measurement of Ability in Reading," *Teachers College Record* 15 (1914): 207–277, esp. 226.

26. Kelly, *Teachers' Marks.*

27. Frederick J. Kelly, "The Kansas Silent Reading Tests," *Journal of Educational Psychology* 7 (1916): 63–80.

28. Frederick J. Kelly, *The Kansas Silent Reading Test.* Studies by the Bureau of Educational Measurement and Standards, no. 3 (1915), 1–38, esp. 10, 28.

29. Yerkes, *Psychological Examining,* 300.

30. For instance, Edward L. Thorndike, "Mental Fatigue, I," *Psychological Review* 7 (1900): 466–488 and 547–549; Naomi Norsworthy, "The Psychology of Mentally Deficient Children," *Archives of Psychology* 1, no. 1 (1906); J. Mark Baldwin and W. J. Shaw, "Studies from the Princeton Laboratory. I. Memory for Square Size," *Psychological Review* 2 (1895): 236–239. (Thanks are due to Marion White McPherson for calling the last items to my attention.)

31. Terman, "Use of Intelligence Tests," 20.

32. Charles W. Odell, *Educational Measurement in High School* (New York: Century, 1930), 41; William A. McCall, "A New Kind of School Examination," *Journal of Educational Research* 1 (1920): 33–46.

33. Pressey and Pressey, *Introduction,* 186.

34. Charles W. Odell, "Another Criticism of Tests Requiring Alternative Re-

Applied Psychology only began publication that year. The uniqueness of this occasion was not lost on the APA's president, Robert Mearns Yerkes, who had requested the conference, and who believed that it would "probably be the most important meeting of the sort ever held." Here was the chance for psychology to shed its esoteric image and prove its intellectual value and practical usefulness to American society. As Yerkes wrote Walter Dill Scott, "I hope we can all get together Saturday night in Philadelphia for a good discussion. The prospects are now excellent that we shall have opportunity to do something important, unless perchance the war should suddenly end."[2]

Unfortunately the gathering at the Walton was severely marred by dissension and the stormy departure of Scott, the profession's foremost applied psychologist, which led to an unharmonious and inefficient organization of psychologists during the remainder of the war. His exit holds significance beyond the displeasure or histrionics of one man, because it threw into question the entire legitimacy of President Yerkes's subsequent actions. Scott never cast his vote to approve the several committee appointments made by Yerkes that evening, which deprived him of a majority of the six council members' votes needed to authorize committee assignments.[3] A more important consequence of the walkout was that for the rest of the war Yerkes and Scott acted independently to modify and implement their respective prewar experiences in mental testing. After the Walton meeting, a gulf deepened gradually between the activities of Yerkes and Scott, who initiated two separate psychology committees for military service during the summer of 1917.[4]

This disunity reflected striking dissimilarities between Scott's and Yerkes's backgrounds, personalities, and approaches to applied science.[5] Scott had devoted the majority of his seventeen years in professional psychology to the useful aspects of his science. From the outset of his career, Scott's interests and associations led him back and forth between the business world and academia. In the first decade of this century he published the first psychologies of advertising and public speaking, and at the beginning of the second decade he shifted his concerns to the psychology of vocational selection and management.[6] Scott's primary interest throughout his career was the process of motivation and how businessmen could affect the behavior of consumers, audiences, and workers through suggestion and argument. Scott began teaching and publishing at Northwestern University in 1902; he became director of the university laboratory three years later and the head of the psychology department in 1909. The same year, Northwestern's business school appointed him professor of advertising and, in 1912, professor of psychology.

Applying the psychology of motivation required certain social skills, which Scott apparently mastered with no difficulty. Possessing these skills was a major factor in helping him gain the first American professorship of applied psychology, at the Carnegie Institute of Technology, in 1916. For instance, when Carnegie psychologist Walter Bingham was considering the different candidates he might appoint to this unique position, he observed that " . . . Scott already has a standing with the business world and a facility in quickly winning the confidence and cooperation of the business men, which would be an extremely valuable asset at the beginning of our work." [7] Even more than his affability, Scott's recent innovative work in the development of "group tests," which employers could use to evaluate "Native Intellectual Ability" (i.e., "quickness of thought") among large numbers of job candidates simultaneously, had been a deciding factor in Bingham's choice. These mass exams were part of a larger "scientific selection" system, which included a method to organize noncognitive human qualities, such as character and manner. Although leading academic psychologists were skeptical about the scientific legitimacy of objectifying subjective evaluations, Scott saw his "Rating Scale for Selecting Salesmen," along with his group tests for intellectual ability, as a very compatible mix of academic method and nonacademic purpose. [8]

In contrast to Scott's career, the first fifteen years of Yerkes's career (as shown in an earlier chapter) had been a period marked by awkward transition, if not crisis. While Harvard president Charles W. Eliot had hired him in 1902 for one of the first modern research positions, which was "independent of all teaching" and allowed him "to devote most of [his] time for years to [his] own research," this privileged situation was altered drastically after the departure of Eliot and the rise of A. Lawrence Lowell to the Harvard presidency in 1909. [9] Lowell led Harvard away from Eliot's focus on pure research as the primary university purpose, returning the school to more traditional professorial duties. For Yerkes, this meant a greater teaching load, less time for his research and prolific publishing, and increased anxiety over institutional support for his program in comparative psychology. President Lowell suggested to him that "the path to professorship lay" in a more human-focused psychology, but Yerkes was reluctant to modify his research to suit the Harvard president. Yerkes remained an assistant professor from Lowell's inauguration until 1917, when the University of Minnesota offered him the same credentials Northwestern had given Scott in 1909: tenure, department chairmanship, and laboratory direction. Although Yerkes denied in his autobiography that Lowell had indeed persuaded him to make his research more useful, Yerkes eventually did redefine his interests in comparative psychology to include more human research; nevertheless, his modifications had little influence on his career at Harvard.[10] Yerkes believed the sources of his rift with Lowell lay in what he called his independent disposition, which bolstered a "whole-hearted commitment to 'pure' as contrasted with 'applied' science." Additionally, these factors caused him to deny that he was making a research transition and to rationalize instead that his new activities in utilitarian human psychology were just as scientific as his earlier work. In 1912, in order to remain at the "intellectual garden of Eden" that was his (1912) Harvard and retain his research idealism, Yerkes began "humanizing" his psychology perspective and course offerings while departing from Harvard half-time to work at the newly opened Boston State Hospital. His early work there involved counseling individual outpatients, but within three years he had also developed an intelligence test to assist in diagnostic procedures. Yerkes promoted this test, the Point Scale for Measuring Mental Ability, as a more effective method of detecting genetically distributed mentality than the established intelligence examination of the day, the Binet test of mental age, which Lewis M. Terman and Henry H. Goddard had adapted for American use.

In all of his studies of animals and outpatients, Yerkes exhibited an interest in the evolutionary development of mind; for example, his and Daniel LaRue's *Outline of a Study of the Self* included a questionnaire that the reader was instructed to fill out and send to Charles B. Davenport's Eugenics Record Office. At the national forefront of the mental testing movement by 1916, Yerkes preferred not to term his work "applied psychology," but referred to it as "human engineering," so that he could have his "pure," evolutionary-based science and use it, too.[11] Whereas Scott was indifferent toward the evolutionary basis of mind and insouciant about pursuing the study of motivation in a utilitarian fashion—indeed, businessmen made suggestions for much of his research agenda—Yerkes predicated the utility of his study of evolutionary mind on the purity of his research.

The disparate origins of Scott's and Yerkes's achievements in mental testing explain their different approaches to wartime psychology. Their interests, methods, career experiences, and professional reputations diverged sharply. Intellectually, Scott was concerned to isolate a number of human qualities to help employers discover the most alert and motivated salesman, whereas Yerkes examined the mentally deficient in order to further an understanding of the evolutionary development of "general intelligence," from invertebrates to lower primates to normal humans. Methodologically, the quest for efficiency motivated Scott to examine en masse, whereas scientific precision moved Yerkes to test his subjects one by one. Scott authored a series of group tests, which permitted the testing of a maximum of job candidates in a minimum of time; Yerkes developed a system of individualized examinations to isolate ontogenetic variations of phylogenetic intelligence. Yerkes believed, with most prewar testers, that tests taken by a group of persons simultaneously in the same room would cause a person's self-consciousness to distract him from demonstrating what Yerkes held to be the essential human quality, general intelligence. As for their careers and personalities, Scott had spent much of the previous fifteen years accommodating psychology to the practical needs of nonacademics, usually businessmen; his amiable, if forthright, character reflected his practical experience. Yerkes, on the other hand, with his part-time departure from Harvard and his disinclination to compromise with Lowell—even though his psychology was becoming more human-oriented, on Lowell's suggestion—displayed the idealistic and uncooperative qualities known to close friends and colleagues alike.[12] As to the question of professional success, Northwestern seemed to advance Scott's position every two years, and a new, well-endowed institute of technology conferred an honor in recognition of his previous career accomplishments; Yerkes's career had stalled at Harvard after 1910, and his appointment at the newly opened psychopathic hospital had almost nothing to do with his original field of animal research. One more quality, self-esteem, cannot be overlooked, even if it is determined by the other four. Scott was confident in his achievements and in his standing as an applied psychologist, while Yerkes's stance on applied psychology, the command of which was most relevant to wartime leadership, was ambivalent, and the ultimate direction of his current career—toward more human psychology or back to animal psychology—was ambiguous. All these differences contributed to the unsteady leadership in American psychology during World War I and to the discrete images of military psychology Scott and Yerkes envisioned during the first weeks of war.

In his speech requesting a declaration of war against Germany, President Wilson asked for universal conscription. The proposal of a national draft was a radical departure from the American voluntaristic tradition of service in war, and, while the April 6 congressional approval of war in Europe followed Wilson's request by four days, debate over conscription lasted over six weeks.[15] When legislation for a national draft was finally passed, on May 18, America's psychologists lacked unified leadership and any workable methods to assist in the massive personnel problems that universal conscription involved. The interval of eleven days from the time the Selective Service Act was approved to the reluctant decision by a committee of America's leading mental testers to construct and administer mass examinations indicated the obvious: the necessity to process quickly millions of soldiers was the mother of the group test invention. While the paternity of the group tests is the subject of another essay, the remainder of this one will address only the question of why American psychologists were so slow in designing the examination device that has become the most influential technology this profession has contributed to American society. National group testing did not originate solely as a result of hasty, eager psychologists seizing a golden research opportunity, as the historiography of the subject generally indicates.[14] For instance, Yerkes, the man who rose quickly and boldly to professional leadership and who had hoped to secure implementation of his own genetic psychological ideals and methods as the dominant wartime psychological purpose, was predisposed *against* group testing; and Scott, the psychological leader who had pioneered in group exam methods before the war and who later became the most influential psychologist among military officials during the war, was excluded from the famous meeting of psychologists in late May at Vineland, New Jersey, where his colleagues developed the notorious group test "Alpha." An overview of the disunified situation of wartime psychological leadership, which was evident as early as April 6, 1917, demonstrated outstandingly on April 21, and soon institutionalized for the duration of the war, can be helpful in understanding the ironic history of the first national group tests of intelligence, whose beginnings are marked more by intraprofessional division than by concerted professional action.

As early as the day Congress declared war, Yerkes demonstrated an appetite for "somewhat dictatorial and headstrong" leadership.[15] In an extraordinary session of a psychology conference at Harvard, Yerkes heard Walter Bingham and others present recommendations on prospective psychological activities in wartime. Bingham discussed Canadian military psychology and the use of tests to detect feeblemindedness among army recruits.[16] It is very likely that Bingham brought up the subject of the methods of group testing developed by Scott and himself during the previous two years. Whatever he may have discussed, it did not prevent his appointment to a special three-man Committee on Military Psychology established that day as the top decision-making body on wartime psychology. Its other members were Yerkes and the previous APA president, Raymond Dodge. It made sense for Bingham, the only APA Council member among the three, to sit on this committee because the Council was the executive body of the APA and because the APA president had to gain the Council's approval of any specialized committees he wished to appoint.[17] This logic aside, however, Yerkes, Dodge, and Robert Ogden moved to dissolve the committee only a few hours later, in the absence of Bingham and those who had witnessed its formation. Yerkes did offer Bingham an explanation for his expeditious actions the following day, asserting that presidential actions taken independently were more legitimate than actions he might take as the presidential member of a committee that had Council representation.[18] Yerkes contradicted this statement in his postwar history and in his autobiography, however, which report that

> On the evening of the same day at an informal conference of the mem-
> bers of this committee (Mr. Bingham's place was taken by Mr. Ogden) it
> was decided that the matter should be placed before the council. . . . This
> temporary committee, whose life was measured by hours, decided to rec-
> ommend that the Council of the American Psychological Association as-
> sume responsibility.[19]

On the day he wrote to Bingham, Yerkes also sent a form letter to
all Council members, requesting Council authorization for the open-
ended power to appoint "such committee or committees from the
Association membership as seem desirable."[20] Two days later, on
April 9, 1917, he moved to acquire the influential recognition of the
National Research Council, asking chairman George Ellery Hale's
support in creating and chairing an NRC committee specifically designed to advance the participation of psychologists in the war. Thus,
after asserting near-dictatorial power within the profession, Yerkes
began communicating extramurally to consolidate his position as
head of wartime psychology.[21]

"One morning about April 10th," Scott later wrote, Bingham and
he "became rather excited about . . . the prospects of the War. . . ."
Whether it was the reception of Yerkes's highhanded correspondence
that stimulated activity at Carnegie Tech's Bureau of Salesmanship
Research is uncertain; nevertheless, Bingham and Scott "decided
that each would dictate a letter independently to Professor Yerkes."[22]
The former of the two wanted back the power he had recently shared
with Yerkes, and, to accomplish this, acted as if he had never received
Yerkes's letter of April 7. Writing as a member of the now defunct Committee on Military Psychology, he mailed a circular to Yerkes and
other psychology leaders simultaneously, making his own suggestions on committee assignments and for plans of action.[23] The letter
Scott sent to Yerkes on April 14 reflects motivations different from
Bingham's, as Scott explicitly recognized Yerkes's leadership of wartime psychology. Appealing to Yerkes's interests, Scott observed that
psychologists could develop and administer general tests to weed out
the mentally incompetent, and that "[i]f all these psychologists were
appointed by you and by a committee appointed by you there would
be no difficulty insecuring [sic] a system more or less competent."
After lending his support to Yerkes's leadership and objectives in intelligence testing, Scott changed the subject. In a separate paragraph,
Scott implicitly staked out a territory of activities for himself, inform-

ing Yerkes of, but not requesting, the possible adaptation of the salesmanship selection devices he, Bingham, and other Carnegie associates had constructed. The "principle" of these rating techniques, Scott said, "could be immediately applied to selecting for *any* position of responsibility in the army."[24] The universal feature of Scott's plan probably caught Yerkes's eye, as only two weeks earlier Yerkes had begun considering the modification of his methods "in connection with the selection of officers, or recruits, as well as in the later state of those who by service have been mentally disturbed."[25] Scott enclosed copies of the selection forms, but did not include a copy of his group test for mental alertness, which suggests Scott's acknowledgment of Yerkes's territory and his willingness to put aside his own interests in intelligence testing.

Scott changed the subject again, to the topic of "special tests to determine fitness" for such positions as artillery man, pilot, etc. in which neither his nor Yerkes's researches were involved, and again deferred to Yerkes: "It seems to me that you should appoint individual men to take up one of these topics."[26] While Scott's letter posed less of a threat to Yerkes's leadership than Bingham's circular, it still represented a second councilor's attempt to share in the formulation of the central purpose of wartime psychology. Yerkes wanted that power vested in himself as president, but he still needed to consider the suggestions of Scott and Bingham, who, with the addition of but one other vote, could block authorization of presidential power.

That night Yerkes was not waiting at home for the responses of Bingham, Scott, or any other members of the APA Council; instead, he boarded a train for Montreal to begin a three-day investigation of "the Canadian psycho-military situation." On this trip he spoke mostly to military doctors about the uses of psychology to assist soldiers who had become mentally ill or crippled. Having gained professional renown in the last three years for the testing system he developed at Boston State Hospital, Yerkes felt much at home during his tour of Canadian hospitals. His interests had been expanding beyond the treatment of the mentally ill or the incompetent, as he had written Carl Brigham of Ottawa two weeks earlier.[27] While visiting with Brigham and others in the northland, Yerkes received a telegram from NRC president Hale, requesting a meeting in Philadelphia on April 14. There and then, Yerkes gained Hale's tentative approval and permission to present a proposal for the formation of a psychology committee at the semiannual meeting of the NRC on April 19, 1917, in Washington.[28] Hale also requested that Yerkes gain consent of the APA Council for the establishment of an NRC psychology committee. Back at Harvard on the 15th, Yerkes opened the replies of the APA Council members to his April 6 request for carte blanche in committee creation. The situation was not favorable for Yerkes. Two members, Roswell Angier and Knight Dunlap, supported him fully; two others, Bingham and Scott, seemed ready to offer their support if Yerkes recognized their suggestions; and the others, Harry L. Hollingworth and Harvey Carr, were not at all sympathetic.[29] Yerkes needed to show Hale and the NRC that he possessed Council support; but because he did not receive it by mail, he abruptly called a meeting of the Council on April 16. He explained only that "[d]evelopments since my letter of April 6 render it evidently desirable," and told Bingham and Scott only that "[m]atters which I must not now stop to state or explain force the calling of a Council meeting. I hope you can both come, for it will probably be the most important meeting of the sort ever held."[30] As noted earlier, their attendance was necessary to create a Council majority and mandate. The next day Yerkes wrote Scott a grateful note, replying to his letter of April 14 and informed him that "Our thoughts have run in very similar lines. Indeed last week I worked out a plan for the examining of recruits very similar to that which you suggest."[31] Yerkes addressed the NRC leadership on April 19, emphasizing the need to recognize the "human factor . . . in our fighting machine," by instituting a committee to "view . . . the man in both Army and Navy from the mental standpoint. . . ." Yerkes suggested studies to examine the "mentally fit and unfit" and mentioned "the far-reaching significance of such studies in the selection of men for special purposes."[32]

Although Scott and Yerkes agreed that wartime psychology should help evaluate the mental abilities of several categories of recruits, their thoughts on how to test them were very different. It was the question of the appropriate style of examining the recruits that caused sparks to fly at the Walton meeting. When Yerkes recommended that all psychological activities be organized under the auspices of the proposed NRC committee and the Army Medical Corps, which was responsible for testing and discharging the mentally deficient, Scott objected vehemently. From his point of view, it was wrongheaded to use only medical diagnostic tests to predict which recruits had leadership qualities, because he did not believe superior mental ability guaranteed competent leadership. Yerkes's medical and evolutionary interests were well suited to the discovery of the unfit, but not to the selection of men with talent and character. Yerkes and everyone else in attendance were ready to unite behind the medical style of testing, as it represented the vanguard of professional psychological technique. Scott's proposal, meanwhile, reflected the questionably scientific, if useful, applications of one practitioner. When Scott recognized his minority position, he excused himself from participation in the rest of the evening's agenda, including the authorization of psychological subcommittees to extend particular services. Yerkes's historical account depicting a group of patriotic psychologists that spoke with a single voice was therefore hardly accurate.[33]

Before I elaborate on the main reason for Scott's departure, it is important to review some important professional divisions among those in attendance, as well as their relationship to Scott. The other Council members present were Bingham, Dunlap, and Angier. Yerkes, APA secretary Herbert Langfeld, and former president Dodge also attended. Although Scott and the others were close in age (35 to 47 years) and shared common experiences, including graduate study in Germany, a number of professional differences divided Scott from the others. The most important of these involved their approaches to applied psychology, which the Walton meeting was, after all, about. Scott had devoted his career to this young field, while all others present had established their career reputations in traditional "pure research" psychology.[34] While utilitarian considerations have always marked American psychology, the self-consciousness of the early professionalizers caused them to view and call their research "pure." Scott was an exception to the rule. Only Bingham—who, as director of the Carnegie Institute's Division of Applied Psychology, had hired Scott to lead Carnegie's Bureau of Salesmanship Research the year before—might also have considered himself an applied psychologist. Bingham understood Scott's interests better than anyone else that night, his "purer" background notwithstanding. He agreed that the psychologists should adapt their interests to the military's needs during their wartime participation instead of expecting the military to accommodate the research ideals of academics. It is not that they were devoid of self-interest, however, as Scott's and Bingham's Carnegie work was utilitarian already, and meeting the army's needs was unlikely to sidetrack their career interests. According to Scott's unpublished account of this meeting,

> Bingham and I presented the practical point of view; we felt that it was a time in which the psychologists of the country would really have an opportunity to do something for the army. It seemed to us that several, if not all, of the other members of the council took a slightly diverse attitude and thought of the occasion, at least in part, as an opportunity to advance the standing of psychology.... I expressed myself very clearly as of the opinion that we should disregard the future welfare of the science of psychology and devote ourselves to the service of the army.[35]

An outline Bingham prepared for his professional autobiography corroborates this view, and hints at the pull of divergent desires in Bingham himself, including urges to promote "pure research" psychology, to promote his own interests in utilitarian psychology, and to do *the patriotic thing*. Under the headings "VIII. World War I" and "The urge to help; but how?" the Carnegie psychologist wrote: "Meeting of the council in the smoke-filled room of a Philadelphia hotel. Midnight. Scott's utter disgust with the shortsighted self-interest revealed. His insurrection not previously told."[36] Ultimately, Bingham chose not to tell of Scott's "insurrection," as the story does not appear in any of the later drafts Bingham left in his abundant collection of papers. The story did find its way into published form, however, in the year prior to the appearance of his autobiographical essay (and his death). This particular account, the official Scott biography, portrays Bingham's attitude as sympathetic with Scott's, which is not unreasonable, considering their partnership at Carnegie and the independence Bingham had shown in his circular to the leaders of the profession less than two weeks earlier. In his copy of this biography, however, Bingham documented further that his position was undecided and that his opinions fell between those of Scott and the others in attendance. In the marginalia he appended to the following passage:

> As the meeting proceeded it became clear to Scott and Bingham that Yerkes and the others were interested primarily in going into the army in order to acquire new psychological knowledge. They seemed to be more concerned with what the army could do for them than with what they could do for the army. Angry, Scott and Bingham walked out in a huff.

Bingham bracketed "Yerkes" and wrote "Dunlap," with an arrow pointing to Yerkes's name. Also bracketed are "the others" and "and Bingham." Denying his own anger and departure, Bingham underlined his name and exclaimed "No!" in the margin beside it.[37] Bingham thus remained at the Walton and in Yerkes's good graces, which permitted his full participation on the mental testing committee during the crucial early period of exam construction. Bingham's diplomacy also allowed that the utilitarian style of Carnegie Tech psychology—and of Scott—would not be without influence upon the idealistic Yerkes and the general plans for testing.

As president of the APA, Yerkes served also as chairman and ex-officio member of the Council. Even if Scott had remained at the Walton, Yerkes was empowered to break any deadlock that might have arisen, such as between the Bingham-Scott and Angier-Dunlap pairings. Nevertheless, Scott's departure deprived Yerkes of the substantive Council support he needed before the National Research Council would bestow its stamp of approval on his leadership. Although it is certain that Scott went his own way, the reasons for his dissent remain for discussion, as does the effect of his departure on the origins of group testing.

Scott left the Walton when he realized that Yerkes was committed to installing a psychological style and purpose that would, Scott believed, severely limit the contribution of the profession. Yerkes insisted that the primary function of the tests was to diagnose mental incompetence, and, according to Scott, Yerkes pressed the medical metaphor further with the proposal that "all of the work should be done under the direction of the Surgeon-General and therefore, under the direction also of the Psychiatrist. I became so enraged at these points of view, that I expressed myself very clearly and left the Council."[38] Scott's plan, and his thinking, had no connection whatever to a concept of testing that was so closely related to individualized psychiatric treatment. A closer look at Scott's and Yerkes's proposals can help explain their mutual alienation.

Yerkes's "Plan for the Psychological Examining of Recruits to Eliminate the Mentally Unfit" articulated the position he had proposed at the Walton. He wrote it on the 26th "(f)or the *Council*" and submitted it to Hale the following weekend in order to secure approval of his NRC psychology committee and to have the NRC deliver it immediately to the office of Surgeon General William Gorgas, an NRC member.[39] Although Yerkes never received the majority Council vote authorizing him to speak for the profession, his assertion of his views as the Council's was consistent with his hope to gain a role for his colleagues that largely reflected his own recent career interests and ideas. The overriding assumption of the "Plan" was that the function of the wartime psychologist should be as an assistant to the military doctor, for the reason that "few medical examiners are trained in the use of modern methods of psychological examining." Yerkes proposed that tests be given to those soldiers whose behavior had been observed at either "exceptional or unsatisfactory" extremes of the normal distribution of human behavior. Of the tested individuals, the mentally normal ("probably 80 to 90% of all") were to return to regular service, the superior "should be systematically examined for indications of their special value in the military organization," and the inferior were to be further scrutinized.

Before turning to Yerkes's approach to the normal distribution of intelligence, we must consider one other aspect of the psychologist's role. The "Plan" proposed that all chief and assistant psychological examiners be commissioned as officers in the Medical Reserve Corps. There was a legitimate purpose in attaining officer status; as Yerkes put it, "that the psychological work may be conducted with proper decorum and with due respect of private for examiner." Yet personal and professional pride were also mixed in with this recommendation.[40] In seeking medical officer status, Yerkes made the quasi-medical experience he had enjoyed at Boston State Hospital into a prototype for the wartime mental tester. Moreover, here he had the opportunity for a doubly prestigious position that was particularly meaningful to anyone whose career had been lacking job security, let alone prominence. Yerkes was not merely "out for himself," however, as his personal status needs reflected those of the overall psychology profession in early twentieth-century America. Here was the chance for psychology as a whole to achieve rank in two of traditional society's most established professions, the military and medicine, while proving itself in war.

Beyond Yerkes's personal ambitions, and consistent with his position as president of the APA, his request for commissioned status reflected the desires of many second-generation psychologists. These men and women had received training as psychologists, and not as physicists, biologists, or doctors, as had most of the first, pioneering professional generation.[41] The differences of training in a society that remained ignorant of the profession contributed to the different priorities of the first two psychology generations. While William James, G. Stanley Hall, and other laboratory founders strove to define psychology as theoretically separate from traditional religious teachings on the soul, Yerkes, J. B. Watson, and others of their generation moved to consolidate the profession by defining psychology as methodologically continuous with the natural sciences. As an "objectivist" researcher at Eliot's university, Yerkes wanted psychology to become a branch of biology. Forced to develop a more applicable meaning for his profession, Yerkes wanted practical psychology to become a branch of practical biology, that is, medicine.[42] The achievement of officer status in the war provided an opportunity to elevate the profession and President Yerkes simultaneously, and not only for reasons of self-promotion. The kind of status sought represented a link to the natural sciences, whose recovery many second-generation psychologists deemed necessary. This drive for preferment and the kind of work Yerkes intended for the military "Psychological Corps," which Scott saw as the concerted exploitation of a national emergency, originated not only from social sources but also from intellectual and methodological concerns, which widened the personal division that abruptly arose between Scott and Yerkes.[43]

The kind of work Yerkes wanted the military psychologist to perform reflected his own intellectual background as well as the testing methodology predominant in the profession. Wanting to study individual differences of intelligence as determined by evolution, and having viewed his work at the state hospital as a research opportunity for the discovery of the continuity between sub- and normal intelligence, Yerkes decided that the purpose of his "Plan" (and of wartime psychology in general) was to isolate and "Eliminate the Mentally Unfit." Yerkes's awareness of Scott's interest in implementing personnel-selection techniques for the discovery of officer material, and of Terman's approach to intelligence measurement as a means for the discovery of genius, make his self-interest patent in the "Plan's" emphasis on the mentally inferior; it was Yerkes's intention to expand the range of testing activities once the preliminary proposal, which represented his own research concerns, was accepted.[44] The lengthy series of tests Yerkes recommended for the diagnosis of the unfit represents not only professional arrogance but an ingenuousness as well—in his assumption that the military might indulge his concerns for the origins of incompetence. Still, Yerkes cannot be held responsible for the most impracticable feature of his proposal, the individualized test, which was the predominant technology before mid-1917. Terman was the most notable advocate of the same examination procedure and environment, no matter that he was more concerned with discovering the variations of intelligence on the other extreme (genius) of the normal curve.[45] Yerkes's "Plan" called for the individualized testing of only as many as 20 percent of all recruits, and specified facilities for the average training camp as including only five examining rooms, each 10 × 12 feet in size, and a "table, flat-top desk, with locked drawers, and two or three chairs." Informed by the camp medical and company officers of cases of extreme behavior,

> ... the Psychological Examiner should summon the men of the Company to appear, one at a time, in his examining room. Each should there be subjected to a short series of mental measurements, the necessary time for which should not exceed ten minutes. The result of these measurements should be a rough estimate of the mental status and chief characteristics of the individual and consequent classification as mentally *inferior, normal,* or *superior.* Special attention should be given to men whose mental fitness had been questioned by medical or other officers.[46]

There was straightforward methodological justification for testing subjects individually; the absence of other subjects and of distractions allowed for the greater isolation of the mental quality—general intelligence—to be tested. On the other hand, a subject forced to take a test in the presence of others might score relatively high because of personal abilities that may have been diluted representations of intelligence, such as concentration amidst noise and self-confidence in a group situation.[47] Many late-twentieth-century survivors of group tests may be surprised to know that the testing examiner was expected to coach his subject, assist the subject throughout the exam, keep the subject's attention on the tasks at hand, and, if necessary, postpone the test if the subject was having the proverbial "bad day."

The methodological solicitude of individualized testing was essential to the investigation of the predominant Anglo-American theory of mind, namely, the conception that a central and innate cognitive entity suffused and determined mental activity in general. Charles Spearman discovered—or reified—this phenomenon, which he called "general intelligence," in 1904. In giving a name to the supposedly unitary entity of intellect (known for short as "g"), Spearman tried to substantiate an assumption widely held by genetic psychologists.[48] If all mental activities were reducible to one, it followed that all mental activities but one were functions of *the* power of intelligence, and that an examiner would want to test in such a way as to isolate it from its several, diverse manifestations so he could measure it. Yerkes proposed such a slow method of mental testing in his "Plan," then, because he felt that various human behavior patterns, including "psychopathic tendencies, nervous instability, and inadequate self-control," were generally dependent upon the presence of one key mental ability. The plan to test individually at least 20 percent of all recruits—not to mention his fancy in May that 100 percent could be tested individually—was laughable from the military's standpoint, especially at this point in the war; but it was very consistent with the methodology and genetic psychological assumptions of current American psychology.[49]

Scott informed Yerkes of his preferences for wartime psychological participation in his letter and enclosures of April 14, 1917. In claiming his sphere of influence, Scott mentioned that he and his Carnegie colleagues could best help out by adapting his "system for selecting men for positions of responsibility"; yet this "would require a cooperation on the part of the psychologists and officials in the army. The Bureau of Salesmanship Research has a group of individuals trained in this particular thing and we would all very gladly volunteer our service to the government."[50] Reflecting his own career background, Scott cast the professional psychologist's role as that of a civilian managerial consultant who could advise the army on a number of topics without having to join or seek rank in it. In response to Yerkes's request for suggestions about appropriate wartime status, Scott showed a lack of concern in the matter. He wanted psychologists to be held in equal esteem with doctors, and he did not seem interested in any opportunities for quasi-medical or any formal military position.

Scott saw the interviewing and rating scales that he sent to Yerkes, and which he hoped Yerkes would bring to the military's attention, as an organized system of common sense. For the system to work, one mental quality was needed—judgment, which Scott assumed was inherent in every person who had achieved a managerial position, and which he believed the rating system could objectify. Thus, before interviewing new applicants, the evaluator, employer, or superior officer was asked to construct lists of his present employees, placing each worker into one of several personality categories. When considering "[h]ow well will [a prospective salesman] impress customers by his appearance and manner?" including "physique, bearing, facial expression; clothing; neatness; voice; cheerfulness, self-confidence; courtesy," the examiner was to compare the subject with his list of five men who possessed this general quality from the degree of "Highest (10)" to "Lowest (2)." The score for the applicant's relative strength of *appearance* was tallied with the estimation of his *conversational convincingness* ("tact, clearness, and force"), *future value to the firm, industry* ("energetic and persevering effort"), *character* ("loyalty, honesty, ambition, thrift, spirit of service, and freedom from drinking, gambling, and other immoral acts"), *overall value,* and *judgment of previous reports.* When Scott and five colleagues developed a "Rating Scale for Selecting Captains" at the end of the first month of war, the list of personal qualities assumed as valuable to the military was not vastly different from that used in the salesmanship context: appearance, military experience, influence over men, regard for authority, vigor, stability (including "courage, imperturbability, and endurance"), judgment, and total value to the regiment. The comparative design of the "man-to-man" rating remained the same, however, as did the accompanying directions.[51]

While Scott's evaluators judged numerous qualities in the subject's character, his objective group tests of intelligence measured a hodgepodge of mental attributes. Scott did not take the opportunity to advocate the adoption of group testing at the Walton meeting, but a consideration of his previous innovations in this area illustrates further the stylistic gap separating him from Yerkes. At the time when mental testing achieved regular recognition in professional journals, around 1910, Scott had established himself as an applied psychologist, specifically in the area of motivation.[52] From his doctoral thesis through his works on advertising and public speaking, Scott was concerned to discover the rational or suggestive ways in which persons cause each other to act. In the second decade of his career, he expanded his interest in exhortation and suggestion to include the isolation of qualities that allowed for the successful inducement of employees as well as customers. Although Scott's interest in motivation remained the prime source of his study of vocational selection, another source was his effective merger of William James's moral psychology with Frederick W. Taylor's efficiency-oriented "scientific management." In an optimistic, popular article of 1911, Scott expressed the belief that the mental habits of white-collar workers could be organized in the same way that Taylor had systematized the physical tasks of blue-collar workers.[53] The way to make thought-labor more efficient, following James's analysis of habit and Taylor's simplification of labor into particularized muscle movements, was to eliminate superfluous thinking, which often accompanied white-collar work in the form of self-consciousness or daydreaming. In order to help employers select more efficient minds, Scott developed an examination to test salesmen for their alertness—that is, for their ability to think rapidly and economically.

The final source of Scott's move to vocational selection was Alfred Binet's work in intelligence testing.[54] He borrowed from the French psychologist's wide range of tests but asserted that his own personal exams disclosed native, not learned, ability. But because his "native mental ability tests" were only one part of his methods, and were continually adapted to the needs of different institutions, Scott never claimed they tested "general intelligence" or any specific cognitive ability. Like Binet, Scott was satisfied that his tests measured "intelligence in general" or judgment.[55] Also like Binet, Scott was not terribly concerned about the complementarity of the several tests he administered to subjects. Interested more in offering the subject numerous opportunities for excellence than in measuring the presence of one general quality in all test takers, Scott defined intelligence loosely, modifying it for the different institutions that hired him. For example, in helping discover suitable prospects "for commercial and industrial positions," Scott defined intelligence as a combination of quickness and accuracy:

> The blank here reproduced is one that has been used with good success in testing salesmen for several organizations. The applicant is given 100 per cent *in speed* if he completes the blank in ten minutes; 0 per cent if he completes it in 60 minutes; 50 percent if he completes it in 35 minutes, etc. He is given a grade of 100 per cent *in accuracy* if he makes no errors. Correspondingly lower grades are given for various mistakes or numbers of mistakes. No attempt has been made to determine definitely the particular mental ability tested by this blank.[56]

The adaptability and pluralism of Scott's intelligence testing allowed him to remain independent within academia, while the reductionism of Yerkes's "general intelligence" program encouraged closer affiliation with biology, or, in the practical context of wartime, medicine. For this reason Scott viewed Yerkes's idea of working "under the direction . . . of the Psychiatrist" as a surrender—not an achievement—of professional prestige. On the level of professional jealousy, Scott was not the only psychologist who was wary of the doctor of neurology, which "psychiatrist" still connoted in 1917; meanwhile, psychiatrists had little to gain from extending recognition to psychologists.[57] Furthermore, working under the psychiatrist meant *slow* person-by-person testing, because a psychiatrist, like other doctors, treated his patients individually. To Scott, this approach seemed the height of foolishness! But to Yerkes, Scott's own version of mental testing, whose definition of intelligence vacillated and which emphasized rapid, mass examining, suggested a different—and unempirical—height of foolishness. Moreover, testing time was not as great a priority as it became a few weeks later.

It was not certain at the time of the Walton meeting whether Congress would enact universal conscription legislation, as the House Military Affairs Committee had reported a bill effectively rejecting compulsory service three days earlier (April 18, 1917). Only during the next month did pro-draft arguments become more persuasive, culminating in the passage of the Selective Service Act on May 18.[58] Lacking this time constraint, Yerkes could project the privileged clinical-research position he had enjoyed at Boston State Hospital in the previous five years onto the general psychological role in the military—that is, developing individualized mental tests under the auspices of the neurologists in the Surgeon General's office. Throughout the month of May, Yerkes indulged his idealization of the psychologist-as-psychiatrist to a fantastic degree, believing that psychologists might receive the opportunity to test every recruit individually.[59] This may appear farcical to us in the late twentieth century, as it did to Scott in 1917, but it is understandable, considering Yerkes's background in genetic psychology and the prevalence of individualized mental testing at the time.[60]

Neither Yerkes nor Scott was finally responsible for the introduction of group testing procedures. The psychologists who finally convinced Yerkes to approve mass examinations, after an "entire" day (May 29) of debate on this issue at Vineland, were Bingham and Terman.[61] The latter's contributions to army Alpha are well known, insofar as Terman developed the group test system worked out in the previous year by his student Arthur Otis.[62] Bingham's achievement was less intellectual than organizational. Having remained at the Walton meeting, although he understood Scott's perspective, Bingham was able to maintain Yerkes's respect and thus salvage the possibility of compromise between Scott's practical efforts and Yerkes's drive to actuate evolutionary intelligence theory in wartime. Bingham never did succeed in reuniting Scott and Yerkes, but the conciliatory role he assumed in late April 1917 mediated the claims of realist and idealist, and furthered the development of mass examinations.

Bingham's letter to Terman two days after the Walton, like Scott's April 14, 1917 letter to Yerkes, represents an open-minded effort to unify America's leading psychologists.[63] It recommended the innovative group format of examinations, which Yerkes would later accept for his Committee on the Psychological Examining of Recruits. The letter also recommended Scott's method of organized subjective evaluations as a means to complement and verify intelligence testing.[64] Most importantly, Bingham noted the recent action of the APA Council and informed Terman that Yerkes would contact him soon regarding the plan to ascertain "the minimum intelligence quotient compatible with efficiency as a soldier." The contemporary reductionist faith in a single, general intellective power is evident here, as Bingham implied that the discovery of a minimum score on a mental test could demonstrate each recruit's "intelligence, stability, resistance to distraction and to panic, and so on." Bingham expressed his support for the "minimum intelligence" plan, which he indicated was Yerkes's and was likely to be accepted by the military. Bingham then changed the subject to a concern he shared with Terman—superior intelligence. He complimented his correspondent by proposing that Terman's testing methods, whose national preeminence Yerkes had recently been challenging with his own Point Scale, be employed in the selection of officers, *if* they could be adjusted to the exigency of examining en masse:

> I myself am particularly interested in the possibility of testing, not for the lower borderline, but for the upper zone of intelligence, for the purpose of discovering men capable of promotion to positions of responsibility and leadership. In that connection I would be very glad indeed to have from you all the suggestions you might care to make regarding the value for this purpose of your extension of the Binet Scale and the possibility of adapting it, in part at least, to methods of group testing.[65]

Bingham believed, then, that individualized testing was a satisfactory means for the isolation of mental deficiency, but inadequate as a device for finding the higher range. His five-year background in mental testing had generally dealt more with intellectual competence than incompetence, but this does not explain why he was less apprehensive about the unscientific environment that was considered unavoidable in group tests.

Two other factors had recently led Bingham to consider intelligence very differently than Yerkes. Hired by the Carnegie Institute of Technology in 1915 to administer the nation's first department of applied psychology, Bingham had had to consider the wide variety of tests that laymen might request, thereby expanding his outlook beyond his previous interest in educational/intelligence examinations.[66] In addition, when he asked Carnegie Institute to appoint Scott as the first professor of applied psychology, he took greater interest in the group tests for selecting salesmen that Scott had developed the year before. Scott's tests of mental alertness could hardly have been considered first-rate intelligence tests, but that was not their purpose. Adapted to the needs of clients, usually business executives, these evaluations measured the discrete mental qualities that, Scott assumed, were appropriate to the different skills of the workplace—for example, salesmanship. Scott did test for "native intellectual ability," but, in keeping with the purpose of employee selection, the inclusion of diverse tests was necessarily emphasized over their complementarity in a larger scale of general intelligence:

> The series of tests employed are adjusted to the general type of applicants and the nature of the service to be rendered. For some positions emphasis is placed on inventive ability, on others tact, on others initiative, on others quickness of thought, etc. The applicant is then graded by a percentage figure indicating the native ability in each of the qualities under consideration; as well as by a single figure to express the entire native intellectual ability *so far as tested.*[67]

The diversity of work-place abilities, and thus vocational tests, was tempting other contemporary psychologists to variegate mentality.[68] Moreover, as noted earlier, Scott's group tests were part of a larger personality evaluation program, which also organized subjective evaluations of noncognitive qualities, including conversational ability and loyalty. Thus Bingham had recently begun to consider the purposes of testing more in a practical context, which encouraged him to consider a plurality of mental abilities, and less in the theoretical context of genetic psychology, which stressed the isolation of a supposedly unitary intelligence.

The movement toward adoption of group testing continued in early May 1917, as Terman responded positively to Bingham's suggestion. Although he had "not tried to adapt the upper tests of the Stanford Revision for group testing," Terman implied that he was moving in this direction, especially in his work with Otis.[69] Bingham reported this to Yerkes on May 10, after suggesting that Yerkes alter a particular weakness in his "Plan . . . to Eliminate the Mentally Unfit." In order to solve the practical and scientific problem of having too little time for each individual test, Bingham reported that "Scott and I hope to be able to help in remedying that objection by helping perfect methods of group testing for the preliminary examination."[70] The proposed mixture of group and individualized tests gained Yerkes's reluctant approval at Vineland later in the month. Yerkes did not invite Scott to this crucial conference on methods, having not forgotten Scott's adamant opposition to the proposed medical style. Bingham amply represented his Carnegie colleague anyway, not only in arguing for a more practical testing format, but also in importing the "general information" section of Scott's salesmanship tests into the content of army Alpha.[71]

A few months later, on August 5, 1917, the War Department implemented Scott's character evaluations and established the civilian Committee on the Classification of Personnel in the Army under his directorship in the Adjutant General's office. Yerkes became a nominal member of the CCPA, but chose not to have his Committee on the Psychological Examining of Recruits subsumed under Scott's direction, continuing instead to seek separate organizational status in the Surgeon General's office. Even though he had received plenty of professional recognition that year, as APA president and chairman of the NRC psychology committee, Yerkes was not interested in any military position that could possibly be construed as auxiliary to another psychologist. During mid-July he had attempted to preempt the acceptance of Scott's methods into the military when he knew they were being given serious consideration.[72] Furthermore, to bring Scott's and other psychologists' work completely under his control, Yerkes requested on July 23 that the military commission him as an officer.[73] His appointment as major in the Sanitary Corps on August 17 caused the work of his committee to become so solidly linked to the Surgeon General's office that no organizational unification, and only a negligible amount of cooperation, is evident between Scott's and Yerkes's committees for the remainder of the war.[74] Ultimately, the army recognized Scott's personnel evaluation devices as far more valuable than Yerkes's intelligence tests and rewarded the efforts of the civilian manager more highly than those of the commissioned medic. At war's end, the War Department made Scott the highest-ranking psychologist and awarded him (and no other psychologist) the Distinguished Service Medal.

While the military's evaluation is not to be underestimated, no individual proved himself *primus inter pares*. Scott's utilitarian background had prepared him well for wartime service, but his distance from the academic mainstream and maverick style nearly caused him to foresake his professional affiliation. Yerkes was not alone in fearing that Scott's plans would trivialize the overall psychological contribution. On the other hand, Yerkes's drive to increase psychology's scientific status by associating it with the Medical Corps threatened to demean the profession's standing. Both men were blind to the ways in which their respective styles might hurt psychology; both still promoted their respective styles one world war later.[75] Bingham, who became the army's chief psychologist during World War II, was a more representative leader in 1917 than either Scott or Yerkes. As mediator, Bingham shared both their interests and served as right-hand man to both; but he is little remembered, due to his selfless preference for working behind the scenes.[76]

In light of the early origins of mass examining, the final war record of the two official leaders of psychological testing is fairly ironic. Scott, who had pioneered in methods of group testing before 1917, was excluded—largely because of his walkout at the Walton—from participation in the construction of army Alpha. An uncooperative idealist among his colleagues on April 21, Scott had more experience in cooperating with practical-minded people (for example, businessmen) than probably any other psychologist. Yerkes, who opposed group tests as a "pure" student of genetic psychology, nevertheless gained greater prominence during the postwar controversy that erupted over the analysis of test results by nationality and race. Finally, the army's minimal concern for and negligible utilization of the group test scores are hardly reflected in the hullabaloo over the examination findings.[77] These ironies raise the question of how the first national group tests might have been constructed if Scott, whose objective in mental testing was more utilitarian and far less wrapped up with the discovery of genetically distributed "general intelligence" than Yerkes, had been allowed greater participation.

NOTES

This paper was first presented at the Seventeenth Meeting of Cheiron, the International Society for the History of the Behavioral and Social Sciences, held in Philadelphia on June 14, 1985, as "Walking Out at the Walton: Psychological Disunity and the Emergence of Group Testing in April 1917." I am indebted to many Cheiron members, especially John C. Burnham, James Reed, Franz Samelson, and Michael M. Sokal, for their many helpful comments. I am very grateful to the following archivists for their assistance: Mary Kay Johnsen (Carnegie-Mellon University), Marion McPherson and John Popplestone (Archives of the History of American Psychology), David Saumweber

(National Academy of Sciences), Bruce Stark (Yale University), Patrick Quinn (Northwestern University), and Timothy Nenninger (National Archives).

1. Donald S. Napoli, *Architects of Adjustment: The History of the Psychological Profession in the United States* (Port Washington, N.Y.: Kennikat Press, 1981), 4.
2. Robert M. Yerkes to Walter Van Dyke Bingham and Walter D. Scott, April 16, 1917; Yerkes to Scott, April 17, 1917, *WDS*.
3. Article II of the constitution of the APA lodged executive power in a council of six members. In addition to these six, the president of the APA was an ex-officio Council member; *Psychological Review* 2 (1895): 150.
4. Scott's Committee on the Classification of Personnel in the Army was established in the Adjutant General's office on August 5, 1917. Yerkes's Division of Psychology was formally established in the Surgeon General's office on January 19, 1918.
5. See Edwin Layton, "Mirror-Image Twins: The Communities of Science and Technology," in *Nineteenth-Century American Science: A Reappraisal,* edited by George H. Daniels (Evanston, Ill.: Northwestern University Press, 1972), for a discussion of the mind-sets of practitioners of science vis-à-vis theoreticians.
6. Walter D. Scott, *The Theory of Advertising* (Boston: Small, Maynard, 1903); idem, *The Psychology of Public Speaking* (New York: Noble and Noble, 1907); idem, *Increasing Human Efficiency in Business* (New York: Macmillan, 1911); Leonard Ferguson, *The Heritage of Industrial Psychology* (Hartford, Conn.: The Finlay Press, 1963), 3–7, for a breakdown of Scott's publications; Jacob Z. Jacobson, *Scott of Northwestern: The Life Story of a Pioneer in Psychology and Education* (Chicago: Mariano Press, 1951), 51–52; Michael M. Sokal, "Walter Dill Scott," *The Dictionary of American Biography,* supplement 5 (New York: Charles Scribner's Sons, 1977), 611.
7. Bingham to Guy M. Whipple, January 21, 1916, *WVB*.
8. Walter D. Scott, "Selection of Employees by Means of Quantitative Determinations," *The Annals of the American Academy of Political and Social Science,* no. 999 (Philadelphia: 1916), 3–4; idem, "The Scientific Selection of Salesmen," *Advertising and Selling* 25 (1915): n.p., in *WVB;* see John B. Watson, "Fake Element in Vocational Psychology," *Baltimore News,* April 26, 1916, in *WVB.*
9. Hugo Münsterberg to Yerkes, December 19, 1911, 6, *RMY;* see Laurence R. Veysey, *The Emergence of the American University* (Chicago: University of Chicago Press, 1965), 248–251.
10. Robert M. Yerkes, "The Scientific Way," *RMY,* 133–134.
11. Robert M. Yerkes and Daniel M. LaRue, *Outline of a Study of the Self* (Cambridge, Mass.: Harvard University Press, 1914), 8; Yerkes, "The Scientific Way," 108, 129–130, 133–134, 150–151.
12. Walter B. Cannon to George E. Hale, April 13, 1917, and James R. Angell to Hale, May 29, 1917, *NAS.*

13. See David Kennedy, *Over Here* (New York: Oxford University Press, 1980), 17–18, 147–149.
14. Daniel Kevles, "Testing the Army's Intelligence: Psychologists and the Military in World War I," *Journal of American History* 55 (1968): 566; Thomas Camfield, "Psychologists at War: The History of American Psychology and the First World War." (Ph.D. diss., University of Texas at Austin, 1969).
15. Angell to Hale, May 29, 1917, *NAS*.
16. Robert M. Yerkes, "Psychology in Relation to the War," *Psychological Review* 25 (1918): 85–86; W. R. Miles to Bingham, April 21, 1917, *WVB;* see report, *Meeting of Psychological Group for Discussion of Relations of Psychology to Defense,* in *NAS*.
17. For his interest in the development of group intelligence tests, see Bingham's contribution to Carl Seashore, ed., "Mentality Tests: A Symposium," *Journal of Educational Psychology* 7 (1916): 231; see above, n. 3, regarding the APA constitution.
18. Yerkes to Bingham, April 7, 1917, *WVB*.
19. Robert M. Yerkes, ed., *Psychological Examining in the United States Army,* vol. 15, Memoirs of the National Academy of Sciences (Washington, D.C.: Government Printing Office, 1921), 7; idem, "The Scientific Way," 167.
20. Yerkes to the Council of the American Psychogical Association, April 6, 1917, *WVB*.
21. Camfield, "Psychologists at War," 85–88. Yerkes claimed later that the NRC sought him out, in "Psychology in Relation to the War," 90–91.
22. Walter D. Scott, "A History of the Committee on Classification of Personnel in the Army," *WVB,* 1.
23. Camfield, "Psychologists at War," 91, brought the likely details of Bingham's letter to my attention. Presumably it is the one to which Scott referred in "A History of the CCPA."
24. Scott to Yerkes, April 14, 1917, *NAS,* my emphasis.
25. Yerkes to Carl Brigham, March 28, 1917, *RMY*.
26. Scott to Yerkes, April 14, 1917, *NAS*.
27. Yerkes to Carl Brigham, March 28, 1917, *RMY*.
28. See Camfield, "Psychologists at War," 90–91, for Hale's skepticism.
29. Ibid., 91–92. Hollingworth was more suspicious of psychologists exploiting the war situation than Scott; see the latter's "A History of the CCPA," 2.
30. Yerkes to Bingham and Scott, April 16, 1917, *WDS*.
31. Yerkes to Scott, April 17, 1917, *WDS*.
32. Third Meeting of NRC (notes), April 19, 1917, *NAS;* "Minutes of the Meeting of the National Research Council Held on Thursday, April 19, 1917 . . . ," *Proceedings of the National Academy of Sciences* 3 (1917): 582.
33. Yerkes, "Psychology in Relation to the War," 91–93, including Herbert S. Langfeld's *Minutes of Special Meeting of the Council of the American Psychological Association.*

34. For the publications of everyone in attendance, see Carl Murchison, ed., *The Psychological Register* (Worcester, Mass.: Clark University Press, 1929), 6–7, 16–17, 59–60, 64–66, 136–137, 210, 291–293.

35. Scott, "A History of the CCPA," 2–3.

36. Bingham, "Outline for Autobiography," *WVB*, folder entitled "Biogr. and Autobiographical Writings & Data Concerning WVB and his Work," box 7, 3.

37. Bingham's copy of the Jacobson (*Scott*, 101–102) is in the open stacks of the Hunt Library at Carnegie-Mellon University.

38. Scott, "A History of the CCPA," 3.

39. Yerkes, "Plan for the Psychological Examining of Recruits to Eliminate the Mentally Unfit," *NAS*, April 29, 1917, Yerkes's emphasis (hereafter, references to the "Plan . . ." will cite its location in Yerkes, "Psychology in Relation to the War," 94–97); Yerkes to Dr. Victor Vaughan, April 23, 1917, *NAS;* Yerkes, War Diary, April 29, 1917, *RMY.*

40. See Yerkes to Vaughan, May 4, 1917, *NAS,* for Yerkes's disappointment about not being allowed a commission in the Medical Corps.

41. See Hamilton Cravens, *The Triumph of Evolution: American Scientists and the Heredity-Environment Controversy, 1900–1941* (Philadelphia: University of Pennsylvania Press, 1978), 193–201; Thomas Camfield, "The Professionalization of American Psychology, 1870–1917," *Journal of the History of the Behavioral Sciences* 9 (1973): 73.

42. See Münsterberg to Yerkes, January 30, 1911, 3, and December 19, 1911, 4, *RMY.*

43. See James Reed, "Robert Yerkes and the Mental Testing Movement," chapter 4 of this volume; also Franz Samelson, "Putting Psychology on the Map: Ideology and Intelligence Testing," in *Psychology in Social Context,* edited by Allan R. Buss (New York: Irvington, 1979), 103–168.

44. See Yerkes to Brigham, March 28, 1917, *RMY;* Yerkes to Scott, April 17, 1917, *WDS;* Yerkes to C. B. Davenport, May 2, 1917, and Yerkes to Bird Baldwin, May 4, 1917, *NAS.*

45. Note Lewis M. Terman's discussion of the "presence of others" in *The Measurement of Intelligence: An Explanation of and a Complete Guide for the Use of the Stanford Revision and Extension of the Binet-Simon Intelligence Scale* (Boston: Houghton Mifflin, 1916), 122–123. Rudolph Pintner, *Intelligence Testing, Methods and Results* (New York: Henry Holt, 1923), 48–50, 138–141, provides a solid, if self-interested, account of the rise of group tests during the period of their novelty.

46. Yerkes, "Psychology in Relation to the War," 96.

47. See Yerkes, "The Role of the Experimenter in Comparative Psychology," *Journal of Animal Behavior* 5 (1915): 258, for a warning that even the tester's presence might spoil the exam.

48. Charles Spearman, "General Intelligence Objectively Determined and Measured," *American Journal of Psychology* 15 (1904): 201–293.

49. Yerkes, who held his own testing technique to be more true to "the laws

of mental development" than Terman's, weighted his exams with the aid of "coefficients of correlation with general intelligence." Yerkes to Carl E. Seashore, February 28, 1916, *RMY*, and Yerkes, "The Binet versus the Point Scale Method of Measuring Intelligence," *Journal of Applied Psychology* 1 (1917): 116.

50. Scott to Yerkes, April 14, 1917, *NAS*, my emphasis. Later that summer, the military would rewrite all of the rating qualities, but the comparative design remained the same.

51. For further discussion of the transition in Scott's evaluation methods, see Richard T. von Mayrhauser, "The Triumph of Utility: The Forgotten Clash of American Psychologies in World War I" (Ph.D. diss., University of Chicago, 1986), 235–256; also see enclosures of Scott to Yerkes, May 12, 1917, *NAS*.

52. The *Journal of Educational Psychology*, which devoted much of its space to testing, began in 1910; the *Psychological Bulletin* began an annual review of "Tests" in 1911.

53. Walter D. Scott, "Habits That Help," *Everybody's Magazine* 25 (1911): 412–417.

54. Scott, "The Scientific Selection of Salesmen," second page (see n. 8).

55. See Alfred Binet and Theodore Simon, *The Development of Intelligence in Children*, translated by Elizabeth S. Kite (Baltimore: Williams and Wilkins, 1916), 42–43; Read D. Tuddenham, "The Nature and Measurement of Intelligence," in *Psychology in the Making: Histories of Selected Research Problems*, edited by Leo Postman (New York: Alfred A. Knopf, 1962), 488–489.

56. Scott, "Selection of Employees by Means of Quantitative Determinations," 4.

57. See Angell to Hale, May 23, 1917, *NAS;* and Charles L. Dana, Adolf Meyer, and Thomas Salmon, "Report of Committee of the New York Psychiatrical Society on the Activities of 'Clinical Psychologists'," *Journal of Abnormal Psychology* 12 (1917): 142–144.

58. The reporting on the draft bill in the *New York Times* became consistently optimistic after April 27.

59. Yerkes to E. R. Embree (Secretary of the Rockefeller Foundation), May 2, 1917, *NAS;* Yerkes, *Psychological Examining*, 299.

60. Angell referred to this plan as a potential "farce" in his note to Hale of May 23, 1917, *NAS*.

61. See Yerkes, *Psychological Examining*, 299.

62. Ibid.

63. Bingham to Terman, April 24, 1917, *WVB*.

64. Serving as administrator of Yerkes's committee during the summer of 1917, Bingham asked camp examiners to secure officer evaluations of recruit intelligence to validate the first tests. See Bingham telegrams to G. M. Whipple, J. W. Hayes, and E. K. Strong, July 25, 1917, *NAS;* also report of statistical unit chief, E. L. Thorndike, in Yerkes, *Psychological Examining*, 316.

65. Bingham to Terman, April 24, 1917, *WVB*.
66. See Bingham, "Some Norms of Dartmouth Freshmen," *Journal of Educational Psychology* 7 (1916): 129–142.
67. Scott, "Selection of Employees," 3–4, my emphasis.
68. Frank Freeman, in his annual review of "Tests," *Psychological Bulletin* 13 (1916): 268–269, reported that testers of vocational abilities were resisting the tendency to consider skills as separate mental powers and instead "placing greatest reliance upon the ability to determine the candidate's general intelligence," thus reflecting Spearman's influence.
69. Terman to Bingham, May 2, 1917, *WVB*.
70. Bingham to Yerkes, May 10, 1917, *WVB*.
71. Yerkes, *Psychological Examining*, 300, 311.
72. See E. L. Thorndike to Yerkes, July 18, 1917, *NAS*.
73. Yerkes to Surgeon General Gorgas, July 23, 1917, CCPA papers, National Archives.
74. Yerkes later sought to merge his military Division of Psychology with Scott's civilian Committee on the Classification of Personnel. Scott diplomatically resisted the merger, but recommended the extension of intelligence testing. See Yerkes to Surgeon General Gorgas, November 5, 1917; Gorgas to Adjutant General McCain, November 7, 1917; Scott to Gorgas, November 14, 1917; CCPA Minutes of Meeting of December 5, 1917, *WDS*.
75. Chester Nimitz to Scott, March 24, 1941, Scott to Nimitz, April 3, 1941, *WDS;* Yerkes to Terman, January 9, 1942, *LMT,* cited in Russell Marks, "Testers, Trackers and Trustees: The Ideology of the Intelligence Testing Movement in America 1900–1954" (Ph.D. diss., University of Illinois at Urbana, 1972), 98.
76. See Millicent Todd Bingham to Terman, August 29, 1953, *WVB*.
77. Samelson, "Putting Psychology on the Map," 142–145.

8

Applied Science and Public Policy: The Ohio Bureau of Juvenile Research and the Problem of Juvenile Delinquency, 1913–1930

In the early twentieth century Americans first forged enduring linkages between the worlds of public policy and scientific expertise. Countless examples of this new development crystallized in American life then. Indeed, this amalgam of policy and expertise has and can be defined as the essence of Progressive reform.[1] Perhaps there were few more interesting examples of this marriage than the development of mental tests by the newly professionalized psychologists. As historian John C. Burnham has rightly insisted, the new mental sciences had much in common intellectually with Progressivism and early twentieth-century public policy.[2] Starting in the early 1900s, such psychologists as Henry H. Goddard and Lewis M. Terman developed their standardizations of Alfred Binet's scaled mental test for American children. The intelligence test and its various derivatives then came into increasingly widespread use in a growing number of public institutions, as in the public schools and, during World War I, in the United States Army. In the first decade and a half of the mental testing movement, almost all psychometricians insisted that the tests measured innate intelligence of groups and individuals. By the later

1920s, of course, they had retreated from this high ground to the extent of admitting that adequate tests of inborn intelligence of groups or races had not yet been devised, but they retained their faith in the tests' general validity and in their ability to measure an individual's native intelligence, which is another way of saying that they believed their technics were a valuable resource for the creation of public policy.[3]

The Ohio Bureau of Juvenile Research provides an illuminating case study of this newly wrought marriage of public policy and psychological expertise. Ohio was a major state, a microcosm of America. By the early twentieth century it had acquired a dynamic network of research institutions and a growing Progressive movement, thus setting the stage for the development of a scientific bureau for social policy. The bureau's champions always insisted that it should function as the scientific and classificatory agency of the state's child-caring institutions and should assist in the development and implementation of the most modern and up-to-date policies for child-saving. Ohio's child-savers, like those elsewhere in the nation, operated from certain assumptions. They believed children constituted a special, vulnerable group in the population whose members should be protected through public policies. Manifestations of this approach were found in the creation of juvenile courts, expansion of involuntary education, enactment of child-labor laws, as well as statutes designed to keep alcoholic beverages from children and to obliterate smut in the mass media. The small band of child psychologists trained and inspired by Clark University's president G. Stanley Hall supported child study as the indispensable scientific adjunct to child-saving and peddled as much of it to child reformers as they could. To the reformers' notion of children as a distinct and separate group in the population, they added the formulation that the child is the father to the man. And indeed they did as much as they could to make this notion a central theme of the new child psychology. In this they were assisted considerably by Alfred Binet, or, more precisely, by the particular interpretations they fashioned of the French psychologist's famous test. Binet's test was one of the first research techniques available to child psychologists for their own specialty that was also useful to the science of psychology more generally.[4]

What gave scientific and policy interest in child welfare a special cachet then was the electrifying promise that science made it possible to engineer a brighter tomorrow. Between the 1870s and the 1920s many Americans in most walks of life acted as if they believed that the causes of the present were to be found entirely in the past. When advocates of child welfare and child science insisted that the child was the father to the man, they were pointing out a tangible way to control the future, for their message was that if children could be trained in just the right way, the future was assured. By saying that the past determines the present, of course, Americans were affirming the omnipotence of tradition and inheritance. From this perspective the psychologists' adoption of the evolutionary point of view and emphasis upon psychobiological inheritance as the clues to human conduct and character made perfectly good sense. This emphasis on the child as the key to the future meant that now the present was a part of the causes of the present, a notion that foreshadowed the reorientation of biological and social theory of the 1920s in mental testing, and in the natural and social sciences and in American culture more generally.[5]

A politician and a scientist created the Ohio Bureau of Juvenile Research. The politician was Democrat James M. Cox, publisher and editor of a Dayton newspaper, who first entered Ohio reform politics in the early 1900s as a cautious advocate of municipal reform, especially in cities other than Dayton. Between 1908 and 1912 Cox served in the U.S. House of Representatives, again occasionally supporting Progressive measures in nation and state. Nineteen-twelve was the *annus mirabulus* of Ohio Progressivism. In that year Progressives engineered a state constitutional convention. At the convention they installed a staple list of Progressive reforms, including women's suffrage, municipal home rule, good roads, the direct primary, the initiative and referendum. Cox ran as a Progressive Democrat for governor and won.

As governor, Cox pushed through a series of laws that were intended to implement and fund the Progressive reforms mandated by the new state constitution. An issue of particular interest to Cox was penal and corrections policy, especially with regard to juvenile delinquency. Like most conscientious Progressive politicians elsewhere in the nation, Cox turned to scientific experts for suggestions on policy matters. Precisely how he came to solicit advice from Henry H. Goddard on juvenile delinquency remains a matter for speculation. Possibly Cox was aware of Goddard's reputation as research psychologist at one of the most prestigious institutions of the day for the mentally retarded, the New Jersey Training School for Feebleminded Boys and Girls in Vineland, and as one of Hall's most famous disciples. Perhaps E. J. Emerick, director of the Ohio institution for the "feebleminded" in Columbus, had recommended his friend and co-professional. Goddard was a Democrat and an advisor to Woodrow Wilson when he was governor of New Jersey. This might have been the link, or perhaps Cox had heard of Goddard's lurid study *The Kallikak Family* (1912), in which Goddard argued that innate mental defect caused antisocial conduct. In any event, the consequences of Cox's consultations with Goddard were neither trifling nor mysterious. In effect, Goddard drew up the plan for the bureau in all its important particulars. Then Cox persuaded the legislature to enact Goddard's plan into law.

Since 1867 the Ohio State Board of Charities had functioned as a state agency with general responsibility for inspirational leadership for all Ohio's state, county, and municipal penal, corrections, and charitable institutions. These institutions remained fully the creatures of the governments to which they were attached, with their own budgets, personnel, policies, and boards of directors. In the late nineteenth century this was a common technique for the coordination of policy among the various levels of government below the federal level. By the early twentieth century, however, the Progressives' vision of a hierarchical, efficient, businesslike policy animated them to push for the considerable expansion of the powers and functions of state government, especially that of the executive branch. Often this resulted in a corresponding loss of power and functions for courthouse and city hall, and in long, bitter conflicts among the interest groups involved. In Ohio a manifestation of this trend was the creation of the Ohio Board of Administration in 1911. This was an issue on which both the economy-minded businessmen and reformers agreed. The board became the central administrative agency for all state charitable and correctional institutions. It had full control over all matters of policy and their implementation. Furthermore, now the board, not the twenty state institutions, requested funds for the institutions from the legislature, and parceled out the funds to the institutions. The State Board of Charities continued to exist, with a circumscribed mandate, and the local institutions functioned as before.[6]

Under the provisions of the act that created the Bureau of Juvenile Research, the agency became the scientific and classificatory arm of the board in the board's campaign to prevent juvenile delinquency and (not incidentally) pare down the costs of the state institutions. The law stipulated that all offenders whom the juvenile courts decided required care in a state institution were defined as wards of the state, and, therefore, were automatically committed to the board which had "sole and exclusive guardianship of such minors." The bureau was thus empowered to administer "mental, physical, and other examinations" to minors thus committed to the board. The board members could demand a complete, written scientific report from the bureau on each child so examined. On the basis of this report, the board could then determine the most appropriate assignment to a state institution for each child. But the board's powers went much further. With the bureau's advice, the board could then transfer any minor from one state institution to another, "whenever it shall appear that such minor, by reason of its delinquency, neglect, insanity, dependency, epilepsy, feeble-mindedness, or other crippled condition or deformity, ought to be in another institution." The bureau was also required to place under observation for extended examination any minor sent to it by any county, municipal, or private institution. Parents and legal guardians could also request these services for their children.[7] Clearly the bureau had great responsibilities, the most important of which was to develop modern and scientific corrections policies for children. In time the presumption among the bureau's supporters was apparently that other public and private institutions would follow suit and implement the new wisdom.[8]

Yet there were problems inherent in the situation. There was a large gap between the bureau's responsibilities and its authority. It could not do more than the board permitted, and was indeed organizationally and legally subordinate to the board. Nor did it have any method, easy or not, of cultivating its own political constituencies. In effect it was the board's lightning rod. The board could create resentment among those allied with or employed at twenty state institutions.

The bureau could then reap the whirlwind. And the bureau stood for a different kind of juvenile corrections policy than the older state institutions. It was expected to promote the prevention of juvenile delinquency by the most modern scientific techniques and therapies. With the apparent exception of the institution for the feeble minded, the state institutions represented the usual custodial approach—no doubt largely because they could do no more due to severe overcrowding and lean budgets. The scientific expertise with which they were familiar was the older medical variety, with its heavy admixture of militaristic discipline. The new psychology that Goddard and his co-professionals were attempting to implement at the better institutions for the feebleminded was often quite suspect to those running the state institutions. It struck them as too permissive.

While at Vineland, Goddard developed his vision of the new applied child science.[9] Central to his scheme was the notion that innate intelligence determined human nature and conduct. As one of Hall's most famous and successful students, Goddard worked out the implications of Hallian hereditarian psychology as he understood them for the problems at hand. Goddard was, of course, an early champion of the Binet test.[10] He also became intellectually and personally close to the famous ideologue of American eugenics, Charles B. Davenport; in this way Davenport recruited Goddard into the eugenics movement.[11] Some of Goddard's most famous early publications, notably *The Kallikak Family* (1912) and *The Criminal Imbecile* (1915), advanced the thesis that criminal conduct, in particular, and antisocial behavior in general, were caused by the inheritance of low mentality in certain types of individuals. Those persons of subnormal or feebleminded intelligence required particular attention. Those with a mental age of less than eight years could not care for themselves and had to be institutionalized. Those between eight and twelve years of mental age, as defined by the Binet test, however, presented a different problem. These were the morons, as Goddard labeled them. They were sufficiently intelligent to take care of themselves in certain routine ways, such as eating, dressing, and perhaps even working in jobs that demanded few skills. Yet they did not possess sufficient intellect to have developed a moral sense, as most normal persons of twelve or more mental years would. Herein lay the cause of much antisocial conduct. The so-called high-grade mental defectives got into trouble because they were just intelligent enough to appear normal and live in society, yet sufficiently substandard that they could not comprehend the difference between right and wrong. For example, Goddard believed that the so-called Kallikak family was comprised chiefly of high-grade mental defectives who were for that reason criminals, degenerates, prostitutes, and other kinds of offenders.[12]

By the later 1910s, however, Goddard had begun to realize that few of the so-called morons were actually predisposed to antisocial conduct. Here his change of heart came from his various experiences at Vineland in attempting to work out techniques and programs for the reeducation of the high-grade defectives so that they could be deinstitutionalized. If they were treated humanely and trained for responsible positions in the community that they could handle, Goddard now concluded, they would turn out to be worthwhile and dependable citizens in civilian society. Thus Goddard had now declared that heredity was not all powerful. Environment and training mattered too. He had said, in other words, that some of the causes of the present were to be found in the present, and some were located in the past.[13] It had not yet occurred to him to reconcile this view with his more general position, which he still maintained, that the most important single cause of antisocial conduct was innate low intelligence. And indeed nor should it have as yet, because he still thought of heredity and environment as distinct rather than interrelated in a larger symbiotic relationship.

In March 1918 Goddard became the bureau's new director after protracted negotiations with members of the Board of Administration.[14] The bureau had operated since July 1914. Yet its prior history, about which he had learned from Harvard psychologist Robert Yerkes, should not have reassured him.[15] The bureau's first director was E. J. Emerick, who retained his position as director of the institution for the feebleminded. Appointed clinical psychologist was Thomas H. Haines, who had studied with Yerkes and Hugo Münsterberg at Harvard before settling into a career of teaching psychology at Ohio State University. Haines joined the bureau because he found little opportunity or encouragement for research at the university. As it turned out, Haines had plenty of time and opportunity for research on the inmates of the state's various institutions. Even so apparently well-connected a man as Emerick could not persuade the legislature to fund the entire program for the bureau as implied in the law. Haines published a number of scientific articles. He also disseminated policy statements on upgrading the state institutions that were sufficiently expensive in their implications that he won no praise, nor perhaps even notice, from the legislature. In 1917 Haines resigned in disgust. He was convinced that the situation was too politicized for any genuinely professional plans ever to succeed.[16] But the board's members persuaded Goddard that the bureau's future was bright indeed. Confident that he had sufficient political support to make the bureau into a first-class child-saving institution, Goddard accepted the position.

He reported for work that May in Columbus. He appointed Dr. Gertrude Transeau, a local general practitioner, as the chief medical examiner. For Haines's position as chief psychoclinician he selected Florence Mateer, one of Hall's later doctoral graduates. Mateer had worked at the Massachusetts school for the feebleminded, which was widely regarded as one of the nation's best. She was as convinced as Goddard that low intelligence was the most important cause of antisocial conduct, including juvenile delinquency. Nevertheless, she too had been working on the practical problem of the reeducation of the high-grade mental defectives. She was quite impressed with the apparent practical efficacy of the conditioned reflex therapy which the Russian physiologist N. Krasnogorski had developed. She had tried it with patients at the Massachusetts school and found potentially useful results.[17] Yet if she was convinced that behaviorist training could change human actions, she still believed that innate mental defect caused antisocial conduct. Mateer's position was not contradictory. When behaviorist psychologists and physiologists ruled out such mental entities of traditional psychology as consciousness, they embraced a model of organic development in which the organism had genetically predetermined anatomical structures that the "right" environmental stimuli would, under certain conditions, "awaken," thus leading to specific patterns of behavior. Thus in this view, inheritance still mattered; environment was assigned a minor role at most, that of the stimulator, or stimulus. The organism was therefore "empty" of all save mute innate structures that, with proper stimuli, would develop "correctly." In a letter to Goddard that spring, for example, she complained indignantly about her visit with Dr. William Healy of the Judge Baker Clinic in Boston. Healy was perhaps the most visible scientist working with delinquents who dissented from the hereditarian interpretation that Goddard, Mateer, and most psychologists accepted. Mateer had visited Healy as a way of touching base and maintaining cordial professional relations, and Healy had responded in kind, she reported; yet "he diatribed that all delinquency is not mental defect, but . . . that environmental factors may play a part." [18]

Over the next two years Goddard and his staff worked hard to implement fully the bureau's mandate. The bureau was in temporary quarters for some time, and then divided between temporary and permanent quarters. Medical and intelligence examinations began almost immediately for those children sent to the bureau. But there were no overnight accommodations on the premises for those who required extended observation for more than a few hours. Hence almost all children received attention for a day or less, except in rare cases in which they could be boarded. Overall, conditions within the bureau were hardly optimal. Space was limited. Often standard medical and dental examinations had to be performed by local doctors and dentists because of the lack of proper rooms and equipment at the bureau.[19] The bureau's external relations and prospects were none too rosy, either. Cox had been reelected Ohio's governor in 1918, but the Republicans captured the legislature. The resulting political wrangling was so bitter that the bureau became the victim of various political conflicts.[20] The chief difficulty was that the board tightened its budgetary and administrative leash over the bureau so much that Goddard thought seriously of resigning. He considered the powerful Republican sweep of Ohio in 1920, with a Republican governor and all but 14 of 150 state legislators in the GOP, as the omen for him to leave.[21] And the bureau's image with the other state institutions was not helpful. When Goddard and his staff visited the state institutions and surveyed the inmates, as mandated by law, they created all sorts of animosities among administrators and their staff who had important political connections. Thus R. U. Hastings, director of the State Boys' Industrial Home, near Lancaster, rapidly became a critic of the bureau. He told Goddard in the fall of 1919 that "it will not be convenient at any time for any [bureau] worker to come to the school to make such examination [sic] of any of our boys."[22] Hastings resented the bureau for several reasons. He feared, not incorrectly, that the new system that the board and bureau had created would result in even more overcrowding in his ill-equipped institution. Understandably, he disliked the loss of authority he suffered at the board's hands, and the bureau was the most obvious and accessible target. In reality both Hastings and Goddard were caught in a situation they could not control.[23]

Indeed, the larger situation depended for the resolution Goddard wished upon the political victory the Republicans won in 1920 and which he so feared. Only then would the one-upmanship between the two parties, if not between the factions within the parties, cease. Yet Goddard could only continue to make policy recommendations to the board and thus indirectly to the legislature, which ineluctably entailed far greater increases in the state appropriations for the board and its institutions than the legislature was willing to grant the Board of Administration. On several occasions, for example, Goddard complained that the number of feebleminded persons in Ohio was several times the number housed in the overcrowded Columbus institution. He insisted that the only solution to the problem was for the state to build more facilities. If there was an issue about which Goddard possessed great expertise, it was this. Naturally, his pleas fell on deaf ears. He was clearly unconcerned, if not precisely unaware, that such a recommendation was expensive and, therefore, politically inadvisable. At considerable political cost, the board did win appropriations for the completion of the bureau's permanent campus in 1917. This was all the board could or would do for the moment.[24] And it should be remembered that Goddard operated at a considerable disadvantage. Many aspects of his position required highly developed political skills and much political capital. Of political skills in that sense he had none. He was a true *naif* in such matters, a trusting, open, and direct man whose talents and expertise rested almost entirely in science, and who did not understand the rules, let alone the nuances, of interest-group state politics. As a newcomer to the state, he had no political influence except that which others would care to confer on him. And few made any political investment in him. Yet in reality even an experienced, powerful, and sophisticated politician would probably have done no better than Goddard. The situation was likely too much to master for any individual appointed to the bureau. By 1920 the bureau was functioning, if only in a political free-fire zone.

By February 1919, the bureau's facilities at the permanent campus were partly completed. Immediately ready for use were the two observational cottages. Herein could be housed those children who required extended observation over a period of days, weeks, or even months. Previously Goddard and his staff could not handle more than a dozen children at once, and they were lucky if they could accumulate a few hours of examination for any child. What was observed and, in that sense, known, was necessarily very limited indeed. This part of the situation was, then, *de novo*. But there was more. Prior to coming to the bureau, Goddard and Mateer, as research professionals, had worked with persons of varying attributes who nevertheless shared one trait in common. All were classified as mentally retarded. Goddard and Mateer had worked with these unfortunates long enough to realize that few, if any, were innate moral degenerates, as some of Goddard's early propaganda had presupposed. By and large they had not worked systematically with a population deemed by the legal system to be criminal or delinquent. While it was true that they did examine children at the bureau who were sent to them by the local juvenile courts, their examinations and observations were inevitably circumscribed. They were well aware that more time for observation and examination was necessary.

It was not until the observational cottages had opened and had been in operation for a period of months that Goddard and Mateer would have had the opportunity, if they wished to pursue it, to think about a population that, no matter how diverse, had one common attribute. The children sent to the bureau were those whom local authorities (and the children's families) had washed their hands of in despair, for various reasons. Rather than being classified as mentally retarded, they had been judged by society as the most difficult, rambunctious, and taxing of the state's delinquent—a mirror image, as it were, of the cream of the state's crop of children. For some time, no one involved imagined that these changes in the bureau and its scientific tasks and responsibilities would make any particular difference or trigger unanticipated results. Such prescience was probably not to be expected. Yet in time the new situation was to function as a tangible catalyst in a transformation in the theory and prevention of juvenile delinquency as Goddard and Mateer thought of these matters as a part, small by itself, of that larger shift of American culture and social thought from the notion that the causes of the present are in the past alone to the newer model of social theory, that the causes of the present are to be found in the present at least as much as in the past.

In April 1919, two months after the cottages opened, Goddard delivered the annual Louis Clark Vanuxem lectures at Princeton University. This was a signal honor for Goddard. It was a sign, if such were needed, of the national recognition he had won over the last decade as one of the leading authorities in his field, which was becoming known as applied or clinical psychology. Goddard was indeed in distinguished company as a Vanuxem lecturer. Among those who preceded him was Thomas Hunt Morgan, the famous geneticist who helped fashion the classical Mendelian genetics and eventually won a Nobel Prize. The next year Goddard's lectures were published under the title *Human Efficiency and Levels of Intelligence*. They represented the culmination of the hereditarian point of view he had developed so far in his career. What he said, then, was of more than passing interest, for it was in fact a transitional statement that looked ahead almost as much as it looked behind.

An efficient society, Goddard declared, would be arranged according to the intelligence, or the mental level, of every individual within that society. Admitting that emotion and temperament were important determinants of behavior, he nevertheless stressed intelligence as the most crucial determinant of the three. Intelligence resulted from the quality of the individual's inborn nervous system, including, of course, the brain. If science were to inform completely the structures and processes of social existence, then the scientist would argue that society should be reconstituted so that each person had the occupation and social status that best reflected his actual mental level. If society were thus constituted, each person would find his proper niche in the social order. From this perspective, Goddard thus defined the delinquent as a straggler in society, as someone who could or would not march in step with his law-abiding fellow citizens. The better and more practical solution to the problem was prevention rather than punishment. The stragglers were not responsible for their actions. Their minds were defective. Ultimately it was easier and more cost-effective to identify juvenile offenders before they became adult criminals than it was to start with adult criminals and attempt to rehabilitate them, for their very persona had become irretrievably criminal. The greatest single cause of delinquency was inborn low-grade intelligence, most of it well within the limits psychologists defined as the range of feeblemindedness.

Goddard had two general recommendations. First, a small proportion of criminals and delinquents were so afflicted that there was no hope of salvation. They were mentally diseased, or psychopathic. The cause was innate mental defect. Permanent incarceration was the only solution. But in the main Goddard was optimistic. Science would lead the way. Thanks to the development of modern psychology, it was now possible to identify most offenders at an early stage and nip antisocial behavior in the bud. Here the Binet test was the indispensable technic. It could easily discriminate among those persons in the general population of above normal, normal, and below normal intelligence. Since almost all potential offenders had below normal intelligence, applied and clinical psychologists could perform this service for society and thus take the first important step toward the virtual eradication of crime and delinquency by means of prevention. He pointed to his own experiments at Vineland as a promising start on the next phase. He had devised programs to train the high-grade defectives to be good and decent citizens. With humane, loving, and respectful treatment they would come to understand that they could make their way in society without being stigmatized as peculiar or worse. Then more precise examinations and observations could determine exactly what they could and could not do outside the institution. Following that, a specific training program could be set up for individuals so that in time they could learn a simple occupation and be released, first on parole, ultimately without conditions. Goddard estimated that perhaps 90 percent of the high-grade mental defectives could be reeducated and prepared for life in society. In turn they would become useful, constructive contributors to the social organization rather than a drain on precious philanthropic and charitable resources. Society needed persons of humble gifts to be hewers of wood and haulers of water. And it served no decent or humane purpose to disparage such persons.[25]

Obviously Goddard had changed a number of important corollaries within his general position. This was no longer the man who wrote about the Kallikaks and the criminal imbeciles and melodramatically claimed that perhaps a large fraction of the national population was of such low grade mentality that civilized society itself was in immediate danger of being engulfed. As late as 1916 he had recommended sterilization of the feebleminded. Now he was silent on the issue.[26] A new phrase had cropped into his vocabulary: the psychopathic offender. He recognized this type at least as early as 1918 in a report to the Board of Administration before accepting the position at the bureau.[27] What he meant by "psychopathic offender" at this point, however, was someone whose mind was so diseased and afflicted by low mental level that he or she was fated to be antisocial. No amount of reeducation would help.

Furthermore, he had put a considerable amount of distance between himself and other champions of psychometrics such as Lewis M. Terman, who insisted that the intelligence quotient, or the relationship of mental and chronological age, was in and of itself a valid yardstick of the intelligence of any child or adult. One had to look at the total person and examine him in terms of his mental level, asserted Goddard. Perhaps there was more than a tinge of professional jealously which explained Goddard's attitude toward Terman.[28] As another of Hall's former students, Terman had by now probably achieved a larger reputation than Goddard because of his version of the Binet test, commonly known as the Stanford-Binet, which had superseded Goddard's insofar as most testers were concerned.

Yet more was involved. Most likely it mattered more. Terman was a Stanford professor very interested in developing the applications of psychological measurement to a variety of research problems. To the extent that he worked with an identifiable research population, it was the children of high or genius level of intelligence who would form the core for the justly famous genius project he was about to launch in the late 1910s. The problems of public policy, clinical examinations of individuals, and therapy for the afflicted were not a major concern for him, like they were for Goddard. And, Terman studied a defined population of one thousand gifted children en masse. The individuals were important *as members of that group.*[29] On the other hand, Goddard and Mateer examined large numbers of children, if perhaps not as many as Terman and his co-workers, but they did so as *individuals,* one by one. It is irrelevant here that they thought of the bureau's charges as classifiable into particular groups, for in a very real sense no matter how important Goddard and Mateer thought their various taxonomies of the children were for explanatory purposes, they were still forced to examine each child *as an individual,* not as but another individual who shared a number of interesting attributes with other individuals in an experimentally defined population. Put another way, Terman's perspective was that of the experimental research scientist collecting data on a predefined group or population, whereas Goddard and Mateer's perspective was necessarily that of the clinician taking one individual at a time. Goddard and Mateer indeed recognized this distinction and thought of themselves as applied psychologists who employed what they thought were clinical methods. Increasingly they examined each individual holistically, from as many different directions as they could imagine.

And indeed, the more Goddard and Mateer studied their charges as individuals, the less important became their traits and actions as members of the predetermined and presumably homogenuous *group* of offenders. What mattered more to them was each child's characteristics and behavior patterns *as an individual.* Goddard and Mateer were coming very close indeed to denying that fundamental premise of American social and natural science of the last half century— namely, that an individual's traits and actions were entirely explained by reference to the "group" to which he or she belonged in the national population[30]

For some time after the observational cottages were opened, however, Goddard and Mateer continued to think of their examinees from a structural point of view, from the posture of original endowment, or the past, as constituting all of the causes of the present. They had not yet clarified the vexing problem of the meaning of group membership for the individual. It was not that they did not occasionally state elements of the newer nostrums of policy and therapy they had devised that indicated that training and environment—that is, the present— could be effective. But they still thought of the structural or historical point of view as the general theoretical explanation, and of their presentist functionalism as different, as policy, as remedy, and as practical solution. Thus, in a report to the board the month the cottages opened, Goddard revealed that of 330 juveniles examined recently, 155 were feebleminded, another 19 were psychopathic, 4 were insane, 2 were insane and feebleminded, and diagnosis had had to be deferred on 62. Clearly, Goddard was thinking of a linear progression of mental levels. He knew well that certain kinds of behavioral functions resulted from such levels.[31] But that was a different issue. In Mateer's official report of the first year's work in the psychoclinic, much the same can be said about her approach. She declared that it seemed that about half of all delinquents were feebleminded or potentially so, and that, at most, a trivial fraction were "insane" or "psychopathic," all as the result of unfortunate inheritance.

By the next September, however, Mateer and her assistants had completed diagnoses on forty-two children in the cottages. The results were the same as before: about half the children were feebleminded. Most of the others were not so easily classified; this clearly bothered her. She used a variety of terms to describe the various children, including psychopathic personality, psychopathic personality developing paranoia, paranoia deferred by psychic epilepsy, and so on. Furthermore, she maintained, not all the feebleminded children were the same. Some were "just straight feeble-minded." Others were more difficult to understand "from the standpoint of behavior, disposition, and diagnosis." And many individual children were simply too baffling to categorize easily. While she was thinking of an ascending number of mental levels as characteristic of the population, she was clearly uncomfortable fitting such children as paranoic or psychopathic in various combinations within this model of the distribution of intelligence.[32]

Obviously Mateer had come to a turning point in her thinking about the problem of juvenile delinquency and its causes. Yet much still remained unclear. The previous year she had published a slashing attack on the casual use of the IQ as a rigid index to human intellect, based chiefly on her work at the Massachusetts school. The IQ was particularly inappropriate for scientific diagnosis of abnormal and subnormal behavior. Intelligence, or the relative lack thereof, did not necessarily explain abnormal or delinquent behavior. She noted, for example, that some children who were classified initially as subnormal, when retested later, made astonishing gains toward, or even beyond, normal intelligence, provided their circumstances had changed dramatically. The real cause of delinquency, she insisted, was some disturbing factor that made the individual personality unstable and then psychopathic. She did not regard this as inconsistent with her more general position that mental defect explained or caused delinquent behavior. In this instance mental defect was not intelligence as such but psychopathic or some other kind of emotional disturbance, presumably within the structure of the individual.[33]

Now Mateer began to attack the problem from a different angle. While tests other than the Binet had been used from time to time, she established a more complicated regime of diagnosis to accompany observation. In succession, the cottage children were given a veritable blizzard of tests and measurements, including a literacy test, the Goddard or Stanford-Binet, the Goddard revision of the Seguin Formboard, the imitation series tests devised by Goddard, the Healy Picture Completion Board, the alternative Binet series and the Kent-Rosanoff association series. Children were also given what Mateer and Goddard believed were complete anthropometric measurements. They were also given tests in regular school subjects. At least from Mateer's eventual standpoint, the single most useful test was the Kent-Rosanoff word association test. Devised in 1910 by Grace H. Kent while she was a psychologist at the Kings Park State Hospital for the Insane in New York State, it was probably the first psychological test designed to diagnose mental illness. It took some time to work with the test and adapt it to the purposes at hand. She noted, with some satisfaction, that the new way of analyzing the child's association response yielded results that "differentiate normal, subnormal, and psychopathic children."[34]

Within two years the bureau's circumstances changed dramatically. One transformation was intellectual. Goddard and Mateer strikingly altered their ideas about the causes and cures of juvenile delinquency. They did not dismiss original nature and mental structure. But they emphasized mental function and social environment as never before. Mental structure and mental function, furthermore, were interrelated in many different ways. Heredity and environment worked together in an inseparable symbiotic relationship. Past and present formed a larger integrated whole.

Goddard and Mateer did not change their ideas in a professional vacuum. Their ideas were congruent with the new approaches invented and disseminated in the field over the next decade, as comparison with the child guidance movement of the 1920s amply demonstrates. Following its founding in 1918, the Commonwealth Fund of New York invested heavily in the mental hygiene movement.[35] The movement's leaders first thought of the problem of antisocial conduct in ways similar in most respects to those Goddard had championed at Vineland. In the early twenties the fund underwrote a new program in mental hygiene aimed toward the scientific prevention of juvenile delinquency. The program shared most of the assumptions on which the original Ohio Bureau of Juvenile Research was predicated. Within the next half dozen years those in the program drastically altered it into one in which child guidance was the central thrust. According to child-guidance workers, it was important to have the individual offender adjust to society's norms; thus they stressed the importance of the environment and of social function. There was considerable overlap between the child guidance workers' assumptions and those of Goddard and Mateer. Indeed Goddard became a revered member of the American Orthopsychiatric Association, the professional organization for child guidance, when it was founded in 1924. The differences between Goddard and Mateer and the child-guidance workers were those of detail and emphasis. Goddard and Mateer worked with juveniles who had severe behavior problems; hence they were thought of as specialists in *abnormal* psychology. Indeed, conventional wisdom on the history of mental testing has drawn a distinction between Goddard, the alleged "hereditarian" who worked with delinquents, and Dr. William Healy, of the Judge Baker Foundation in Boston, Goddard's supposed "environmentalist" professional nemesis. In reality, by the late 1910s and early 1920s the differences between Goddard and Healy were minimal, primarily those of emphasis, style, and prior ideological reputation. Both focused on the individual. Both discussed the influence of original nature and environment. And Healy himself provided much of the intellectual leadership for the Commonwealth Fund's program in child guidance as it evolved from its initial point of view to its later one in the 1920s.[36] Thanks to an interesting and peculiar chain of circumstances, best understood as a response to the larger shift of American culture itself, the child-guidance workers quickly moved from juvenile delinquency per se to an interest in the so-called normal or "everyday" child who suffered from mild behavior problems in the family, such as talking back to parents, intimidating siblings or playmates, wetting beds, or perhaps indulging in the solitary vice.[37] Hence the child-guidance workers came to be defined as specialists in *normal* child psychology. Furthermore, if chronology per se is taken as an indication of priority of scientific discovery, Goddard and Mateer worked out the implications of the assumptions of the new age just then dawning in American culture in their field first, several years before the Commonwealth Fund's professionals were able to do so.[38]

It was Goddard who first publicized the results of the bureau's new stance in several professional journals and in a popular book in 1920 and 1921.[39] He and Mateer now insisted that it was not the moron, the high-grade mental defective, who presented the greatest menace to the social order. After all, they had shown in their own work with such unfortunates that with proper professional institutionalization, a high-grade mental defective could be trained for civilian society in a few years. They knew there were not enough good institutions for mental defectives. Their optimism, such as it was, arose from their hope that because science had shown how to educate the high-grade defectives, society would eventually provide enough institutions. If as many as nine of every ten of the morons could be saved, feeblemindedness was obviously not the only, or even the most important, cause of antisocial conduct. Its real cause was the affliction of the psychopathic personality. While some morons might develop that condition for various reasons, psychopathy, not feeblemindedness, was the real problem. A clear distinction had to be drawn between the subnormal and the abnormal mind.

Goddard and Mateer argued that the army psychological tests indicated that 10 percent of the examinees had a mental age of ten or less. As the tests were the first mass examinations of the general population, presumably they were broadly representative of that population. Herein lay the first difficulty. If one took the tests as the only valid measure of intelligence, this meant that 10 percent, or even more, met one major criterion of feeblemindedness as defined by the professionals, that is, subnormal intelligence as defined by the tests. Yet they thought there was a more important criterion of mental defect than mental age—whether the individual could get along in society. The results of the army tests simply flew in the face of accepted conventional wisdom in the field, for no expert had ever believed that mental defectives constituted more than one or two percent of the general population, Goddard and Mateer insisted. Thus they criticized the tests as technics of science. As yet they still assumed that mental defect was usually inherited. Clearly, they had shifted their emphasis from analysis of mental structure and, therefore, inheritance, to discussion of the possibilities of changing mental function and social action. In one sense this flowed from their social roles as applied or clinical psychologists immersed in the practical problems of diagnosis and in the alteration of behavior in particular individuals.

But more was involved. Mateer had done an enormous amount of work with the children in the observational cottages, and with those examined in field surveys as well. While a fair proportion were feebleminded according to various tests, many were not. The new distinction Goddard and Mateer now made was between those who were *subnormal* mentally (which could mean absolute mental defect or simply low normal intelligence) and those who had diseased minds, who were abnormal or *psychopathic.* Psychopathic children could be found at all levels of intelligence as measured by standard tests, ranging from borderline imbecile to genius. Furthermore, standard intelligence tests could not reveal the condition of psychopathy. This distinction explained many problems that had arisen in previous work in which family members—including those in the famous Kallikak family—apparently did not meet the functional definition of feebleminded but were nevertheless obvious miscreants and threats to the social order. It also accounted for the astonishing educability of many mental "defectives." What distinguished the mental defectives from the psychopaths were their intelligence and conduct. The mental defectives had minds that developed normally to a certain level and then stopped. The psychopaths were found at various mental levels, mostly above feebleminded or low normal levels. But the psychopaths had diseased minds that were abnormal emotionally, and therefore morally. They were not mentally subnormal. Obviously, simple linear diagrams of ascending mental levels were inadequate to distinguish between those who were subnormal and those who were abnormal.

Consider the discussion of 1,603 inmates Goddard and Mateer had examined closely in county children's homes. Before they had worked out their new differentiation between the subnormal and the abnormal mind, they simply administered standard tests and taxonomized the examinees by mental level alone. By this yardstick, they found that many were feebleminded, many others had no clear diagnosis, and a handful suffered from psychopathy. With their new notion of the subnormal and the abnormal mind, their analyses took a different tack. Mateer constructed a table for the 1,603 children, one tabulation for mental level, the second for mental function. In the first, approximately 49 percent were located in the feebleminded to low normal levels, 36 percent could not be classified and were labeled "deferred diagnosis," and the rest were clearly located in the normal to bright normal mental levels. In the second tabulation, however, the resulting picture was far different. Almost one third of the feebleminded had no behavior problems. They were simply mentally defective. The vast majority classified as having behavior problems and suffering from psychopathy functionally had either normal or bright normal intelligence. Structure and function were different if interrelated. Put another way, it was clearly inadequate to conclude analysis and interpretation by saying that all of the causes of the present were to be located in the past. Now it was necessary to say that some of the causes of the present were to be found in the present (environment or function) as well as in the past (heredity or structure).

Mental defect and antisocial conduct were independent of one another from a causative point of view, although clearly the two could be associated in particular individuals. Yet science had shown this was tragically unnecessary. The individual's environment and social function could be changed. Not only were past and present the causes of the present, but the present could override the past in the majority of cases. As Mateer pointed out in her discussions of the children in the cottages, who were manifestly among the bureau's most obnoxious clients, it was important to distinguish quality as well as quantity of mind. By quantity of mind she meant the kind of emphasis on IQ for which Lewis Terman was so well known; by quality of mind she meant behavioral and mental function.

The real key to juvenile delinquency, then, was not the moron but the psychopath. The psychopath presented many more serious dangers to society than the moron ever could. Most psychopaths were far more intelligent than the morons. They were more effective in the havoc they wreaked on society. Now the psychopathic personality became so important in Goddard and Mateer's prescriptions for public policy that they recommended that separate psychopathic institutions be created. Psychopaths presented different problems for science and society. They had to be treated separately from other problem groups. Goddard and Mateer insisted that even the psychopathic children had hope for a brighter and better tomorrow. There were three kinds of psychopaths. In some instances the psychopaths' minds deteriorated rapidly, the result of biological or physical factors such as innate defect or congenital syphilis. Other psychopaths were stabilized. But most could be improved or even cured if appropriate professional care and attention were lavished on them. Clearly a handful were sufficiently intractable to require permanent institutionalization. More could be cured by medical treatment. Probably the majority suffered from prior emotional traumas. With the right therapy they could be made well. Goddard was the eternal optimist: science would lead the way to a better future. The psychopath as a social problem became primarily resolvable through special education and therapy. "Juvenile delinquency," he exclaimed, "can largely be eradicated."[40]

With this claim, Goddard was perforce attacking the notion that delinquents constituted a predefined and predetermined *group* in the national population. He allowed that this might be true if social technology and public policy did not attempt to "solve" the problem of juvenile delinquency. What he argued, however, was that each delinquent was also an *individual,* not merely a member of a group—delinquents—whose behavior and character would always be "delinquent" as the ineluctable consequence of being classified as a member of that group. If most delinquents could be reformed and made into constructive, normal citizens, then traditional scientific analysis was, at best, inaccurate and social policy prescription was misdirected. It is notable that Goddard had come very close to attacking the fundamental methodological premise of American evolutionary natural and social science as it had developed in scientific and social-policy ideology since the later nineteenth century. That premise, of course, was that individuals in the national population were best described, analyzed, and interpreted by reference to the *group* in the national population to which they "belonged," or, in other words, to their "evolutionary past." Of course it had been the artificiality of social convention and scientific ideology that had created this concept of a natural hierarchy of inferior and superior groups in the national population in the first place, whether such groups signified socioeconomic class, ethnic nativity, color of skin, religious identification, sex, or such categories as "delinquent" or "genius." In effect the man who had become famous in the early 1910s for propagandizing that scheme was now turning it on its head, and loudly proclaiming that it was careless science and callous social policy.

It is doubtful that Goddard perceived the broader implications of his message. His was not a thoughtful or reflective mind, and, even so, it is highly unlikely that he would have grasped the underlying meaning of his arguments. It was not simply that he was too busy with the details of everyday existence. In reality it was that the assumptions he attacked were too deeply imbedded in the very perceptual and explanatory structures of the larger American culture for few, if any, to recognize clearly. Yet even if no one involved in public policy or applied science could recognize the deeper implications of what he said, Goddard had inadvertently committed a great offense by undercutting the whole notion of group, and, therefore, of class, sex, race, religion, and other "groups." Since the 1830s Americans had used changing notions of the meaning of group identity for the individual to reconcile the severe tension between their sincere if circumscribed commitments to such ideals as "democracy," "equality," and "individualism," on the one hand, and their grim determination to maintain white, middle-class hegemony over the "other" groups in the national population. In other words, by implying that the lines of class and caste in American society and culture were artificial, not natural, Goddard was playing with fire.[41]

And, as Goddard was to discover, if never to understand fully, he was caught up in the midst of a political maelstrom. The Ohio Bureau of Juvenile Research was swept up in a sudden transformation of state politics as well.[42] The Republican landslide in 1920 had broken the eight-year logjam between the two parties over the valuation formula for state taxes. In turn, the new Republican governor, Cleveland attorney Harry L. Davis, had masterfully sidestepped this perilous issue. He had occupied the safer, not to say higher, ground of wholesale reorganization of state government, which, he insisted, would bring economy and efficiency. He let the legislators and their constituencies exhaust themselves over the taxation issue.[43] No sooner was Davis in his office than he replaced all board members with his own. He instructed his appointees to prepare a much larger budget for his proposed Department of Public Welfare under which all board institutions would be managed. He planned for the bureau to assume all its mandated functions, and for new state institutions for the insane and the mental defectives. Thus he embraced Goddard's recommendations as fully as he dared.[44] Some interest groups forced modifications here and there in his larger reorganization scheme, as when the banking industry won informal control over the new commerce department and Ohio State University alumni obtained a million dollar appropriation to construct Ohio Stadium.[45]

If matters had depended merely on the traditional patterns and foreseeable vicissitudes of Ohio politics, it was possible that the legislature might have assented to Davis's plans and Goddard's hopes to the extent of providing a new skeletal form for the Bureau of Juvenile Research. Doubtless the fleshing out of that institutional structure was problematic under the most auspicious political and budgetary circumstances. Such circumstances did not exist in Ohio in the early 1920s thanks to the ravages of inflation and political infighting.[46] An ineluctable consequence of the new marriage of public policy and scientific expertise now came into play, contention and rivalry among those professional groups whose members sought exclusive claim to the scientific interpretation of social policy issues and problems. Those who had been the professional opponents of the bureau, of Goddard and Mateer, and of the science they represented now intervened. Critics allied with the state and county institutions outside Columbus joined powerful doctors and alienists throughout the state to throttle the bureau. The bureau's enemy heartily disliked its new-fangled psychologizing because it was not medical science and because Goddard and Mateer had been openly—and indiscreetly, therefore—critical of the "warehouse" mentality and quasi-militaristic regimens the state and county institutions seemed to represent. Above all, Goddard, Mateer, and the bureau were quite literally beyond their control within the framework of the usual operations of the state institutions and of professional politics. Those who were cognizant of the new and seemingly permissive approach Goddard and Mateer were suddenly peddling in Ohio politics were outraged even more. Although sufficient documentation is lacking to provide a full portrait of the bureau's opponents, it may be inferred that they were driven by the totality of their collective professional identities, and whatever personal animosities they may have harbored, to attack the bureau by thrusting themselves into the legislative process. And, quite beyond the bureau as a threatening entity, there was also the problem of the new Department of Public Welfare that the governor had proposed, which would centralize all state and county organizations even more than the Board of Administration.[47]

It soon became evident that some of the bureau's most noisy and bitter opponents were employees within the agency itself. In April the new budget was about to be approved.[48] At that point eleven staff members resigned. Their leader was Gertrude Transeau, the chief physician. Transeau resented Mateer on personal grounds.[49] She also believed the new psychology was a substantially inferior science to the medical expertise she represented.[50] But the pot boiled even more. Many county and state institutional administrators chafed at Goddard's salary, which was several thousand dollars higher than theirs. That his bureau might be fully funded and operational intensified their bitterness. A full-scale public brouhaha resulted within the legislature and in state politics. Mateer resigned. The legislature slashed Goddard's salary 47 percent. The budgets for the bureau and the state institutions were put on proportional levels, thus implying that all institutions in the state system were equally valid if not identical in function and scope of operations. The revised blueprint for the new department mandated horizontal, not vertical, relationships among the distinct and indivisible elements of the larger whole, thus dramatically overturning Governor Davis's plan. At the ensuing public hearings, not surprisingly, the legislative committee exonerated Goddard of the ineptitude his professional enemies had alleged.[51] After all, the bureau's professional opponents had won as much as they thought they could, and only a few legislators had strong views about Goddard one way or the other.

The bureau's professional enemies satisfied themselves that they had won the war. Within a year Goddard retreated to a professorship at Ohio State University. Doctors and alienists assumed control of the bureau. Within the new Department of Public Welfare the bureau was redefined as an ancillary service agency for the state system and, indeed, for all who desired its expertise. Its staff offered medical, dental, and psychological diagnoses to the department's wards, including those referred by the juvenile courts. Administrators at state, local, and private child institutions could ask for the bureau's services. Nor were its services centralized in Columbus. The bureau offered field clinics throughout the state in response to local initiatives, thus taking account of the multiple and various needs of the many different local communities that constituted the larger entity of Ohio.

By the mid-1920s the Bureau of Juvenile Research was no longer the technical hemisphere within the administrative brain of the Ohio Board of Administration in Columbus that Cox and Goddard had designed only a dozen years before. And for that matter, the larger hierarchical pyramid of state and county institutions, with the board at the pyramid's apex, as defined in 1911 and 1913, no longer existed. Davis had wanted to strengthen Cox's pyramid through the new Department of Public Welfare to reinforce the premise of vertical integration in public enterprise. The result was not only a new name and a new structure, but an institutional network predicated upon notions of horizontal integration of distinct yet interrelated parts, and of the decentralization rather than the centralization of power and authority.[52]

Clearly there were multiple layers of historical action and discourse. On the most obvious level, as George S. Addams, a leading Cleveland juvenile court judge, explained the whole affair, Goddard and the new psychology were the real targets of the attack. Doctors who neither knew nor cared about the mind, psychology, mental tests, psychopathy, and the like thought the new psychology was quasi-scientific if not irrelevant; indeed, "some small minded doctors are jealous of him [Goddard] and think a medical man should be at the head of the Bureau."[53] On the level of concrete events, Addams was correct.

Ultimately, the victory of the bureau's enemies was incomplete. The bureau's major professional function of scientific diagnosis of problem children operated as the budget allowed. Ironically, the institutionalization and regularization of the bureau's responses to local constituencies throughout the state helped legitimate its purposes more than would have been possible under the older arrangements. Nor was the new department's legal control over children who were committed to the state institutions any less than that of the old board. The bureau's facilities in Columbus were gradually enlarged. The new psychology was not eliminated, even though Goddard's immediate successor, E. M. Baehr, probably would have wished that. Even if after the investigation of the bureau Baehr could publicly praise Gertrude Transeau's statement that successful psychological diagnosis could not begin until doctors, alienists, and dentists had completed their work with the children—and thus indicate his true allegiances and affiliations—the new psychology was still an indivisible and integral part of the bureau's mixture of scientific services. Indeed, the bureau's scientific ideology was not very different from that of Goddard and Mateer or even of the mainstream of the child guidance movement.[54]

Yet by any professional's criteria, the situation was hardly promising. The bureau never received the funds to implement the enlarged functions Goddard's opponents said they wanted when they criticized the bureau as too narrowly conceived. The field clinics remained few in number and occasional, not to say eccentric, in operation. In the mid-1920s Baehr was replaced by Goddard's old ally E. J. Emerick, who promoted the new psychology as much as he could at the bureau. Even his presence could not remove the fear among the bureau's original supporters that it would always be subject to unwholesome and unscientific political pressures. Thus in 1930 Emerick retired from state service at the bureau and at the institution for mental defectives. Alma W. Patterson, a member of the university's board of trustees and enthusiast of the child guidance movement, asked Ohio State University president George W. Rightmire if now the bureau could be transferred to the university. As such, she argued, it could be reconstituted as an agency that would promote the science and therapy of child guidance. President Rightmire consulted with numerous individuals, including Goddard, Dean George F. Arps, a leading psychologist in his own right, and certain professionals in the community. Goddard and other university faculty strongly opposed the transfer. They insisted it would bring unwelcome political influences to bear upon the university, and would undercut the university's appropriations. In addition, it was entirely inappropriate: the bureau was not an educational institution. It served rather the purposes of public welfare. Goddard's counsel was evidently crucial. President Rightmire gently told Patterson that the transfer could not be implemented.[55]

Since the 1870s professionals in America had insisted to those in public life that social policy required the values of technical expertise, namely objectivity, rationality, and selflessness, not to mention the professional services of the experts themselves. By the early twentieth century this campaign was yielding results for professionals in many distinct areas of expertise. It was to be expected that not all such campaigns succeeded according to the most sanguine projections of their leaders and followers. Contention and half loaves, not linear progress, was the real experience of most of the professions, their own accounts of these struggles notwithstanding. From one perspective, that of concrete events, the short and unhappy life of the Ohio Bureau of Juvenile Research was a cautionary tale, a telling demonstration, if such were needed, of the insight that professionalism was largely interest-group politics clothed in modern dress. The new professionals in American life merchandized technical expertise as the pure, selfless product of the new post-1870 professionalism, and, therefore, a magnificent benefaction for the publics of America and the policies the political system invented in the name of those publics. Yet the bureau's history enables us to peer beyond this ideological façade and understand that expertise was in no small measure a political instrument of high utility—save, perhaps, when competing professional groups carried their competition into full public display.

From a more remote perspective, however, the bureau's history illustrates the transformation of American culture from one age to another. Between the 1870s and the 1920s American culture functioned on certain patterns of thought and conduct. The most important of these for present analysis were the establishment of nationally articulated standards of worth and value, the creation of hierarchical blueprints of centralized authority, and the self-conscious invention of a unified national culture predicated on developmental, linear—historical—models. The new psychology of Hall and his disciples was fully a manifestation of those larger patterns, as was the emergence of large-scale vertically integrated firms following the return of prosperity in 1897. So too was the Progressive movement, a broad-based response to the age, an attempt to provide efficiency, centralization, and rationality in public life. Starting in the mid-1910s, the fundamental patterns of American culture underwent a massive shift that was complete by the early 1930s. In the new formulation, the national or larger whole assumed a new importance. Indeed, now the whole constituted a system greater than the sum of its parts. A substantial modification came in the substitution of horizontal for vertical relationships among the parts, those distinct yet interrelated elements of the whole. In science and in social policy, indeed in every aspect of American culture and society, this transformation took place, silently if unevenly, on a level of human experience that few if any could perceive at the time.[56] Evidence of this massive cross-sectional shift can now be recognized, as so amply indicated by the seemingly disparate manifestations in the 1920s of corporate decentralization along functional lines, the indeterministic models in the sciences that assumed the functional indivisibility of past and present, the abandonment of three dimensional for n-dimensional perspectives in the visual arts, and the rise of cultural pluralism, cultural relativism, and cultural and political regionalism in social thought and public policy. If on a concrete level the bureau's history is well apprehended as a conflict among interest groups attempting to gain public authority and legitimacy, nevertheless those involved were apparently swept up in a major transformation of American culture from one age to another they dimly and fleetingly realized if at all.

NOTES

I wish to acknowledge, with thanks, the assistance, comments, and suggestions of the following scholars: John C. Burnham, Alan I Marcus, Robert M. Mennel, Steven L. Schlossman, Michael W. Sedlak, Michael M. Sokal, and Leila Zenderland. I also wish to thank Dr. John Popplestone, Director, and Dr. Marion White McPherson, Associate Director, Archives of the History of American Psychology, University of Akron, and Mr. John Miller, University of Akron Archives, for their courteous and effective assistance in working through the papers of Henry H. Goddard at the Archives of the History of American Psychology. I am also grateful to Drs. Popplestone and McPherson and to the Archives of the History of American Psychology for permission to cite from the Goddard papers.

1. See, for example, the highly suggestive works of Barry D. Karl: "The Power of Intellect and the Politics of Ideas," *Daedalus* 86 (Summer 1968): 1002–1035; *Charles E. Merrian and the Study of Politics* (Chicago: University of Chicago Press, 1974); and (with Stanley N. Katz), "The Ameri-

can Philanthropic Foundation and the Public Sphere, 1890–1930," *Minerva* 19 (1981): 236–270.

2. John C. Burnham, "Psychology, Psychiatry, and the Progressive Movement," *American Quarterly* 12 (1960): 457–465.

3. For a discussion of the history of mental testing, see Hamilton Cravens, *The Triumph of Evolution: American Scientists and the Heredity-Environment Controversy, 1900–1941* (Philadelphia: University of Pennsylvania Press, 1978), 56–88, 224–265.

4. The standard biography of Hall is Dorothy Ross, *G. Stanley Hall: The Psychologist As Prophet* (Chicago: University of Chicago Press, 1972). A perceptive synopsis of the history of American child development is Robert R. Sears, *Your Ancients Revisited: A History of Child Development* (Chicago: University of Chicago Press, 1975).

5. See Cravens, *The Triumph of Evolution,* passim. Other studies that make much the same point in somewhat different language and with different historical phenomena include John Higham, *Strangers in the Land: Patterns of American Nativism, 1860–1925* (New Brunswick, N.J.: Rutgers University Press, 1955); Stow Persons, *American Minds: A History of Ideas,* rev. ed. (Huntington, N.Y.: Robert E. Krieger, 1975 [1958], 237–382; Henry D. Shapiro, *Appalachia On Our Mind: The Southern Mountains and Mountaineers in the American Consciousness, 1870–1920* (Chapel Hill: University of North Carolina Press, 1978); idem, "The Place of Culture and the Problem of Identity," in *Appalachia and America: Autonomy and Regional Dependence,* edited by Allen Batteau (Lexington: University Press of Kentucky, 1983), 111–141; Merle Curti, *Human Nature in American Thought: A History* (Madison: University of Wisconsin Press, 1980), 186–416; Cravens and John C. Burnham, "Psychology and Evolutionary Naturalism in American Thought, 1890–1940," *American Quarterly* 23 (1971): 635–657; Mark H. Haller, *Eugenics: Hereditarian Attitudes in American Thought,* paper edition (New Brunswick, N.J.: Rutgers University Press, 1984 [1963]).

6. This discussion of Progressivism in Ohio is based upon Hoyt Landon Warner's *Progressivism in Ohio, 1897–1917* (Columbus: Ohio State University Press for the Ohio Historical Society, 1964), 232, 312–432. For the relationship between Cox and Goddard, see pp. 406–407, 419 n. 52, 432. Whatever might be said of Warner's interpretation of "Progressivism" or even of his focus on conflict among professional politicians, his work is exhaustively documented. I could find no contemporary tangible link between Cox and Goddard in *HHG;* yet it is quite apparent in reading Goddard's correspondence while at the Bureau of Juvenile Research that Goddard knew the governor.

7. A printed copy of the bill, "House Bill No. 214, An Act to Supplement Section 1841 by the enactment of supplemental sections 1841–1, 1842–2, 1842–3, 1842–4, 1842–5, 1841–6, 1841–7, and relating to the 'Ohio Board of Administration,'" may be found in folder 5, box M37, *HHG.*

8. For example, see Thomas H. Haines, "The Ohio Plan for the Study of Delinquency," *Popular Science Monthly* 86 (1915): 576–580, which quotes the bill creating the bureau.

9. For information on Vineland, see Leila Zenderland, "The Debate Over Diagnosis: Henry Herbert Goddard and the Medical Acceptance of Intelligence Testing," chapter 3 of volume; Bird T. Baldwin, "The Psychology of Mental Deficiency," *Popular Science Monthly* 79 (1911): 82–93; Lucy Chamberlain, "The Spirit of Vineland," *The Training School Bulletin* 19 (1922–1923): 113–120; Edgar A. Doll, ed., *Twenty-Five Years: A Memorial Volume in Commemoration of the Vineland Laboratory, 1906–1931* (Vineland, N.J.: Publication of the Training School, 1932); Joseph B. Byers, *The Village of Happiness: The Story of the Training School* (Vineland, N.J.: The Smith Printing House, 1934.)

10. See, for example, Henry H. Goddard, "Four Hundred Feeble-Minded Children Classified by the Binet Method," *Pedagogical Seminary and Journal of Genetic Psychology* 17 (1910): 388–397; Goddard and Helen F. Hill, "Delinquent Girls Tested by the Binet Scale," *The Training School Bulletin* 8 (1911): 50–56; Goddard, "Two Thousand Normal Children Measured by the Binet Measuring Scale of Intelligence," *Pedagogical Seminary and Journal of Genetic Psychology* 18 (1911): 232–259.

11. See, for example, Henry H. Goddard to Charles B. Davenport, March 15, May 5, May 7, July 18, July 26, July 31, October 1, October 18, October 25, November 21, and December 9, 1909; Charles B. Davenport to Henry H. Goddard, March 18, April 29, May 7, May 24, July 9, July 21, July 24, July 28, August 5, August 14, September 7, October 2, October 26, and November 26, 1909; all in Henry H. Goddard file, Charles B. Davenport papers, Library of the American Philosophical Society, Philadelphia. In light of the thesis of the present essay, it is interesting to note that Goddard and Davenport continued to correspond until Goddard went to the Ohio Bureau; then the correspondence stopped.

12. Henry H. Goddard, *The Kallikak Family: A Study in the Heredity of Feeble-Mindedness* (New York: The Macmillan Company, 1912); idem, *The Criminal Imbecile: An Analysis of Three Remarkable Murder Cases* (New York: The Macmillan Company, 1915).

13. See, for example, Henry H. Goddard, *School Training of Defective Children* (Yonkers, N.Y.: World Book Company, 1915); idem, "Educational Treatment of the Feeble-Minded," in *Modern Treatment of Nervous and Mental Diseases*, 2 vols., edited by William A. White and Smith E. Jelliffe, (Philadelphia: Lea and Febiger, 1913), vol. 1, 143–194; idem, *Feeble-Mindedness: Its Causes and Consequences* (New York: The Macmillan Company, 1914); idem, "The Possibilities of Mental Hygiene in Cases of Arrested Mental Development," *The Training School Bulletin* 15 (1918): 67–72.

14. Henry H. Goddard to S. D. Porteus, April 17, 1918, folder "Correspondence PQR," box M615; Henry H. Goddard to H. S. Riddle, February 21, 1918, folder, "AAD," box M33; D. S. Creamer to Henry H. Goddard, Febru-

ary 26, 1918, folder "AA1," box M33; H. S. Riddle to Henry H. Goddard, February 27, 1917, folder "AA1," box M33; all in *HHG*.

15. Henry H. Goddard to Robert M. Yerkes, December 7, 1917, and Robert M. Yerkes to Henry H. Goddard, December 14, 1917, author folder 190, *RMY.*

16. See author folder 200, *RMY,* for full documentation on Haines's experiences at Ohio State University and the bureau. Examples of Haines's policy recommendations are Haines, "The Ohio Plan for the Study of Delinquency," 576–580; idem, *The Increasing Cost of Crime in Ohio,* Ohio Board of Administration, Publication No. 10, June 1916 (Mansfield: The Press of the Ohio State Reformatory, 1916); idem, "The Feeble-Minded Situation in Ohio," *Ohio Bulletin of Charities and Corrections* 23 (1917): 29–36.

17. Florence Mateer, *Child Behavior: A Critical and Experimental Study of Young Children by the Method of Conditioned Reflexes* (Boston: Richard G. Badger, 1918), 73–215 et passim.

18. Florence Mateer to Henry H. Goddard, April 24, 1918, folder "AA2," box M33, *HHG.*

19. See, for example, Henry H. Goddard et al., *The Bureau of Juvenile Research: Review of the Work, 1918–1920,* Ohio Board of Administration, Publication No. 19, February 1921 (Mansfield: Press of the Ohio State Reformatory, 1921), passim; Henry H. Goddard, "First Report of the Bureau of Juvenile Research: The Ohio Board of Administration," October 17, 1918, folder "Correspondence #2," box M31.1, *HHG.*

20. See, for example, *The Ohio State Journal* (Columbus), March 7, March 8, March 26, March 28, May 1, May 9, June 9, June 19, and June 20, 1919. See also *The Columbus Dispatch,* March 30, 1919.

21. See, for example, Harry Maddy to Henry H. Goddard, June 9, 1920, folder "Correspondence #1," box M31.1; G. H. Transeau to Henry H. Goddard, February 27, 1919, folder "Correspondence #2," box M31.1; Henry H. Goddard to Ohio Board of Administration, January 7, January 12, January 17, 1921, and Harry Maddy to Henry H. Goddard, January 11, 1921, both in folder "Correspondence #1," box M31.1; Henry H. Goddard to Ohio Board of Administration, April 28 and July 18, 1919, and Harry Maddy to Henry H. Goddard, August 4, 1919, both in folder "Correspondence #2," box M 31.1. See also [Henry H. Goddard], "Bureau of Juvenile Research: Budget for 1919–1921 . . . ," n.d., 3-page typescript, folder "AA3," box M33; Henry H. Goddard to Ohio Board of Administration, November 21, 1919, and April 10, 1920, folder "Correspondence #2," box M31.1. Goddard expressed his desire to resign in Henry H. Goddard to Mr. [Frederick] Burk, June 17, 1920, folder "Miscellaneous (2)," box M35.2. All in *HHG.* See also *The Ohio State Journal* (Columbus), June 20, 1919.

22. R. U. Hastings to Henry H. Goddard, September 15, 1919, folder "Bureau Juvenile Research," box M31, *HHG.* See also Margaret E. McNamara to Henry H. Goddard, September 8, 1919, folder "Bureau of Juvenile Research," box M31, *HHG,* for another instance.

23. No less an authority than the famous Los Angeles juvenile judge, Dr.

Miriam Van Waters, told Goddard that it was her understanding that Ohio's political problems were hopeless. See Dr. Miriam Van Waters to Henry H. Goddard, February 16, 1921, folder "AA4 #2," box M33.1, *HHG*.

24. See, for example, *The Ohio State Journal* (Columbus), March 3, March 27, June 19, and June 20, 1919.

25. Henry H. Goddard, *Human Efficiency and Levels of Intelligence* (Princeton, N.J.: Princeton University Press, 1920), passim.

26. In fact, Goddard dealt with sterilization opportunistically and changed his mind several times in the 1910s and later depending on his thinking about its medical and political practicalities. See, for example, Henry H. Goddard, "Menace of the Feeble-Minded from the Standpoint of Heredity," *Boston Medical and Surgical Journal* 175 (1916): 269–271. See also Henry H. Goddard to A. A. Merrill, January 5, 1916, and A. A. Merrill to Henry H. Goddard, January 10, 1916, folder 5, box M37; Henry H. Goddard to The Editor, *The Ohio State Journal*, February 10, 1922, and Henry H. Goddard to F. B. Kirkbride, October 10, 1933, folder "R-M55," box M32; all in *HHG*.

27. Henry H. Goddard to Ohio Board of Administration, January 3, 1918, folder "Correspondence #2," box M31.1, *HHG*. On the history of the idea of psychopathy, see Henry Werlinder, *Psychopathy: A History of the Concepts, Analysis of the Origin and Development of a Family of Concepts in Psychopathology* (Stockholm: Uppsala Studies in Education, Serial No. 6, 1978). I am indebted to Professor John C. Burnham for this reference.

28. For example, Henry H. Goddard to Lewis M. Terman, November 25, 1918, folder "AA1," box M33, *HHG*.

29. See, for example, Lewis M. Terman et al., *The Stanford Revision and Extension of the Binet-Simon Scale for Measuring Intelligence* (Baltimore: Warwick and York, 1917), passim; see also Lewis M. Terman et al., *Genetic Studies of Genius* vol. 1. *Mental and Physical Traits of a Thousand Gifted Children* (Stanford, Calif.: Stanford University Press, 1926), and subsequent volumes.

30. See, for example, Arnold Gesell, Henry H. Goddard, and John E. W. Wallin, "The Field of Clinical Psychology," *Journal of Applied Psychology* 3 (1919): 84–87; Florence Mateer, "The Future of Clinical Psychology," *Journal of Delinquency* 6 (1921): 283–293. For a discussion of the changing meaning of group identity for the individual, see Hamilton Cravens, "History of the Social Sciences," in *Historical Writing on American Science: Perspectives and Prospects,* edited by Sally G. Kohlstedt and Margaret W. Rossiter, *Osiris,* 2d series, vol. 1 (1985), 183–208.

31. Henry H. Goddard to Ohio Board of Administration, February 27, 1919, folder "Correspondence #2, box M31.1, *HHG*.

32. Florence Mateer, "Annual Report, 1918–1919: Department of Clinical Psychology," 48-page typescript, September 13, 1919, folder "BJR #2," box M31.1, *HHG*.

33. Florence Mateer, "The Diagnostic Fallibility of Intelligence Ratios," *Peda-*

gogical Seminary and Journal of Genetic Psychology 25 (1918): 369–392. See also her skeptical essay, "The Moron as a War Problem," *Journal of Applied Psychology* 1 (1917): 317–320.

34. Mateer, "Annual Report, 1918–1919, Department of Clinical Psychology," passim. On the Kent-Rosanoff test, see Grace H. Kent and Aaron J. Rosanoff, "A Study in Association in Insanity," *American Journal of Insanity* 67 (1910): 317–390.

35. Still the best and most perceptive account in print of the Commonwealth Fund's work with the mental hygiene movement in creating the program in juvenile delinquency, later the child guidance movement, is Roy Lubove, *The Professional Altruist: The Emergence of Social Work as a Career, 1880–1930* (Cambridge, Mass.: Harvard University Press, 1965), 85–117 et passim. See also Norman Dain, *Clifford W. Beers: Advocate for the Insane* (Pittsburgh: University of Pittsburgh Press, 1980), passim, for an excellent discussion of the mental hygiene movement from the standpoint of one of its major founders. The development of the Fund's activities can be followed in Commonwealth Fund of New York, *Annual Report,* 1922–1930.

36. See, for example, Lewellys F. Barker, "The First Ten Years of the National Committee for Mental Hygiene, With Some Comments on Its Future," *Mental Hygiene* 2 (1918): 557–581; National Committee for Mental Hygiene, *Twenty Years of Mental Hygiene, 1909–1929; First Distributed at the Twentieth Anniversary Dinner Held at Hotel Biltmore, New York City, Evening of November Fourteen, Nineteen Hundred Twenty-Nine, Under the Auspices of the National Committee for Mental Hygiene and of the American Foundation for Mental Hygiene* (n.p., 1929), passim; George K. Pratt, "Twenty Years of the National Committee for Mental Hygiene," *Mental Hygiene* 14 (1930): 399–428; Lawson G. Lowrey and Victoria Sloane, eds., *Orthopsychiatry, 1923–1948: Retrospect and Prospect* (New York: American Orthopsychiatric Association, 1948), 53–86 et passim; George S. Stevenson and Geddes Smith, *Child Guidance Clinics: A Quarter Century of Development* (New York: The Commonwealth Fund, 1934), passim; Lawson G. Lowrey, ed., *Institute for Child Guidance Studies: Selected Reprints* (New York: The Commonwealth Fund, 1931), provides easy access to a representative sample of technical papers in child guidance. See also Hamilton Cravens, "Child-Saving in the Age of Professionalism, 1915–1930," in *American Childhood,* edited by Joseph M. Hawes and N. Ray Hiner (Westport, Conn.: The Greenwood Press, 1985), 424–432.

37. A representative general statement of the child guidance approach as it had developed by the later 1920s is Smiley and Margaret Gray Blanton, *Child Guidance* (New York: The Century Company, 1927), passim.

38. Goddard and Mateer had worked out their new argument by December 1920; the child guidance movement did not fully emerge until more than three years later.

39. Henry H. Goddard, "Feeble-Mindedness and Delinquency," *Journal of Psycho-Asthenics* 25 (1920): 168–176; Goddard et al., *The Bureau of Juvenile Research: Review of the Work, 1918–1920*, 1–3, 5–50; Goddard, "The Problem of the Psychopathic Child," *American Journal of Insanity* 77 (1920): 511–516; idem, "In the Light of Recent Developments: What Should Be Our Policy in Dealing With the Delinquents—Juvenile and Adult?" *Journal of Criminal Law and Criminology* 11 (1920): 426–432; idem, "The Sub-Normal Mind Versus the Abnormal," *Journal of Abnormal Psychology* 16 (1921): 47–54; idem, *Juvenile Delinquency* (New York: Dodd, Mead, and Company, 1921), 1–12, 27–48, 67–120, et passim. See also Florence Mateer, "The Future of Clinical Psychology," *Journal of Delinquency* 6 (1921): 283–293. The discussion of their ideas in the following passages in the text is drawn from these materials.

40. Goddard, *Juvenile Delinquency*, 120.

41. See Cravens, "History of the Social Sciences," 183–208.

42. Much of Goddard, *Juvenile Delinquency*, has thinly veiled references to the bureau's political problems in Ohio politics and professional disputes from Goddard's point of view as of late 1920.

43. *The Ohio State Journal* (Columbus), March 1, March 2, March 5, and April 22, 1921; *The Columbus Dispatch*, December 17 and December 20, 1920, January 3, January 10, and January 12, 1921. See also *The Columbus Dispatch*, March 7, March 8, March 9, March 10, March 11, March 12, March 13, and March 15, 1921. State politics had become so polarized and stalemated over the issue of state taxation that the legislative session that began in January 1919 could not adjourn until February 1920, a full thirteen months later; the issue was not resolved. From the standpoint of one of the themes of this essay, it is interesting to note that the conflict was between those who wanted a single valuation standard for calculating state taxes and those who wanted different functional standards of valuation depending on the uses of property, such as residential, agricultural, industrial, and so on. Ultimately those who championed the latter scheme prevailed.

44. See *The Ohio State Journal* (Columbus), March 10, March 11, March 13, March 15, and March 23, 1921, for evidence that these conflicts involved longstanding regional economic competition among urban centers in the state. See also Henry H. Goddard to Ohio Board of Administration, January 12, 1921, folder "Correspondence #1," box M31.1, *HHG; The Columbus Dispatch*, March 16, 1921.

45. *The Ohio State Journal* (Columbus), March 10, March 11, and March 23, 1921.

46. See, for example, Mrs. Charles Axline to Henry H. Goddard, January 20, 1921, folder "Bureau of Juvenile Research," box M31, and "Minutes of Mass Meeting at Bureau of Juvenile Research," March 1, 1921, 2-page typescript, box M38, both in *HHG; The Ohio State Journal* (Columbus), March 8 and March 31, 1921; *The Columbus Dispatch*, March 17 and March 18, 1921. See also *The Columbus Dispatch*, March 30, 1919.

47. See, for example, *The Ohio State Journal* (Columbus), March 8, March 18, and March 31, 1921; *The Columbus Dispatch*, March 10, March 13, March 16, March 17, March 18, March 25, March 27, March 28, March 30, March 31, April 1, April 3, April 4, April 7, and April 8, 1921.

48. *The Ohio State Journal* (Columbus), April 6, April 12, April 18, April 19, April 20, and April 27, 1921.

49. "The Eleven" to Ohio Board of Administration, April 4 and April 7, 1921, folder "Bureau of Juvenile Research," box M31; Henry H. Goddard to Ohio Board of Administration, April 5, 1921, folder "Correspondence #1," box M31.1; [Henry H. Goddard], "Who Are the Eleven Who Resigned in a Group From the Bureau of Juvenile Research?" two typescript pages, n.d.; Henry H. Goddard, "Resignations From the Bureau of Juvenile Research," four typescript pages, n.d.; Florence Mateer to Henry H. Goddard, April 17, 1921, folder "Bureau of Juvenile Research," box M31; all in *HHG*.

50. See, for example, Transeau's comments on the new psychology in her part of the bureau's first report; Goddard et al., *The Bureau of Juvenile Research: Review of the Work,* 3. There she said that the psychologist "needs to have all these unknown [medical and physical] quantities removed or evaluated before he can be sure of his psychological analysis of the case," and, further, she implied that the doctor would be more humanitarian than the psychologist.

51. *The Ohio State Journal* (Columbus), April 27, April 28, April 29, April 30, May 17, May 29, June 2, and June 3, 1921; Florence Mateer to Henry H. Goddard, June 24, 1919, Willie Stephens to Henry H. Goddard, June 8, 1921, Florence Fitzgerald to Henry H. Goddard, July 5, 1921; all in folder, "Bureau of Juvenile Research," box M31, *HHG*.

52. See, for example, E. M. Baehr, *The Bureau of Juvenile Research: Review of the Work, 1920–1922,* State of Ohio, Department of Public Welfare, Publication No. 23, December 1922 (Mansfield: Press of the Ohio State Reformatory, 1922), passim; E. J. Emerick, *The Bureau of Juvenile Research,* State of Ohio, Department of Public Welfare, Publication No. 27, September 1927 (Mansfield: Press of the Ohio State Reformatory, 1927), passim. A useful sketch of E. M. Baehr, who succeeded first Mateer and then Goddard in the early twenties, can be found in Cecil Striker, M.D., ed., *Medical Portraits* (Cincinnati: Academy of Medicine of Cincinnati, 1963), 20–25.

53. George S. Addams to D. S. Blossom, June 14, 1921, folder "BJR," box M31, *HHG*.

54. Baehr, *The Bureau of Juvenile Research,* passim.

55. Alma W. Patterson to George F. Arps, June 2, 1930; Evelyn Brewster to Henry H. Goddard, June 4, 1930, with attachment; George F. Arps to Mrs. Alma W. Patterson, June 3, 1930; George F. Arps to Julius F. Stone, June 4, 1930; George F. Arps to George W. Rightmire, June 4, 1930; all in folder "AA4 #1," box M33.1, in *HHG*. Also George W. Rightmire to George F. Arps, July 15, 1930; George F. Rightmire, "Memorandum. Conference

with Doctor E. J. Emerick Concerning the Bureau of Juvenile Research, October 17, 1920," 2-page typescript; "Bureau of Juvenile Research," 4-page typescript, n.d.; George W. Rightmire, "Bureau of Juvenile Research, Some Facts," 8-page typescript, October 21, 1930; [Henry H. Goddard], "Memorandum: October 22, 1930, Bureau of Juvenile Research," 7-page typescript; George W. Rightmire to "Honorable Secretary of State," October 24, 1930 [sent to Secretaries of State in fifteen states]; George W. Rightmire to Honorable H. S. Atkinson, November 25, 1930, and attachments; H. S. Atkinson to George W. Rightmire, November 21, 1930; Mary Irene Atkinson to H. S. Atkinson, November 17, 1930; George W. Rightmire Records, 3/f/27, "Bureau of Juvenile Research"; all in University Archives, The Ohio State University, Columbus.

56. For a fuller elaboration of this argument, see Shapiro, "The Place of Culture and the Problem of Identity," 111–141; Hamilton Cravens, "The Wandering IQ: American Culture and Mental Testing," *Human Development* 28 (1985): 113–130; Alan I Marcus, "The City As A Social System: The Importance of Ideas," *American Quarterly* 37 (1985): 332–345.

NOTES ON CONTRIBUTORS

HAMILTON CRAVENS is professor of history at Iowa State University, Ames, Iowa, where he teaches in his department's graduate program in history of technology and science. He also teaches courses in American social and cultural history. He received his Ph.D. in history from the University of Iowa in 1969 and has taught at the Ohio State University, the University of Washington, and the University of Maryland, College Park. Among his publications are *The Triumph of Evolution: American Scientists and the Heredity-Environment Controversy 1900–1941* (Philadelphia: University of Pennsylvania Press, 1978), *Ideas in America's Cultures: From Republic to Mass Society* (Ames: Iowa State University Press, 1982), and numerous articles on the evolutionary sciences and social technologies in American society and culture. Among his recent publications are "Child-Saving in the Age of Professionalism, 1915–1930," in *American Childhood*, edited by Joseph M. Hawes and N. Ray Hiner (Westport, Conn.: The Greenwood Press, 1985), 415–488, "The Wandering I.Q.: American Culture and Mental Testing," *Human Development* 28 (1985): 113–130, and "History of the Social Sciences," in *Historical Writing on American Science*, edited by Sally G. Kohlstedt and Margaret W. Rossiter, *Osiris*, 2d series, vol. 1 (1985), 183–207.

HENRY L. MINTON is professor of psychology at the University of Windsor, Windsor, Ontario, Canada. He received his Ph.D. in clinical psychology from Pennsylvania State University in 1962, and has taught at the State University of New York at Albany and at Miami University. His research in psychology has focused on personality and individual differences, and while preparing a textbook on differential psychology (individual and group differences) about ten years ago, he became interested in the historical development of the nature-nurture controversy. This interest has led to his current research in the history of mental testing. He has written a biography entitled *Lewis M. Terman: Pioneer in Psychological Testing*, (New York University Press, 1988).

JAMES REED is associate professor of history and dean of Rutgers College at Rutgers University, New Brunswick, New Jersey. His study of the birth control movement in the United States, *From Private Vice to Public Virtue* (Basic Books, 1978), is now available in a paperback edition as *The Birth Control Movement and American Society* (Princeton University Press, 1983). His interests have shifted from sex to intelligence, and he is now preparing a biography of Robert M. Yerkes.

FRANZ SAMELSON is a professor of psychology at Kansas State University, Manhattan, Kansas. He is a social psychologist with a Diploma in Psychology from the University of Munich and a Ph.D. from the University of Michigan in

Ann Arbor. His work on attitudes and social influence, together with some puzzlement about trends in the discipline, led him into historical studies in the late 1960s. Dissatisfied with what he has called the "origin myths" of psychology's textbooks, he came to believe in the need for a more "critical" history of psychology. His major interest in the interplay of the academic discipline with its surrounding society is expressed in a number of articles and chapters on early intelligence testing and its social ramifications, the growth of behaviorism, and the development of such social-psychological concepts as authoritarianism.

MICHAEL M. SOKAL is professor of history in the Department of Humanities, Worcester Polytechnic Institute, Worcester, Massachusetts, and Executive Secretary of the History of Science Society. He has edited *An Education in Psychology: James McKeen Cattell's Journal and Letters from Germany and England, 1880–1888* (MIT Press, 1981) and compiled (with Patrice A. Rafail) *A Guide to Manuscript Collections in the History of Psychology and Related Areas* (Kraus, 1982). He has written extensively on the history of psychology and the history of American science. An advisory editor of *Isis* and a member of the book review board of the *Journal of the History of the Behavioral Sciences,* he recently completed a history of Sigma Xi, The Scientific Research Society. He is now preparing a full biography of James McKeen Cattell.

RICHARD T. VON MAYRHAUSER is assistant professor of History at Slippery Rock University, Slippery Rock, Pennsylvania. He recently completed graduate study in American history at the University of Chicago with a dissertation entitled "The Triumph of Utility: The Forgotten Clash of American Psychologies During World War I." His research interests generally concern the redefinition of human nature in industrialized and secular America, and focus on the careers in psychology of Walter Dill Scott and Walter Van Dyke Bingham.

LEILA ZENDERLAND is assistant professor of American Studies at California State University, Fullerton, California. Her interests in the history of the social sciences in America represent part of a larger concern for American cultural history, and she has edited a volume entitled *Recycling the Past: Popular Uses of American History* (University of Pennsylvania Press, 1978). Her current major work in progress deals with Henry H. Goddard's role in the American intelligence-testing movement.

Index